Democracy and Human Rights

Essays in Honour of
R. Radhakrishna and G. Raghava Reddy

Democracy and Human Rights

Essays in Honour of R. Radhakrishna and G. Raghava Reddy

A. Ranga Reddy

SERIALS PUBLICATIONS
NEW DELHI (INDIA)

First Published - 2009

ISBN: 978-81-8387-291-1

Published by

SERIALS PUBLICATIONS
4830/24, Prahlad Street, Ansari Road
Darya Ganj, New Delhi-110002 (India)
Phone : 23245225 Fax : 91-11-23272135
E-mail: serials@satyam.net.in

CONTENTS

Section–III
University Education

Section–IV
Environment Protection

Section–V
Democracy and Human Rights

FOREWORD

I am delighted to be associated with this book which is being brought out in honour of two well known economists of India Professor R. Radhakrishna and Professor G. Raghava Reddy. Professor Radhakrishna has made significant contributions to diverse areas of development such as poverty, rural labour markets, food security, nutrition, social policy, etc. I have had the privilege of close personal as well as professional association with him for the last several years. Although I have had not the fortune of knowing Professor G. Raghava Reddy personally, I have learnt about him though several friends as a very good teacher who has taught and guided a large number of Economics students in Andhra Pradesh.

I am very happy that Dr. A. Ranga Reddy has brought out this book in honour of Professor Radhakrishna and Professor Reddy. The book, which is based on Dr. Ranga Reddy's previous papers, deals with some of the important themes of policy discourse on Indian development such as globalization and agricultural development, industrial development, higher education, environment and human rights and democracy. The canvass of the papers are very wide and range from global to national to local. Some of the papers provide useful insights in the working of the local economy and its interactions with the larger process of globalization.

I congratulate Dr. A. Ranga Reddy for this endeavour which, I hope, will be useful for not only students of Economics but also for all those interested in development issues. I am thankful to him for associating me in honouring the two eminent economists.

Alakh N. Sharma
Director
Institute for Human Development
and Editor, Indian Journal of Labour Economics

30 January 2009
New Delhi

PREFACE

The objective of human being is to carry the good Peoples' activities and abilities to the coming generations, so that they can learn a lesson for improving their quality of sacrifices and services to others. To fulfill this, I ventured in that direction for bringing a volume.

By virtue, Late Prof. G. Raghava Reddy, was a evergreen friend, Philosopher and guide to all young scholars and to me also. He felt that nothing is impossible on this earth, provided you had a will. Prof. R. Radha Krishna is a multi-faceted personality-a disciplinarian, writer, builder and visionary. He is an inspirer of many students, scholars and always looking for their par excellence. Dr. Reddy an architect of me in achieving the highest degree, where as Dr. Radhakrishna taught me the Art of living.

Wholeheartedly I express, a sense of gratitude to both of them for accepting to bring a volume in their honour. I am extremely grateful to all editors of journals acknowledging my request of using their papers for a volume. In fact, I am indebted to Dr. Alakh N Sharma, Editor, Indian Journal of Labour Economics for writing a foreword, amidst of his busy bee schedule.

Last but not least, I am ever thankful to Shri S.K. Jha and his sons, Serials Publications, New Delhi for bringing a volume in very attractive and memorable way.

Prof. A. Ranga Reddy

Prof. R. Radhakrishna

1992 Oct.10	: Born
	: M.A Economics, M.Sc. Statistics, Andhra University
Ph.D. Economics	: Gokhale Institute of Politics and Economics Poona University, Pune.
1963-64	: Pre–Doctoral Research Fellow, Gokhale Institute, Pune
1964-67	: Doctoral Research Fellow, Gokhale Institute
1969-70	: Lecturer in Econometrics, Marathwada University, Aurangabad
1971-80	: Professor, Sardar Patel Institute of Economic& Social Research Ahmadabad
1980-85	: Professor& Head, Dept of Economics, University of Hyderabad
1985-94	: Director, Centre for Economic and Social Studies, Hyderabad
1994-97	: Member Secretary, ICSSR, New Delhi
1997-98	: Sr. Fellow, CESS, Hyderabad
1998-2001	: Vice Chancellor, Andhra University, Visakapatnam
2001-2007	: Director, IGIRD, Mumbai
Awards and Honours	: 9
Assignment/Membership with International Organisations	: 11
Membership in Committees Constituted by Government	: 25
Other Assignments	: 43
Monographs/Books	: 18
Research Papers	: 60
Ph.D and M.Phil Guidence	: 24 Ph.Ds, 10 M.Phils
Presently	: working at Hony Professior at CESS, Hyderabad For details: *E-mail rkrokkam@gmail.com*

Late Prof. G. Raghava Reddy

1937, Jan. 26	: Born Papireddigariplli–Chittoor District
1959	: PUC, S.V.Arts College, Tirupati
1960	: B. A. (Hons)/M.A. Economics, Sri. Venkateswara University, Tirupati
1960-63	: Regular Ph.D, Sri.Venkateswara University, Tirupati
1964-65	: Lecturer in Economics, Wrangal
1965-72	: Lecturer in Economics, S.V.U. Engg. College, Tirupati
1972-77	: Lecturer in Sri.Venkateswara University P.G. Centre, Kavali
1978-80	: Reader, Nagarjuna University, Guntur
1981-1997 Jan	: Professor& Special officer, S.V.U.P.G.Centre, Kavali, Nellore District.
1995	: Executive Council Member, S.V.University, Tirupati
M.Phils/Ph.Ds	: 33 Ph.D, 70 M.Phils
Research Papers	: 130
Books	: 10
Organisation of National Seminars	: 20
Major Research Projects	: 6
Visiting Professor	: 50
Evaluation of theses	: 200
Social Service	: Social forestry Scheme at P.G.Centre, Kavali
Died on	: November 14, 2003 at Tirupati.

Section–I

Agricultural Development

1

IMPACT OF GLOBALISATION ON INDIAN AGRICULTURE

Introduction

Globalisation is the process of integration of economies across the world through Cross-border flow of factors, products and information.

The Universal economic liberalisation which gathered momentum in the last two decades of the twentieth century, reinforced and enforced by the World Trade Organisation, seems to have made globalisation irreversible and un-stoppable. "All institutions have to make global competitiveness a strategic goal. No institution, whether a business, a university or a hospital, can hope to survive, let alone to succeed, unless it measured up to the standards set by the leaders in its filed, any place in the world".[1] Globalisation, of course, is not a new phenomenon. The period 1870 to 1914 experienced a growing trend towards globalisation. The new phase of globalisation which started around the mid-20th Century became widespread, more pronounced and over changing since the late 1980's by gathering momentum from the political and economic changes that swept across the Communist Countries the economic reforms in other countries, the latest multi-lateral trade agreement which seeks to substantially liberalise international trade and investment, and the technological and communication revolutions. Globalisation may considered at two levels, viz., at the macro level and at the micro-level.

Drivers of Globalisation

The world economy has been emerging as a global or transnational economy. Globalisation is a process of development of the world into a single integrated economic unit. The transnational economy is a borderless world economy characterised by free flow of trade and factors of production across national borders. "In the mid-1970s-with the OPEC; and floating of the US dollar-the world economy changed from being international to transnational. The transnational economy is characterised by money flows rather than trade, money and capital markets increases, market maximisation rather profit maximisation, trade become function of investment, decision making shifts from national State to regional blocs, genuine organised information and entire world turns into a single market for production".[2] Globalisation represents the increasing integration of the world economy based on five inter-related drivers of change. They are international trade, financial flows Communications, technological advances and population modility.[3]

Stages of Globalisation

Normally, a firm passes through different stages of development before it becomes a truly global corporation. Typically, a domestic firm starts its international business by exporting. Later it may establish joint ventures or subsidiaries abroad. From an international firm it may then develop into a multi-national firm and finally into a global or transnational one. Ohmae identifies five different stages in the development of a firm into a global corporation. A domestic company moves into new markets overseas, company takes over activities on its own. Domestic based company begins to carry out its own manufacturing, at overseas. The company moves towards a genuinely a global mode of operation."[4]. This is what Akio Morita of sony has termed as global localisation.

Benfits of Globolisation

Foreign Capital, if properly utilisation, can make substantial contribution to the economic development of a nation. A classical example is the communist China. Productivity grows more quickly when countries produce goods and services in which they have comparative advantage. Living standards can go up faster. Increase in competition would make companies more cost and quality conscious, and innovative. Global Competition and imports keep a lid on prices, so inflation is less likely to derail economic growth. Liberalisation and global competition enhance consumer choice and consumer surplus. An open economy spurs innovation with fresh ideas from abroad. Export jobs often pay more than other jobs. Unfettered capital flows give the country access to foreign investment and keep interest rate low. Globalisation opens up enormous domestic and global opportunities for firms in developing countries. Despite discriminations of the global economic order against them, there are chances of developing countries benefiting from trade.

Survival of the Fittest in Globalisation

Globalisation brought number of challenges for the individuals, firms and Countries. Certainly, globalisatioin will doom the future of those who fail to meet these challenges effectively. (a) In a competitive environment, a firm can survive only if it is efficient. Cost efficient is to be promoted either cutting size of labourers or other inputs. (b) Attracting foreign investment is a real challenge, as is evident from the fact that the FDI in flow of India is far below the target. (c) Liberalisation increases the economic inequality. Even in China, the liberalisation has created many islands of affluence. The fast growth of China economy has reduced poverty. Naisbitt points art that there were as estimated 200 to 270 million Chinese living in absolute poverty in 1978 and their number came down to 100 million by 1985.[5] (d) small and medium firms often have some edge over the large ones in respect of standardised products or technologies. The new patent regime should be expected to help the Indian industry by promoting it to give added thrust to R & D and enabling Indian firms also to develop patented products (e) The domestic and Cross-border M & As Pose a serious Challenge to governments in ensuring fair competition. (f) Liberalisation will be successful only if the policy is proper and clear and there is the required political mandate, will and boldness. Lack of clarity regarding privatisation; lack of boldness to implement labor law reforms, downsizing, bureaucratic hurdles and so on are retarding India's reform process. Lack of clarity in policies and delays can make the situation worse instead of realising the objectives of liberalisation. Eg. Tata steel had bagged corus for 12.1 billion[6].

Impact of Globalisatiion on India

With the new economic policy ushered in 1991, there has been a change. Globalisation has in fact become a buzzword in the Indian firms now and many are expanding their overseas business by different strategies.[7]

Negative Factors

The Indian business suffers form a number of disadvantages of globalisation like bureaucratic culture not encouraging, high costs of many inputs, poor infrastructure facilities, obsolescence technology resistance to change, poor quality image, supply problems, small size, lack of experience, limited R & D, growing competition and trade barriers. There is a view that globalisation is another from of imperialism, to exploit the resources of developing countries.[8]

Positive Factors

There are number of favourable factors for globalisation. India had enough human resources, wide based industrial business, growing entreprenuership, growing domestic market, niche markets, expanding markets, transnationalisation, large number of Non-resident Indians, encouragement of economic liberalisation, cut throat competition, global strategies.[9]

II

Moving Towards Corporate Agriculture

India has to support one sixth (1 billion) of world population in the 2 per cent of land area (247 M. ha) and one per cent of global precipitation (400 M ha. m).

India is endowed with a natural wealth of diversified soil types heterogeneous climate conditions and biodiversity. This variability together with abundant sunshine and equitable temperature regimes provides conditions for round the year cropping and to adopt diversified farming system to include livestock, tree crops, horticultural crops and aquaculture to ensure food security and prosperity to country men. (3) The other side inherited scarcity and poverty from the colonial rule. Through systematic planning to harness natural resources and technological development, Indian Republic surged ahead from scarcity to self-sufficiency, marginal surplus on food front in new millenium. The apprehensions of Thomas Malthus about the human ability to produce food to match the needs of human numbers, fortunately, did not come true. [10]

Globalisation and economic liberlisation has direct impact on production process, commercialization of agricultural products and social structure, it is capital intensive and offers opportunities for educated youth to participate. To compete with global market, cost reduction and quality improvement in production system will be indispensable; consequently shrinkage in labour and grater expectation on labour productivity. In future, corporate will play a lead role in Indian agriculture, effective partnership building will be warranted to bridge/reduce the severe disparity between rural and urban population. Agribusiness should strike a partnership with farmer for covering his produce to satisfy market needs. This type of inter dependence between the farmer-Customer-Corporate would Constitute a socio-economic matrix (ITC,. Pepsi, Mother Dairy etc. are examples).

Agri-business

It is a profit-motivated enterprise that involves providing agricultural supplies and or the processing marketing and distribution of agricultural materials and consumer products.

Agri-business Companies provide input supplies to the production agriculturists. The production agriculturist produce food, fibre etc, and the output is taken by agri-business companies that process, market and distribute the agricultural products. Many services are needed in agriculture, transportation, storage, refrigeration, credit, finance and insurance. Agri-business manufactures furnish farmers with supplies and equipment needed to produce and protect their crops. Hundreds of agri-business trade organisations, committees and conferences, educate, promote, advertise, coordinate for their agricultural products. Millions of people are employed in agri-business through out world. To uplift kisan, give him fishing road and teach him how to fish. Otherwise he is bound to turn into a Naxalite. Blood revolutions in Russia and China were started by just such disagrunted farmers.

Precision Farming

Presently, the average farm worker supplies over 150 persons with food and fibre. Annual consumption of food is 600 kgs per person, production is 50 tonnes of food. This productivity frees others from food production and pursue careers in science, medicine, computers and many other fields.

Precision farming combines crop planning, including tillage, sowing, chemical application, harvesting and post harvest processing of the crop. The five major objectives of comprehensive precision farming are–increased production efficiency, improved product quality–more efficient chemical use, energy conservation, soil and ground water protection. Precision farming requires the use of digitally, geographically referenced date in cropping operations.

Most of agri-business is small business. When it comes to jobs small business is not small in the number of people they employ. Entrepreneurs are people who have vision, diligence and persistence to flow through. An entrepreneur is a person who accepts all the risks pertaining to forming and operating a small business. A business succeeds only when it fills an economic need. Determine what type of business is needed. Many new business succeed they provide a product of service that others need for which they are willing to pay.

Agro-Industries in India

Agro–industries are considered an extended arm of agriculture, but in India it has not received as much attention as agriculture, while agriculture contributes about 18 per cent of India's GDP the value added by the processing industry is only 8 per cent of total food production. The size of the domestic market is Rs. 350,000 crores (Rs. 350 billion). An average Indian spends 53 per cent of his/her income on food. The domestic demand of processed food in not only huge but is growing fast it tandem with the economy. If more income are to be generated in the rural areas to improve the lot of farmers, it is imperative to accelerate the growth of the agriculture sector and agro industry segment.

The focus on value addition in agri-sector is vital for comprehensive development of the rural economy. Since food processing industry creates job, demand for agri raw materials, leads to diversification and commercialisation of agriculture, enhancing the income of the farmers and creating surplus for export of agro-foods. The broad-based development of food proceeding industry will improve both the social and physical infrastructure of rural India. Some of the critical areas that require immediate attention are strengthening the infrastructure like cold storage, improving the production process in the agriculture sector, relaxing or removing stringent laws and regulations, and ensure reliable power supply.

Bio-village Development

Rural environment is to be changed. Globalisation is a capital intensive and has vast scope for better-educated personal. An inefficient and outdated technology farmer may not sustain in agriculture. The new technology and better distribution networks allow farmers to succeed in agriculture. Agriculture is to be adopting industrial approaches. New technologies such as no-till or minimum till, precision farming, drip irrigation and genetically altered crops are attempts to increase profitability, stability and sustainability. It is estimated that assuming India's share in world exports improves from 0.5 per cent to 1.0 per cent, trade gains may conservatively be placed at 2.7 billion US dollars per year. Although agricultural exports are increasing in value terms, their share in India's total exports declining. It declined from 33 per cent in 1980 to 13.5 per cent in 2000-01.

India is also losing competitiveness because the very step increase given to administer prices and rising administrated prices have not only resulted in weakening India's competitiveness they have also resulted in creating the dilemma of moaning stocks of food grains along with persistence of large scale poverty. High prices have tended to price out the poor from the market.[11]

Further, Lester Brown has predicted that India may have to import 50 million tonnes of food grains and China over 20 million tonnes by 2030. These estimates are based on the basis of three major criteria, increasing population, increasing purchasing power and increasing degradation of life supporting systems. The first two will increasing the demand for food. The last one will reduce potential to produce the food we require. This is why partnership between all sectors assume great importance care of nature counters care of civilisations.

Bio-village programme is pro-nature, pro-poor, pro-women development paradigm. It seeks sustainable agriculture and rural development by concurrently attempting to mitigate the twin concerns of the present times, namely, creeping degradation of the resources base and persistence or rural poverty. Technologies and interventions are needed, which are ecologically compatible, economically viable and socially acceptable.

Technology empowerment, Agri-export zones contract farming through corporate culture, organised rural force, intellectual property Rights, Biotechnology, Information technology were new agencies entered into agriculture sector for farmers growth.[12]

A Threat to Sustainable Ecology

Ecology is the science of the distribution, abundance and activity of life. It is the science of environmental awareness, ethics, stewardship and remediation. The distribution of organisms and agricultural system is dictated by global and attitudinal climatic belts of temperature and by availability of water soil types and other organisms. The community, its physical environment and the interaction between organisms and the physical environment comprise the ecosystem, which some scientists regard as the basic of ecology. Community can be measured by their bio-diversity. Gentleman farmers are likely to increase conversation of rare endangered species. It is estimated that 60,000 species will be eliminated in the fore see able future and 50,000 will be at risk of extinction in the next half a century.

Sustainable development was defined by weed (1983) to mean development, which meets the needs of the present generation without jeopardizing the needs of future generations.

In fact, of the 304 Million ha. of cultivated land in India as much as 175 million ha.. Suffer from environmental degradation–wind and water erosion - water logging, salinity, alkalinity caused by reservoirs and water rise and mis-management of soil and water resources. Further, green house gases remain in the atmosphere for decades for centuries. The Co_2 concentration has increased from 290 ppm hundred years ago to 350 ppm and likely to increase to 440-500 ppm by 2100. Co_2 emission has to be cut. The global increase in Co_2 and other green house gases may enhance the lower atmospheric temperature by 1.5^{0}C to 4.5^{0}C by the year 2030. This will result in the melting of Pole ice Caps and rise in sea level. Such an increase in sea level will cause flooding in many coastal wetlands. 10-15 *per cent* arable and productive coastal land will be lost. Ecology protection and promotion are must for global community to avoid natures havocs and disasters. Modern agriculture, technology, training to farmer community, social moisture water management, credit supply leading, marketing, price mechanism, global markets are to be pushed into agriculture sector and forced to shift, marginal, small medium farmer to non-agriculture areas.

Conclusion

The objective of globalisation is to bring cheap and quality goods and services to all people of globe in one market, so that welfare for all is ultimate achievement, provided, people are efficient with modern technology then only the fruits would go to that area. In fact, Indian agriculture is not so advanced. It has to improve its nature and extent through corporate farms, Agri-business, Agri-industry, Ecological protection, Bio-village development, so that it can removed rural poverty and promoted employment opportunities. Globalisation is to be taken as an opportunity to flourish with prosperity of agriculture and its based industries. Certainly, Indian farmer would become a global trekker and enjoy the flavour of different markets, prices and goods.

Notes and References

1. Peter Drucker, (1999), Management Challenges for the 21st Century, Harper Business, Newyork, p. 61.
2. Peter R. Drucker (1990), The New Realities Mandrin, London.
3. John, D. Sullivan (2000), Preparing in the Global Economy, *Economic Reforms Today*, November 1.
4. Kenchi Ohmae (1991), The Borderless World, Fontana, London.
5. John Naisbitt, (1994), The Global Paradox, Nicholas, Barely Publishing, London, p. 186.
6. P. M. Thomas, S. Sen R.R. Sriram (2007), Iron Willed. It is a Steel Plated Victory, *The Economic Times*, 3, p. 1.
7. G. S. Bhalla (2004), Globalisation and Indian Agriculture (19) Academic Foundation, New Delhi.
8. Sitaram Yechury, Globalisation; Impact of Indian Economy for Desh Bhagat Yadgar Committee Seminar.
9. S. Subramanian (2004), Globalisation and Sustainable Agriculture.

10. R. Maria Saleth (2004), Agricultural Strategy for a Globalising Economy; Continuing and Changing, edited by C. G. Krishna Swamy, SR Keshava, Ravi M. Tirlapur, Better Expression G'lobalisation Better Expression, Dept. of P.G' Studies and Research in Economics Bangalore, University, Bangalore.

11. Jagadish Bhagawathi (2007), Out Souring is as Good or Bad or any Kind of Trade, *The Economic Times,* Jan. 29.

12. Joseph Stiglitz (2002), Globalisation and its Discontents, Penguin Books, New Delhi.

2

IRRIGATION OF RAYALASEEMA "BEGGER THY NEIGHBOUR POLICY" IN ANDHRA PRADESH

The paper highlights backwardness of Rayalaseema's Irrigation situation in the scenario of Andhra Pradesh economy.

Andhra Pradesh is a river State and an agriculture economy, which is based on dichotomy in between irrigation and rainfed agriculture. The total surface water of entire river systems of the State is estimated to be of the order of 2764 TMC at 75 per cent dependability. This breaks up into 1480 TMC from Godavari River system, 811 TMC from the Krishna, 99 TMC from the Pennar and the rest from 37 other Small rivers. We had surplus water of 745 TMC in Godavari and Krishna water was fully harnessed through projects. Unfortunately, investment on large water resources development projects is presently seen as a panacea. Earlier projects lost their installed capacity in mid-way. Another giant project of linking Ganga-Cauvery is on pipe line. Users should be encouraged to aim at greater efficiency and productivity, through integrated use of soil moisture, local and exogenous water.

At present, a shift is needed from the present approach of equating water resource development to creation of new resources by rain water harvesting and construction of storage reservoirs. Importance needs to be given to sustainability, productivity enhancement and efficiency of water-use. Local resources by themselves are often inadequate in rainfed areas to provide for food security. Further, due to land degradation and sub-optimal water use, it is difficult to provide the water needed to create the marketable surplus of food grains and pulses. Integration of local resources of water and land can enhance the benefit from external water by optimizing the storage options through the limited use of irrigation water over extensive area for extended commands as well as new projects[1].

Irrigation alone cannot bring prosperity to any area. There is a big sector of landless poor in the affluent Coastal Andhra districts and other areas, they go in search of work during seasonal agricultural operations in K.C. Canal, Nizamsagar and other projects in the backward areas of Rayalaseema and Telangana regions. Many such people have also migrated to Hyderabad, in search of better income and employment and vice versa[2].

Struggle for Irrigation

In Andhra Pradesh, out of 133.113 lakh acres of cultivated area, from irrigation department sources lakh acres (133.113–(14.90+7.75) = 110.5 lakh acres, 14.90 lakh acres under Panchyat Raj Departments irrigation tanks and 7.75 lakh acres under Andhra Pradesh State Irrigation Development Corporation (APS IDC) and the balance is rainfed. (2.92-133.113=158.887) lakh acres. In all irrigated sources 46% of land is irrigated[3].

The regions of Rayalaseema and Telangana have experienced drastic shifts in the composition of irrigation. By the 1980's well irrigation had become the dominant source of irrigation replacing tank irrigation in Rayalaseema and Telangana. The larger part of rainfed area is affected by frequent droughts. As the droughts increase, the struggles for 'water' and Politics of water have intensified in recent times. The water struggles are fought at different levels. The regional struggles of Telangana and Rayalaseema for more water are being intensified, including a demand for separate "State of Telangana". "Recently, the 'War' between the farmers of Kurnool District and Mahabub Nagar district at Rajolibanda

Diversion System (RDS) are in effect fought between the close relatives separated only by the district boundaries and Tungabhadra river of course, the water 'war' between Andhra Pradesh and Karnataka is never ending.

There are number of studies linking rain-fed areas and poverty, irrigation development and poverty reduction, irrigation development and industrial development. All studies generally subscribe to the theory that irrigation development has strong influence on the overall growth and regional development.

Most of the farmers suicides are reported from drought prone areas especially small and marginal farmers. Anantapur tops the list of farmers suicides as a result of frequent droughts. The drought hit farmers are in the web of perpetual cycle of indebtedness and poverty for generations and are unable to get out of it. Only some assured irrigation could provide a farmer with ability to cope with such a pathetic situation.

When Telangana, Coastal Andhra political leaders are continuously fighting for their share of river waters and stabilising their ayacuts, Rayalaseema faction political leaders never voiced their resentment. Of course, gocd droughts are fortunes for their vote bank but not stability in politics and regional greenery. Possibly, the history of Rayalaseema made them immunised not to go for development of irrigation projects. A brief analogy is given below.

A Brief History of Rayalaseema

Satavahanas ruled Rayalaseema during 400 B.C. Kings were Vaishnavites but queens professed Buddhism. At 600 A.D., feudalism had been with high taxation and harsh punishments. Chalukyas, Kakatiyas and Reddy rulers reigned during 680-1450 AD with Vengi, Warangal (Orugallu), Rajamahendravaram, Kondavidu as capitals. Both Kannada and Telugu had a homogenous language. Muslims conquered and ruled Telugu land and people-Bahamani and later Kutbshahi sultans of Golconda and still later the Nizams of Hyderabad with their vassals of Kurnool, Adoni, Cuddapah and Acrcot Nawabs.

Vijayanagara Rule

Rayalaseema means, the area (*seema*) ruled by the *Rayas* (rulers) of Vijayanagara Empire. It consisted of the present districts of Anantapur, Chittoor, Kadapa, Kurnool and Bellary which is now in Karnata State. Under their glorious rule particularly of Sri Krishnadevaraya (1509-1529), Rayalaseema received systematic canal linked Tank irrigation and flourished with *navadhanyas*[4] and *navaratnas*. Unfortunately, Vijayanagar rulers besides a very large standing army, had also encouraged military chieftains of *palems* known as *Palegars*. These *Palegars* ruled at times extremely cruel. Due to this situation some dignified and rich families migrated from Rayalaseema. Under anarchism and promiscuity, poets and reformers emerged leading to a very rich folklore and literature based on the life and work of Pothuluri Veerabramham, Poet Vemana, Bala Nagamma and Lakshmamma and so on.

Under British Rule

In 1800 A.D Nizam had given Rayalaseema districts to the British East India Company as *Ceded Districts* because of his inability to pay the amount due to the Company's subsidiary forces. During 1800-1807 A.D. Thomas Munro, as Principal Collector, had given golden rule to Rayalaseema people by supressing eighty *palegars* and extended *Ryotwari* System. Under the British crown, after 1857 AD, the worst famine known as the *Dhatu Famine* during 1876-1878. It took a toll of 40 per cent of people, who died for want of food. Arthur Cotton and Mackenzy were architects of Kurnool-Cuddapah Canal in 1872 A.D. for Inland water ways (later found uneconomical) and irrigatational purposes including drinking water.

Sri Bagh Pact

In 1937, at Madras, at the Sri Bagh residency of Kasinathuni Nageswara Rao, there was an gentleman agreement among Rayalaseema and Coastal Andhra leaders. The objectives of Sri Bagh pact was to start a Post Graduate Centre of Andhra University, Waltair (established 1926) at Anantapur, the surplus water available in Krishna river have to go Rayalaseema and political capital or High Court is to be given to Rayalaseema. Of course, capital was given for very short period of three years 1953-56 and shifted to Hyderabad from November 1, 1956. Potti Sreeramulu, a great patriot, went for fast unto death from October 19, 1952 died on Dec. 15, 1952. N.G. Ranga, Krushikar Party asked Coastal Andhra and Rayalaseema leaders to go for making Tirupati as Capital.

Rain Shadow Area

When comparing other two regions, a distinctive feature of Rayalaseema was low rainfall around 500 m.m., which transformed entire development under backwardness. 75 per cent of cultivated lands was under rainfed. 1954 Tungabhadra project was started to construct, which gave 20 per cent water and 80 per cent power to Rayalaseema. Unfortunately, much of assured water is being enjoyed by Coastal Andhra and Telangana regions, the uncertain and un-reliable surplus water from Srisailam Hydel Project was allotted to the poorest Rayalaseema region. Telugu Ganga was started in 1989, much of water was planned to go for irrigation of Nellore District and Madras for drinking water. In 1992, Galeru-Nagari was conceived. On flood water of Krishna , Srisailam Right Branch Canal, Hundri niva (lift irrigation), Galeru-Nagari and Telugu Ganga were planned to develop and distribute to Rayalaseema region, which will be a permanent dream. It shows the other two regions suppressed the voice of Rayalaseema people under their brutal force both in Parliament, Assembly. Rayalaseema region may not get assured irrigated water, unless there was a miracle of political will.

Planning Expenditure

State had given top priority for irrigation development in Andhra Pradesh. Irrigation is the only medicine and tonic for disease of chronic droughts. The following table provides a bird's eye view of state budget under planning.

The Table 1 has given a picture that under planning period 18-96 lakh acres was brought under irrigation in all sources and pre-plan and annual plans the area irrigated was 31.682

lakh acres, in total 50.642 lakh acres for the year 2003-04. The expenditure column in percentage.

Table 1
State Plan Irrigation Created and Expenditure

Plan	*Irrigation Potential Created (Lakh Acres)*	*Expenditure (In Percentage)*
I Plan years (1951-56)	0.845	22.58
II Plan years (1956-61)	1.452	34.75
III Plan years (1961-66)	1.408	35.32
IV Plan years (1969–74)	2.80	22.82
V Plan years (1974-78)	2.67	31.58
VI Plan years (1980–85)	2.53	26.80
VII Plan years (1985-90)	1.42	24.23
VIII Plan years (1992-97)	0.61	18.44
IX Plan years (1997-2002	2.38	18.84
X Plan years (2002-2004)	1.175	-
Total	18.96	-

Sources: 1. Government of Andhra Pradesh, Economic Survey 2004-05, p. 169.
2. Veethshanam, (A Telugu monthly) 2005, Can achieve Irrigation projects-in Effective planning? Nov. 15, p. 16.

Further it explains that upto III Five Plan, State spent one-third of its budget for irrigation. Later, except V Five Plan, the funds devoted for irrigation was declined. Especially under Telugu Desam Party rule, it reached to bottom level. Of course, again after Congress came to power on May 14th, 2004 has given mega or lion's share for irrigation, such as completing 26 Projects with Rs. 46,000 crores, escalation of cost structure became a stumbling block for irrigation. In fact, the I Plan was given irrigated water cost per hectare was Rs. 1060, whereas in VII Plan it was Rs. 50,000, i.e., almost raised around 47 times.

There are about 80,000 tanks in the State, of which Telangana has 44 per cent followed by Coastal Andhra 38 per cent and Rayalaseema 18 per cent. Interestingly, the region with the highest dependence on ground water (Rayalaseema) has the lowest number of tanks. In fragile resource region, ground water irrigation has become privy to large farmers, denying rights to small and marginal farmers[5].

Further, integration of Tank restoration with watersheds, check dams, water harvesters and pits would not only strengthen the ecological base but also, get the Community's sustainability. The changes in the distribution acres repercussions. (1) Repercussions well irrigation is concentrated in the fragile resource regions. More important, private people mostly financial irrigation, while canal and tank irrigation are financed by the state. This aggravated regional inequalities. (2) Development of well irrigation is less favourable to small and marginal formers when compared to canal tank irrigation due to high capital intensity[6].

Irrigation Spread

Assured irrigated water is a basic life input for sustainable agricultural development. Naturally, river side, delta areas got opportunity to change their agricultural methods and prospered well. Unfortunately, chronic drought prone areas were still suffering for want of irrigation water. The following table explains the area irrigated by different source scenario of Andha Pradesh.

The Table 2 reveals that out of 55.48 hectares of gross area irrigated in the state, 23.6 per cent was the area shown more than once during 2001-02. West Godavari district had the large extent of gross area irrigated in the state with a share of 10.18 per cent of total gross area irrigated followed by East Godavari with 8.06 per cent share.

In Andhra Pradesh, cheapest input is canal irrigation. In Coastal Andhra in *kharif* crops, more than 50 per cent area was irrigated in 5 districts, out of 9 districts. The other four districts had above 30 per cent canal irrigation. Area of non-food crops in Coastal Andhra were below 10 per cent. It received lion share of 49 per cent of area irrigated.

In Rayalaseema district canal irrigation except in Kurnool District, all are negligible. But much of irrigation was based on ground water, which was around 60 per cent. Agriculture was shifted to non-food crops, which was uncertain and risky, so that more suicides had taken place in this region. State policies like cheap rice, cheap power, ground water policies

Table 2
Net Area Irrigated by Sources, District-wise-2001-02

District	Canals	Tanks	Tube-well/ other/ other sources	Total in (hectares)	Area Irrigated more than once	Total food crops (in per cent)	Total Non-Foods crops (in per cent)
Coastal Andhra							
Srikakulam	55.0	34.0	11.0	1,67,036 (100.0)	6.0	96.0	4.0
Vizianagaram	31.0	56.0	13.0	1,154,16 (100.0)	22.0	95.0	5.0
Visakapatnam	38.0	24.0	38.0	91,332 (100.0)	41.0	97.0	3.0
East Godavari	68.0	8.0	24.0	2,61,965 (100.0)	71.0	95.0	5.0
West Godavari	56.0	0.5	43.50	3,35,318 (100.0)	68.0	91.0	9.0
Krishna	77	5.0	18.0	2,93,485 (100.0)	36.0	98.0	2.0
Guntur	82.0	2.0	16.0	3,68,956 (100.0)	5.0	93.0	7.0
Prakasam	36.0	16.0	48.0	2,04,971 (100.0)	4.0	87.0	13.0
Nellore	31.0	31.0	38.0	2,38,445 (100.0)	13.0	93.0	7.0
Total				20,76,924 (49.0)			
Rayalaseema							
Chittoor	1.0	22.0	77.0	1,75,438 (100.0)	28.0	80.0	20.0
Cuddapah	12.0	10.0	78.0	1,52,071 (100.0)	19.0	65.0	35.0
Anantapur	21.0	11.0	68.0	1,43,366 (100.0)	24.0	67.0	33.0
Kurnool	37.0	6.0	57.0	1,65,938 (100.0)	25.0	63.0	37.0
Total				6,36,813 (15.0)			
Telangana							
Mahabubnagar	10.0	4.0	86.0	163,606 (100.0)	28.0	71.0	29.0

Contd...

District	Canals	Tanks	Tube-well/ other/ other sources	Total in (hec-tares)	Area Irrigated more than once	Total food crops (in per cent)	Total Non-Foods crops (in per cent)
Ranga Reddy	4.0	4.0	92.0	71,904 (100.0)	22.0	89.0	11.0
Hyderabad	-	-	-		-	-	-
Medak	2.0	6.0	92.0	130,209 (100.0)	44.0	97.0	3.0
Nizamabad	15.0	11.0	74.0	168,313 (100.0)	59.0	96.0	4.0
Adilabad	32.0	28.0	40.0	76,112 (100.0)	23.0	91.0	9.0
Karimagar	25.0	11.0	64.0	2,62,858 (100.0)	47.0	88.0	12.0
Warangal	1.0	19.0	80.0	3,02,001 (100.0)	18.0	64.0	36.0
Khammam	30.0	22.0	48.0	1,55,068 (100.0)	8.0	88.0	12.0
Nalgonda	32.0	7.0	51.0	1,94,060 (100.0)	40.0	95.0	5.0
Total				1524131 (36.0)			
Andhra Pradesh	37.0	13.0	26.0	42,37,868 (100.0)	36.0	87.0	13.0

Source: GOAP; Statistical Abstract of Andhra Pradesh 2003, pp. 33.

were further put this region under more stress and strain. It got only 15 per cent area under irrigation in the state.

The Telangana region, with the exceptions of Khammam and Nalgonda districts, all other district had less than 30 per cent canal irrigation. Eight districts depended on ground water, which was highly fluctuated and unpredictable. Mahabub Nagar and Warangal districts went for around 30 per cent non-food crops, which also suffered under suicide shocks. In the state, 36 per cent of irrigated area was found in it

The south-western part of Andhra Pradesh, Rayalaseema was comparatively highly backward both in irrigation and agriculture than Telangana and Coastal Andhra, simultaneously income income and employment levels also. In fact, State has to apply location- specific policies, than homogeneous policies to make it sustainable. Equal rights on water distribution for all is a basic ethics. This moral code failed over Rayalaseema region after independence especially Sri Bagh pact, 1937, Bachawat Tribunal Award and State Governments. The two rich regions–Coastal Andhra and Telangana–are working tirelessly denying water rights to Rayalaseema due to weak socio-economic, political and cultural leadership eg: Pothireddipadu Head Regulator height issue. It proved that Rayalaseema *begger thy neighbour policy* in Andhra Pradesh irrigation politics the above facts proved that coastal Andhra and Telangana political leaders are interested to see Rayalaseema as beggar also for irrigated water.

Krishna Water Distribution Dispute: Bachawat Tribunal

In 1960, Maharastra, Orissa, Karnataka states had raised river water dispute. After prolonged dialogue and formation of States, in March 23, 1963 Centre brought an award that under Krishna 800 TMCs to Andhra Pradesh, 600 TMCs to Karnataka and 400 TMCs to Maharastra. Again in April 10, 1969, the tribunal changed its verdict, in such a way that Karnataka 700 TMCs, Maharastra 600 TMCs and Andhra Pradesh 800 TMCs had to be utilised. Surplus water can be used by Andhra Pradesh. This award should have been reviewed after May 31, 2000. Meanwhile, Karanataka State had raised the height of many projects like Almatti and led to chronic water dispute.

Godavari River Water Tribunal Award

During Dec. 19, 1975-August 7, 1978, State for Andhra Pradesh was interested to construct Ichampalli project. According to Tribunal, the Andhra Pradesh can avail 1495 TMCs water. Down stream projects like Penuganga, Lendi were considered as projects, whereas Pranahita project will go with Andhra Pradesh Government.

Under ioint venture, Tungabhadra Project was started in 1956 and gives water to 86, 617 hectares covers Anantapur, Kadapa and Kurnool Districts. Somasila on Penna in Nellore

District was started and covered an area of 56,295 hectares. Yeleru project was launched with Rs. 335 crores, finished the first stage and stabilized ayacut of 44,200 hectares. Polavaram on Godavari, covering an area of 2.9 lakhs hectares, still environmental impact assessment report has not come. Srisailam project, Telugu Ganga, Singur project, Priyadarshni Jurala project, Nizamsagar, Gannavaram Acquiduct, Sunkesula barrage, Pothireddipadu lift, Pulichintala, Alaganur Balancing Reservoir, Galeru-Nagari canal project, Hundri-niva Sujalasravanthi, Bhima lift Irrigation are in different stages.

Issues like the lack of capital, managerial deficiencies, shortage of leadership, failure of efficient political will, bad governance entailed the pace of the projects not to move fastly. By all means, by channeling water resource in right way to field can raise the yield rate upto 50 to 60 per cent higher[7].

As water levels are falling rapidly, there is a big shift has come up that in future marginal, small farmers may not get irrigated water resources, only medium and large farmers would enjoy. Much of water budget and amounts had been used for diverting water to industrial development, hydel power and drinkable water distribution to Urban areas, than farmers. In fact, in the State, 55 per cent of irrigated water is going to roots of crops and rest is in drainage. Water Users Associations have to play effective role in distribution of water, cropping pattern, pricing of water, water budgeting; which are still infant stage in understanding water democracy. Scientific irrigation schedules must be based on a through understanding of soil-water-Plant-atmosphere relationship[8].

Irrigation Projects and Oustees

In all irrigation projects, three issue are to be taken up carefully–designing project at particular location, construction of project with adequate capital and evacuating people to ensure intact ecology with the storage capacity of project. Vacating villages and tribals, submerging forest land, flora and fauna missing and environmental destruction would be considered seriously by State. Among them the most important issue is vacating people by force became a burning problem. So that many environmentalists like Vandanasiva, Medha Patkar, Sundarlal Bahuguna and opposition party leaders were stressing more on giving packages to oustee households, who are victims for large scale movement of men and materials from plateaus to plains. Minimum facilities are to be given for displaced people under any project, before construction.

Self-reliance Model of Anantapur District Irrigation

A Study in Anantapur District is briefly highlighted. In a family of 5 members, 2 children were studying Intermediate course. They own an ordinary mud-house and cattle-shed requiring some maintenance every year. The farmer is neither to traditional nor progressive and cultivates "less risky crops" like paddy, Ground-nut and sunflower. The dry land owned by him is not considered. It is arrived that Rs. 35,000/- per family was required for minimum level of subsistence (MLS). Rs. 400/- per person per month was required for food security alone i.e Rs. 24,000/- per annum for a family of 5 towards food expenditure alone. The other costs of health, education, house repairs, repairs and maintenance of agri-equipment would make up for Rs. 35,000/- MLS. One acre wet under irrigation even with three crops per year is inadequate to meet a family's MLS. The deficit is ranging from Rs. 8,300 to Rs. 19,600. Therefore, it suggests that having one acre under irrigation even with 3 crops per year is inadequate to meet a family's MLS. whereas 2 acres and 3 acres of irrigated land and with the possibility of 3 crops in a year, the projected surplus is Rs. 17,600/- and Rs. 42,400 respectively. So, 2 acres of wet land would provide some cushion for saving or making some capital investment on agriculture. However, the study indicated that mostly such a surplus went in for treatment of sickness as one or the other in the family fell sick every year. 30 per cent of the debts in a family are said to have been on account of sickness. Whereas 3 acres of wet, possibility of 3 crops provides a family with comfortable surplus over MLS. The farmer could afford for higher education, higher health needs, functions like marriage, purchase of luxury goods like T.V., motor cycle etc.

It is rarely possible to have three crops in a year in drought prone areas like Anantapur.

Of course, 2 crops a year situation of 3 acres scenario just crosses the MLS household and has a marginal surplus of Rs. 5,612 and 4 acres scenario provides a surplus of about Rs. 19,000 over the years chronic indebtedness has become an integral part of the rural households in drought prone regions. Excessive indebtedness in recent years had been driving the farmers towards long term or permanent migration. And some farmers have been resorting to suicides. This phenomena is not only limited to marginal and small farmers, but also spreading to medium and large farmers. Due to increasing input costs and falling output prices among farming community, the debt trap is covering more farmers[9].

The rich Districts are stabilising their ayacut while backward Rayalaseema is undergoing chronic droughts. The following is an illustration of Polavaram.

Polavaram Project: A Link between Krishna and Godavari

The project is to be built on Godavari, near Polavaram village in West Godavari, is expected to irrigate 7,21,000 acres in the districts of Krishna, West, and East Godavari and Visakapatnam. The project cost is estimated at Rs. 8,188 crores and another Rs. 4,500 crores for resettlement and rehabilitation. The project obtained site and environmental clearance recently and work already has begun on the Right and left canals and the spillway.

Irrigation and Revenue officials tentatively put the figure of displacement at a whopping 1,95,000 people–a majority of them Koya and Kondreddi tribes, making it one of the biggest shifting of indigenous people in the country for an irrigation project. The number of villages to be submerged is put at 280 in all, 209 in Khammam, 42 in East Godavari and 29 in West Godavari District. Twenty more villages in Chattisgrah and Orissa could be submerged. Such dams perpetrate cultural genocide of tribals. The Government offer of land, resettlement and rehabilitation packages were thin with poor track record from Nagarjunasagar. B.V. Raghavulu, CPI(M) politi-bureau member said that what is the worth of a project that submerges

2,00,000 acres of fertile land, uprooting 2,00,000 Advasis and creates a new ayacut in an agriculturally well developed region. By dam impact, tribes have started "Vertical migration" back to the hilltops occupying large chunks of forest. The non-Adivasis of the villages to be submerged echo similar sentiments, a farmer raised sugarcane that yield a high 60 tonnes an acre and tobacco eight to 10 quintals. Should we leave all this and go to a new place? People are already feeling the pinch, that is, relatives from other areas look to us, with pity, no new house construction or repairs, no work for a mason. The Project when completed would gobble up 3,500 hectares of forest area some of it typical to the eastern 'Ghats[10]'

By transferring Godavari Water to Krishna, to make Krishna, Guntur, Khammam Districts to stabilise ayacut. Therefore, it is a hope that Rayalaseema can avail more Krishna river water at Srisailam on to on-going Rayalaseema Projects.

Supplementary Support for Irrigation

Fortunately, State had given preference to short term, low cost, community associated minor irrigation tanks, watersheds, lifts, check dams by using different institutions. They are as follows.

A.P. State Irrigation Development Corporation

In 1974, State introduced Andhra Pradesh State Irrigation Development Corporation (APS IDC) to support lift irrigation, Tube wells, infiltration wells. It all started with good beginning but not worked for longer period, due to non-recovery of overdues and high establishment costs.

Andhra Pradesh State Ground Water Development

It had supported the Integrated Tribal Development Agency also, which was established to help Scheduled caste & Tribes, Backward caste farmers, like marginal and small farmers by extending financial cooperation, Technological support and extension activities to exploit ground water. It identifies levels of ground-water availability and also suggests grey areas. Scarcity of funds made it to grow slowly.

Panchayatraj Institutions

It had extended helping hand to 80,000 irrigation sources. By this institution around 14.90 lakhs acres were brought under *ayacut*. It maintains flood control, Tank maintenance. Lack of funds this institution is not effectively functioning in the State.

Cyclone Emergency Reconstruction Project

In May 1990, due to heavy rains and cyclones, many irrigation resources in Coastal districts were destroyed. State went to seek financial help from the World Bank. Though its financial estimate was Rs. 42 Crores, but spent only Rs. 10 crores.

Drainage Canal Schemes

Due to bad drainage facilities; delta districts crops were under low yield. Therefore, Krishna, Godavari, Nellore Districts were badly need of drainage canal facility. The total canal was 10,123 Kms under drainage with World Bank funds. State was interested to do drainage facility by collecting those loans spent through drainage cess, So that it brought two Acts in 1985, 1986 years. It is on snail walk.

Command Area Development Authority

It's Objectives are to maintain the level of land, soil health, canal management, *warabandi*, water management, planning, supervision. So that with scientific methodology the cultivation will be controlled and expanded for high yield rates the objectives were defeated and disturbed.

Water Users Associations (WUAs)

Andhra Pradesh is the first State, which introduced Water Users Associations through legislation in 1997. The Objective is to maximise irrigation potential improving efficiency and stakeholder participation. Under this Act, 10292 WUAs were formed. WUAs elections where conducted in March 2003 for 80 per cent of these minor irrigation systems. It has realised some positive results. Many WUAs Presidents have become money making ventures, than extending irrigation potential.

Conclusion

Unfortunately, Rayalaseema before independence suffered under Sultans, feudal lords, British and presently with State government's uneven policies. Where ever plenty of water was their civilizations flourished. When water shortage is there, the society faces all types problems like factionalism, growing hunger, immeasurable poverty, jungle of unemployment. Arthur Cotton, is the father of irrigated projects, who introduced Kurnool-Kadapa Canal. Irrigation alone cannot solve agriculture and rural problems. But irrigation can solve many lingering problems and integrates development. Rayalaseema had suffered under chronic droughts and famines. Comparing other two regions with Rayalaseema's irrigation scenario, it is at low ebb. The irrigation spread is around 15 per cent, which is highly negligible to overall development. The other two regions–Telangana and Coastal Andhra-were completing existing projects, denied the rights of Rayalaseema like Sri Bagh Pact, Bachawat Award, even after fifty years of independence. The hypothesis is that minimum three acres and two wets irrigations can make a household of five members to sustain. Godavari water is to be transferred from Polavaram to Krishna for Prakasam Barrage, then Krishna river water can be diverted to Rayalaseema projects from reservoir of Srisailam. Besides long term projects of Rayalaseema districts, encourage short term projects like watersheds, check dams, water harvesters, sprinklers, drips and awareness campaign will improve the condition. The two elderly brothers should not show step mother policies over continuously suffered youngest brother–Rayalaseema. Let extend helping hand to Rayalaseema's irrigation.

Notes and References

1. K. R. Daley (2003), Integrated Development and Management of Local Resources and Exogenous Water, National Seminar on Water, CESS, Hyderabad, July 30-31 p. 12.
2. T. Hamumantha Rao (2003), Multipurpose Utilisation of Godavari River and the Relevancy of Interlinking of Rivers, CESS, July 30-31, p. 23.

3. Government of A.P. (2005), Economic Survey 2004-05, p. 61.
4. A. Ranga Reddy (2003), The State of Rayalaseema, Mitta Publication, New Delhi.
5. V. Ratna Reddy (2003), Irrigation: Department and Reforms *Economic and Political Weekly,* March 22-29, p. 1181.
6. V. Ratna Reddy (2003), Irrigation: Development and Reforms Andhra Pradesh: Economic Reforms and Challenges Ahead CESS, Hyderabad.

Vidyabhusan (2005), Comprehensive Irrigation Projects in Effectiv Planning, *Veekshanam,* Nov. 15, pp. 16-18.

8. S. S. Prihar & B. S. Sandhu (1987), Irrigation of Field Crops, NCAR New Delhi, p. 5.
9. Y.V. Malla Reddy (2003), Irrigation and Poverty Among Farmers Micro-perspective, CESS on National Seminar on Water durin July, 30-31, pp. 59-65.)
10. K. Venkateswarlu (2006), Issues: Displaced Development, *Th Hindu,* Magazine, Jan. 8.

3

AGRI–INDUSTRY NEEDS MORE CORPORATE INVESTMENT

In India, 65 per cent of the population living in rural area and around 10 crores households are depending on agriculture as a livelihood. The need for rural industrialization can be hardly over emphasized. Since it has been endowed with vast and varied natural, human and man-made resources, exploration and exploitation of these resources can contribute substantially to economic development. A large number of unemployed and under employed people may have to found jobs in activities other than direct cultivation of land and growing crops. This is because the land-man ratio in many parts of our country is already such that engaging more workers on land may not prove very productive i.e., disguised unemployment. Apart from the need for creation of non-form employment opportunities in rural areas to reduce the pressure on land and also to provide a deeper and wider base for the rural economy. The scope and prospects of development of rural industries particularly, agri-based industries are to be addressed.

Review of Literature

Rural development is a pre-requisite for the structural transformation of an economy. This can be achieved by taking industry to the rural areas on a large scale. Agri-based industries in countryside hold great promise to bring about substantial improvement in the quality of life of rural people. Agri-based industries is that the share in the total production of all the industries is nearly 50 per cent. These industries also represent about 23 per cent in terms of total value added in our country. According to an estimate by the United Nations Food and Agriculture Organization (F.A.O.) these industries account for about half of the total value added in developing countries. Liberalization measures encourage the rich to become richer but should not leave the poor to become poorer. Siman Kuznets also confirmed the contribution of agriculture to economic growth through Agri-based industries[1]. According to British economist schumacher advocated a programme of balanced developed between industry and agriculture, and saw the potential for industrial achievements to make rural people's lives less arduous and their livelihoods more production, secure and sustainable[2]. Japan took a pragmatic view of its large agricultural base and made the best use of it. When modernization of agriculture threw out a large agricultural population as surplus not required in agriculture, it was utilized by starting and encouraging agricultural industries using a sort of intermediate technology and tools. The agriculturists also did not go to distant places in search of employment. Job was provided in around their places of residence. Only a quarter of them depend upon agriculture. Thirty five per cent of them have part time jobs in manufacturing industries and about 40 per cent primarily rely on agricultural industries[3]. Coir industry in kerala is the second to agriculture as a source of employment in this state. There is a technological change in Coir sector through indigenously developed technique in that adversely affecting the employment potential of the sector[4].

Balance of Agriculture and Industry

We have bear in mind that there cannot be prosperity in agriculture without prosperity in industry. Interlining of these two sector has one more angle, that is, the continuous investment in land and adoption of improved techniques of production decrease the demand of labour working on form lands. Absorption of surplus labour thus released is possible only if simultaneously industries are set up in the rural sector. It is estimated that the rural labour force shown an increasing trend from 199.60 million in 1992-93 to 270. 50 million during 2001-02.

Conversion of paddy into rice, production of *atta* from wheat, preparation of pickles from mangoes, lemons etc., baking of bread and biscuits and making fruit juices are a few examples. However, in the early 1980s, the Government of India felt the need for sustain and organized efforts to give a boost to this sector. With the twin objectives of reducing wastage of, and adding value to farm produce and setting up of an exclusive Dept. of food Processing, Industries in the Ministry of Agriculture[5].

Agri-based industries can be identified as those processing industries which use large quantities of agricultural the raw-materials as its inputs. In order to bring about industrialization in a developing economy, promotion of agri-based industries forms an integral part of overall developmental strategy.

In Andhra Pradesh the industry wise data on working of factories under the factories Act during 2002 shows that there are 30, 747 factories in the state. Highest number of 13, 737 i.e., factories are under the industry group of manufacture of food products and Beverages[6].

Inter-locking of Agriculture and Small Industry

The process of agri-industrialization owes itself to the rising pace of agricultural commercialization and the expanding volume of surpluses that build the supply chain between agriculture and industry. Many of the Agri-industrial enterprises come up right in the villages themselves some of which, depend on the size, location and connectivity of the village, may be small scale modern factories or processing mills. Commercial surpluses from agriculture give rise to a whole chain of industrial activities in the rural areas themselves. Most conspicuous examples are wheat flour and rice milling, oil extraction, cotton processing and ginning, sugarcane processing, leather tanning and leather products, dairy and poultry products, wooden furniture and fixtures and on.

Rising income levels in rural areas have their own impact on industrial output and employment, the benefit of which must partially accrue to the rural people themselves. The standard examples of the demand-driven local industrial activities are making of shoes and other leather products, Pottery, rope making, handlooms, black smithy, carpentry, making of Jewellery and other wearing apparels, sweet meat making, dairy and poultry products, wheat flour and rice milling, raw sugar, beverages and tobacco products and so on[7].

In 2000-01, in rural India, more than 99.0 per cent of manufacturing units and nearly 90.0 of manufacturing employment, were in the un-organized segment alone.

About the relationship between the rate of growth of agricultural output and that of gross value added in individual food processing sub-sectors, four scenarios stand out clearly.

Chart 1

First Scenario	*Second Scenario*	*Third Scenario*	*Fourth Scenario*
1. Preservation fruits and vegetables 2. Curing-roasting, grinding blending of coffee 3. Manufacture of prepared animal/ bird feeds 4. Manufacture of starch 5. Manufacture of soft drinks and syrups 6. Beverages-tobacco.	1. Dairy products 2. Canning - preserving of fish 3. Grain milling 4. Processing and blending of tea	1. Slaughtering preparation-preservation of meat 2. Manufacturing and refining of sugar 3. Indigenous sugar *boora, Khandasari and gur,* sugar confectionery	1. Distilling, rectifying and blending of spirits 2. Manufacturing of malt liquors and malt 3. Manufacture of cigars

After all, agri-industry does also operate under a policy frame work, and it is possible that, in spite of a robust growth of the incoming agricultural commodities, the industry faces an unfriendly policy regime that does not allow it to pick up all that agriculture can deliver.

Private Sector Partnership

One of the widely expressed concerns is that public investment in agriculture is steadily declining. It is claimed that the burden of subsidy faced by the government has limited the scope for public investment. It is also to be appreciated in the market economy, public sector alone cannot fill the investment. Improving the climate for private investment and employment is very much essential.

Corporate sector entry into agriculture using information technology and by providing market access to products has proved very successful in recent years. The e-choupal of ITC, Kisan Sanchar of TATA, Agribusiness of Godrej, Shulakh of Mahendra and Rural Malls of shriram are some example. Other corporate houses like Bharati, Pepsi, Reliance and the like have also entered the agriculture sector. This has improved the services such as extension and input supply, market linkages including market intelligence and better prices[8].

Indian farmer slowly moving towards corporate linkages. Market analysts are terming this opportunity in agriculture as the next big growth driver, with demand coming not only from the domestic market but also from overseas. In fact, the opportunity for growth is immense with less than 1.5 per cent of the food undergoing processing in the country. This is miniscule compared to Thailand, Malaysia and Brazil where it is as much as 65- 75 per cent. The segment, with immense potential, is projected to growth at a high double – digit rate. A study conducted by Mc kinsey and the confederation of Indian Industry (C11) pegs the turnover of the total food market at approximately Rs. 2.5 lakh core. Retailing in general and food retailing in particular is one of the high-growth sectors. Food retaining is to grow 10 fold in five years. For a lot of Indian companies, this may pose a good business opportunity.

In fact, both Reliance and retailing giant pantaloon are learnt to be in the process of partnering with farmers to source food grams, fresh vegetables, fruits and processed foods directly. Similarly, Bharati, which is in talks with several foreign retailer, including Tesco, to foray into food retailing can derive synergies from its subsidiary field fresh foods, a 50:50 joint venture with the Rothschild group. Field fresh, which started of with an investment of Rs. 250 crore, could become the supply lime for Bharati's proposed retailing business. The company has been working with farmers in Punjab, Jammu & Kashmir, has been Himachal Pradesh and Uttaranchal to source apples, Kinnos, litchis, cherries and tomatoes among other products. This post folio may soon increase to include grapes, mangoes, and bananas[9].

Liberalization: Ready to Eat

India's 25 crore strong middle class is looking towards packaged and convenient food products. On one side growing urbanization and changing food habits, the demand has been ever raising for ready to mix or eat products. Since liberalization, food market turnover was Rs. 2,50,000 crores, out of which value added products that include convenience foods comprise Rs. 80,000 crores. The size of the semi-processed and ready to eat packaged food industry is over Rs. 4,00 crores ($1 billion) and is growing at over 20 per cent annually. Higher awareness of quality has led to a growing demand for packaged foods even for basic ingredients like salt, atta. Only segment where processing has been all these years is tomato ketchups, jams and fruit squashes. This too has largely been more less an urban phenomenon.

India is the world's second largest producer of fruit and vegetables, but hardly 2 per cent of the produce is processed. India is the land of spice producing all varieties worth over Rs. 3,500 crores ($ 900 million) amounting to 25-30 per cent of the world's production, which is processed for value-addition and exports. It grows 22 million tonnes of oil seeds covering most of the varieties. Other important plantation products includes tea, Coffee, Coca and cashew.

India has large marine products and processing potential with varied fish resources along the 8041 km. Long coastline, 28000 km of rivers and millions of hectares of reservoirs and brackish water. India's livestock population is the largest in the world with 50 per cent of world's buffaloes and 20 per cent of cattle, but only about one per cent of total meat production is converted to value added products. India is the largest milk producer and about 15 per cent of the total milk production is processed through the organized sector.

Towards Agri-trade

Under special agricultural produce scheme, Government of India encouraged export of fruits, vegetables, flowers, minor forest produce, dairy, poultry and their value added products produced and processed by exports. The proportion of Agri-exports to total exports came down from 11.9 per cent in 2003-04 to 10.2 per cent in 2004-05. The import of Agricultural and allied products during 2004-05 was at US $ 381.1 crore as compared to US $ 370-82 during 2003-04[10].

The Table 1 gives an impression that one-third of exports are Rice and marine products and also foreign exchange. Whereas in imports, vegetables oils has taken lion share of two third and next are pulses and cashew nuts.

In total exports, for the year 2004-05 year agri-exports are 10.2 per cent only and imports are 3.5 per cent. Under globalization and World Trade Organization regime, a change in agriculture development and diversification is needed. It means, more investment is to be invested over agricultural revolution.

Eleventh Five Year Plan (2007-2012)

The stage is being set for large scale entry if corporates in agricultural sector. The government may formulate a comprehensive contract farming to accelerate agricultural sector growth. Corporate investments as one of the major vehicles in introducing crop diversification, creating market linkages and established cold chains. It is to encourage

Table 1
Agricultural Exports and Imports 2004-2005.

	Exports			*Imports*	
Item	*Crores of US $*	*Percentage share of Agri-exports*	*item*	*Crores of US $*	*Percentage share of Agri-exports*
Tea & Coffee	62.14	7.8	Cereals	2.49	0.7
Rice	147.82	18.5	Pulses	38.25	10.1
Wheat	32.23	4.0	Milk and Cream	0.29	0.1
Sugar & Molasses	3.32	0.4	Cashew nuts raw	39.11	10.4
Tobacco	27.75	3.5	Fruits and nuts ex.	23.53	6.2
Spices	39.93	5.0	Sugar	21.24	5.6
Cashew	52.00	6.5	Oil seeds	0.57	0.2
Sesame	14.75	1.8	Vegetables oils (Fixed edible)	239.39	63.4
Niger seeds	1.35	0.2	Others	16.24	3.43
Guargum meal	14.60	1.8	*Agricultural imports*	381.11	100.0
Oil meal	69.01	8.6	Total Imports	10,706.97	-
Fruit & vegetables	36.17	4.5	Agri-imports as % of total imports	-	3.5
Processed Foods (Fruits and vegetables)	34.42	4.3			
Meat and Meat preparation	38.60	4.8			
Marine products	126.76	15.8			
Others	99.32	12.5			
Agricultural Exports	800.17	100.0			
Total Exports	7820.53	-			
Agri-exports as % of total exports	-	10.2			

Source: Govt. of India (2006) Economic survey 2005-06, p. 172

small farmers to come together and enable them for crop diversification. A legal frame work will be made to boost up contract farming[11].

Conclusion

India lives in Bharat. No Salivation for India with out revolutionary changes in Indian agriculture and farmers mind set. Traditional products of paddy to rice, tomato to Ketchup, Mangoes to pickles to ready made quality mixes/foods become part of high and middle income households, who are around 25 crores in this country. Corporate entry into agriculture and rural economic scenario, with information technology has been proving very successful. Agri-exports in total exports of India was 10 per cent for the year 2004-05, which is quite insignificant. There is a big potential for agriculture, which is to be scientifically explored to meet the challenges of world Trade organization and developed countries. Nonetheless, Corporate capital as to enter into agriculture sector in a big way, without hunting marginal and small farmers.

Notes and References

1. Siman Kuznets (1971), Notes on stages of Economic Growth as a System Determinant, in Comparison of Economic Systems, p. 24, 3.
2. E. F. Shumacher (1973), Small is Beautiful: A Study of Economics as it People Mattered, p. 161.
3. A. Ramaswamy (1969), Rationale of Agri-Industrial Integration in India, *Khadigramodyog,* Vol. 15.
4. Dr. M. K. Ramachandram (2004), Economics of Agri-based Industries in Kerala *W.S.R.* to Bamboo and Coir (Unpublished Thesis). M.G. University, Kottayam, p. 279.
5. B. S. Padmanabhan (2001), Food Processing Set for Quantum, *The Hindu Survey of Industry,* p. 284.
6. DES, Govt. of A.P. (2005), Statistical Abstract, A.P., p. 196.
7. G. K. Chadha (2005), Agriculture and Rural Industrialization in India: Recent Development and Future Choices, edited by CESS Silver Jubilee Seminar on *Perspectives on Equitable Development: International Experience and what can India learn?* Hyderabad.

8. Dr. S. Rajakuthy (2005), Mixed Bag of Results, *The Hindu Survey of Indian Agriculture*, p. 198.
9. Neha Kaushik and Dharini Nagarajan (2006), The Opportunity in Green, *The Hindu Business Line*, Band line p. 1.
10. Govt. of India (2006), Economic Survey 2005-2006, p. 171.
11. Subash Narayan (2006), Corporate can Make Agri Foray, *The Economic Times*, June 27.

4

SUSTAINABLE AGRICULTURAL DEVELOPMENT FOR ORGANIC FARMING: AN INEVITABLE PHASE NEEDED

Still, Agricultural Development is a backbone for this great country, inspite of 22 per cent contribution to Gross Domestic product and 58 per cent took livelihood in Rural India. Two-third sown area is under recurring droughts and famines. It has recommended that pro-poor rural and agricultural development should be promoted by increasing investments in rural infrastructure and agricultural research and development (R & D). Social safety nets should be re-oriented to create more employment in rural areas, and the human resource base should be strengthened through education, nutrition and empowerment of women. Better physical infrastructure should be built, Water Management and institutions should be reformed and water pricing system should be designed on the basis of water rights to cope with increasing scarce water supplies for agriculture[1].

Sustainability of Agriculture

National Commission on Farmers feels that a 3-pronged strategy needs to be introduced to ensure the economic well being and nutrition security of rural families. First, families possessing assets like land, livestock or fish ponds will have to be assisted to enhance the productivity of their resource endowments in an environmentally and economically sustainable basis. *Second,* nearly a third of the rural population and a large proportion of women earn their livelihood through wage employment, who needs empowerment. The *third* group are rural artisans working in the secondary and tertiary sectors of the economy. Their skills will have to be mobilised to enhance the competitiveness of agriculture through value-addition to primary products and diversification of livelihood opportunities. The three pronged strategy consists of improving the productivity of land, labour, water, livestock and enhance the skills of families and labourers in the secondary and tertiary sectors of the rural economy. So that they are able to assist in improving agricultural efficiency and competitiveness and in ending the prevailing mismatch between production and post-harvesting technologies[2].

There is increasing feminisation in families with small and marginal holdings, due to out migration of men. The proposed conferment of land rights to women will help to redress this distressing situation. Meanwhile, joint *pattas* will have to be issued to make women eligible for institutional credit.

The green revolution was mainly directed to increase the production of food grains. It did not affect initially the production of commercial crops or cash crops such as sugarcane, cotton, jute, oil seeds. Later there was a considerable improvement in the production of cash crops. As a result of the green revolution, the crop pattern in India has undergone two significant changes. The output of cereals has risen at the rate of 3 to 4 per cent per annum but the output of pulses has remained stagnant.

The new technology and modernisation of agriculture has strengthened the linkage between agriculture and industry. Agriculture modernisation has created a larger demand for inputs produced and supplied by industries to agriculture and thus the backward linkage has also become quite strong. In this way, the linkage between agriculture and industry has got strengthened. In fact, new agricultural technology has made the farmer market oriented. The farmers are largely dependent on the market for the supply of inputs and for the demand for their output. Many inputs-like credit size, cost of seeds, price of mechanisation have increased, because of superiority of traditional technology.

Growth in Agriculture

Agriculture and allied sector value added registered a growth rate of 9.1 per cent in 2003-04, reflecting the growth in physical production and remunerative prices of agricultural goods. The growth rate of the sector for 2003-04 was one of the highest in recent years, and only marginally lower than the previous high of 9.6 per cent achieved in 1996-97[3]. The farm sector, which grew by 1.1 per cent last year, could even surpass 3 per cent this fiscal. 3-3.5 per cent may be next year. The average growth rate for Tenth five year plan will be 2 per cent[4].

Capital Formation

In Indian Agriculture (2006), capital formation was on the decline in the share of agriculture sector. Capital formation in GDP from 1.9 per cent in the early 1990's to 1.3 per cent in the early 2000s is a matter of concern. This declining share was due mainly to the stagnation or fall in public investment in agriculture, particularly since the mid-1990s. However, there is indication of a reversal of this trend of late with the public sector investment in agriculture attaining a 5 year high in 2002-03.

Agri-Trade

Agricultural exports increased from $ 5.9 billion in 2001-02 to $ 6.7 billion in 2002-03. However, as a percentage of total mercandise exports, the share of agri-exports declined from 13.5 per cent in 2001-02 to 12.8 per cent in 2002-03. Marine products, contributing around 20 per cent of the total agri-exports, is amongst the dominant items of the agri-exports of the country. The exports of food grains have picked up considerably in recent years, accounting for around 20 per cent of the agri-exports.

The imports of agricultural products increased to $ 2.8 billion in 2002-03 from $ 2.3 billion 2001-02. The share of agri-imports in total merchandise imports increased from 4.5 per cent to 4.6 per cent over the same period. Edible oil, which accounts for almost two-thirds of the total agri-imports.

Marketing of agricultural produce is the most important activity for the farming community, particularly for those who are small producers and have small surpluses for marketing. To benefit the farming community from new market access opportunities, the internal agricultural marketing system in the country needs to be integrated and strengthened. Union Ministry of Agriculture is interested to amend the State APMC Act to encourage development of competitive agricultural markets in the private and cooperative sectors, and de-regulation of marketing system to promote private investment in marketing infrastructure. A model law will come into force like establishment of direct purchase centres, consumers/ farmers markets for direct sale, prohibition of commission agency, contract farming, standardisation of product, training farmers.

Eco-friendly Horticulture

It is recognized as an important avenue for diversification in agriculture in an eco-friendly manner through efficient land use, optimum utilisation of natural resources and creation of employment opportunities, particularly for unemployed youth and women. The sector was given a boost by enhancing its outlay from Rs. 1000 crore in the Eighth Plan, to Rs. 1,454 crore in Ninth Plan and further to Rs. 2,105 crore in the Tenth Plan. India got leadership in the production of many commodities like mango, banana, coconut, arecanut, cashew, ginger, turmeric and black pepper. India accounts for 10 per cent of the world fruit production with first rank in the production of banana, Sapota and acid lime. India is also the largest producer of milk, the fifth longest producer of eggs and seventh largest producer of meat. It is necessary to improve cold storage and refrigerated transportation, processing, quality control, package facilities and develop efficient marketing and export networks to optimize the production and export potentialities in respect of these products[5].

Livestock an Fisheries

Economic survey plays an important role in the economy and in the socio economic development of the country. Livestock sector produces 86.4 million tones of milk, 41.7 billion eggs, 52.1 million Kgs of wool, 4.94 million on tones of meat and 6.2 million tones of fish in 2002 2003. The sector provides regular employment to 11 million in principal status and 9 million in subsidiary status. Women constitute 69 per cent of the labour force in livestock sector as against 35 per cent in crop farming. The livestock and fishery sector contributed 6.5 per cent to total GDP (5.4 per cent from livestock and 1.1 per cent from fisheries in 2002 03[7].

Awareness Campaign on Organic Farming Dhule District, Maharastra Experiment

There are mounds of compost and under a large tree is a 'laboratory'. They makes a bio-spray called "top 10" using 10 kinds of leaves, and various other concoctions using cow dung, egg shells, powdered gravel, etc. They have a large variety of produce on farm, including an orchard of guavas intercropped with drum-stick trees.

Now farmers are learning to re-cycle waste, recognise the value of certain insects, the importance of birds, using seeds untreated with chemicals and new ways of handling pests using home made preparations.

While organic farming in Maharashtra is not as highly developed as an Uttaranchal, it is growing. Since 2003 about 5,00,000 hectares is under organic farming. The Dhule district alone, more than one lakh hectares is under organic farming, with about 2,500 hectares certified as organic. About 3,50,000 farmers are growing organic produce now all over Maharashtra[6].

In an effort to spread greater awareness organic farming among the masses, Karnataka government plans to introduce lessons in the primary and secondary school curriculum. The Dept. of Agriculture is taking up the matter with the help of Department of education to include in lessons in the Science book from next academic year. At present, now the Agriculture

Dept. has drafted contents of the lessons on organic farming. As of now only, the Agriculture Universities offer causes at the degree level and post graduate levels in organic farming. The Ministry of Agriculture is planning to bring same 17,600 hectares under organic farming in the State during current year[7]. Due to increase in suicidal cases among farmers, the centre has revised insurance policy to the forming community.

Agricultural Insurance

National Agricultural Insurance Scheme (NAIS)

In place of the Comprehensive Crop Insurance Scheme (CCIS), government introduced a new scheme entitled "National Agricultural Insurance Scheme (NAIS) from Rabi 1999 2000 season. The scheme is available to all farmers (both loanee and non loanee) irrespective of their size of land holdings. It envisages coverage of all the food crops, oilseeds, horticultural crops, in respect of which past yield data are available for an adequate number of years. Already eleven crops, viz., annual banana, chillies, cotton, ginger, jute, pineapple, onion, potato, sugarcane, tapioca and turmeric, have been covered under the scheme. All other annual commercial/horticultural crops will be placed under insurance cover in due course of time subject to availability of past yield data. The premium rates are 3.5 per cent of sum insured for bajra and oil seeds, 2.5 per cent for other kharif crops, 1.5 per cent for wheat, and 2 per cent for other rabi crops, while actuarial rates are changed in the case of commercial/horticultural crops. Small and marginal farmers are entitled to a subsidy of 50 per cent of the premium, which is shared on 50 : 50 basis by the central and state governments. The premium subsidy will be phased out over a period of 5 years.

The scheme is operating on the basis of 'Area Approach' i.e., defined areas for each notified crops for wide spread calamities, and on an individual basis for localized calamities such as hailstorm, landslide, cyclone and flood. At present, the scheme is being implemented in 23 states and 2 union territories[8].

Farm Income Insurance Scheme (FIIS)

In order to target the two critical components of a farmer's income, namely yield and price, through a single policy instrument, the Department of Agriculture and Cooperation formulated the Farm Income Insurance Scheme (FIIS). The scheme was conceived to provide income protection to the farmers by integrating the mechanism of insuring production as well as market risks. It has been taken up on pilot basis in Rabi 2003 04 in 18 districts of 12 states for wheat and paddy. Slowly it will be appropriately fine tuned as necessary of course, insurance schemes were not succeeded.

10th Plan Priorities

It had several areas of priorities. The most important is raising the cropping intensity of existing agricultural land. The first area is public investment in irrigation which has fallen significantly over succeeding plan periods, which is to be revived and also water management. The Accelerated Irrigation Benefit Programme is potentially important instrument for providing resources to state governments in support of ongoing irrigation schemes. The *second* priority must be development of other rural infrastructure that supports all rural economic activities. The *third* area is the development and dissemination of agricultural technologies. *Fourthly,* serious thoughts needed to be given to the issue of declining public investment in agriculture. *Finally,* there is need to diversify Indian agriculture both geographically and over time[9].

Conclusion

Sincere efforts that state have to promote organic farming. The Government should not subsidize pesticides and chemical fertilizers, while simultaneously promoting organic farming. A combination of spreading awareness, more commitment infrastructure are necessary to ensure that farmers do not lose our on the new revolution.

It is found that organic farming leads to sustainable development. Land, labour, capital and organisation are to be used rationally for sustainable approach of nature. Capital formation is found very meagre in post economic reforms period. Integration of cropping pattern, horticulture, livestocks, insurance protection, state intervention have to go directly to enhance the organic farming system in total for sustainability farming. Uttaranchal is leading in this farming follows other states.

Notes and References

1. G.Venkataramani (2005), Making a Smart Economy, *The Hindu, Survey of Indian Agriculture*, 2005, p. 6.
2. Prof. M. S. Swaminathan, (2005), Sustainable Farming: Three Pronged Strategy Needed, *The Hindu, Survey of Indian Agriculture*, p. 8.
3. Govt. of India (2004), *Economic Survey*, 2004, p. 155.
4. Press Trust of India, (Farm Sector, poised to growth 3 per cent) *The Economic Times*, 9th Feb. 2006.
5. Ministry of Finance Economic Survey, 2003-2004, p. 169.
6. Meena Menon (2005), Success Stories: Dhule: Organic Revolution, *The Hindu, Survey of the Environment*, p. 138.
7. Mahesh Kulkarni (2006), Organic Farming Lessions in School to Catch'em Young. *The Economic Times*, Feb. 7.
8. Govt. of India (2004), Economic Survey, 2003-04, p. 162.
9. Prabhakar Deshpande (2006), Thought for Food. *The Economic Times*, Feb., 15.

5

IMPACT OF GLOBALISATION ON INDIAN INFORMAL HOME WORKERS

Introduction

Globalisation is the process of integration of economies across the world through Cross-border flow of factors, products and information.

The Universal economic liberalisation which gathered momentum in the last two decades of the twentieth century, reinforced and enforced by the World Trade Organisation, seems to have made globalisation irreversible and unstoppable. "All institutions have to make global competitiveness a strategic goal. No institution, whether a business, a university or a hospital, can hope to survive, let alone to succeed, unless it measured up to the standards set by the leaders in its filed, any place in the world".[1] Globalisation, of course, is not a new phenomenon. The period 1870 to 1914 experienced a growing trend towards globalisation. The new phase of globalisation which started around the mid-20th Century became widespread, more pronounced and over changing since the late 1980's by gathering momentum from the political and economic changes that swept across the Communist Countries the economic reforms in other countries, the latest multi-lateral trade agreement which seeks to substantially liberalise international trade and investment, and the technological and communication revolutions. Globalisation may considered at two levels, viz., at the macro level and at the micro-level.

Benfits of Globolisation

Foreign Capital, if properly utilisation, can make substantial contribution to the economic development of a nation. A classical example is the communist China. Productivity grows more quickly when countries produce goods and services in which they have comparative advantage. Living standards can go up faster. Increase in competition would make companies more cost and quality conscious, and innovative. Global Competition and imports keep a lid on prices, so inflation is less likely to derail economic growth. Liberalisation and global competition enhance consumer choice and consumer surplus. An open economy spurs innovation with fresh ideas from abroad. Export jobs often pay more than other jobs. Unfettered capital flows give the country access to foreign investment and keep interest rate low. Globalisation opens up enormous domestic and global opportunities for firms in developing countries. Despite discriminations of the global economic order against them, there are chances of developing countries benefiting from trade.

Survival of the Fittest in Globalisation

Globalisation brought number of challenges for the individuals, firms and Countries. Certainly, globalisatioin will doom the future of those who fail to meet these challenges effectively. (a) In a competitive environment, a firm can survive only if it is efficient. Cost efficient is to be promoted either cutting size of labourers or other inputs. (b) Attracting foreign investment is a real challenge, as is evident from the fact that the FDI in flow of India is far below the target. (c) Liberalisation increases the economic inequality. Even in China, the liberalisation has created many islands of affluence. The fast growth of China economy has reduced poverty. Naisbitt points art that there were as estimated 200 to 270 million Chinese living in absolute poverty in 1978 and their number came down to 100 million by 1985.[5] (d) small and medium firms often have some edge over the large ones in respect of standardised products or technologies. The new patent regime should be expected to help the Indian industry by promoting it to give added thrust to R & D and enabling Indian firms also to develop patented products (e) The domestic and Cross-border M & As Pose a serious Challenge to governments in ensuring fair competition. (f) Liberalisation will be successful only if the policy is proper and clear and there is the required political mandate, will and boldness. Lack of clarity regarding privatisation; lack of boldness to implement labor law reforms, downsizing, bureaucratic hurdles and so on are retarding India's reform process. Lack of clarity in policies and delays can make the situation worse instead of realising the objectives of liberalisation. Eg. Tata steel had bagged corus for 12.1 billion[6].

Impact of Globalisation on India

With the new economic policy ushered in 1991, there has been a change. Globalisation has in fact become a buzzword in the Indian firms now and many are expanding their overseas business by different strategies.[7]

Negative Factors

The Indian business suffers form a number of disadvantages of globalisation like bureaucratic culture not encouraging, high costs of many inputs, poor infrastructure facilities, obsolescence technology resistance to change, poor quality image, supply problems, small size, lack of experience, limited R & D, growing competition and trade barriers. There is a view that globalisation is another from of imperialism, to exploit the resources of developing countries.[8]

Positive Factors

There are number of favourable factors for globalisation. India had enough human resources, wide based industrial business, growing entreprenuership, growing domestic market, niche markets, expanding markets, transnationalisation, large number of Non-resident Indians, encouragement of economic liberalisation, cut throat competition, global strategies.[9]

II

Informalisation of Home Workers

92 per cent of able workers were in informal sector, who do not have secured minimum wages, pension benefits, insurance, congenial working conditions, work agreements, and compensation for loosing limb or life. Much of illiterate and ignored workers were concentrated in Rural India. Government had done a little for their welfare. Agriculture is in private sector and Industry extends a little, the service sector is done well. Industrial growth in 1980s being much more rapid than in the proceeding 15 years period, was characterized by "Jobless growth". In the 1990s there was an increase in employment in the registered manufacturing sector but or decline in employment in un-registered manufacturing.

Informalisation of the labour force

In Pakistan, in rural areas, 73 per cent of all economically active females and 68 per cent of such males, were in the informal sector; in urban areas, 61 per cent of all working women, and 64 per cent of such men, were in the informal sector. In India, as much as 80.3 per cent of the non-agricultural labour force is in the informal sector (with the remaining 19.7 per cent in the formal sector). The shares of the informal sector, though still large in South-East Asia, are not as significant as in India. Half of Indonesian and Thai non-agricultural labour force is in the informal sector, while in the Philippines, the share reaches 63.8 per cent.

The most interesting feature is feminisation of informalisation of the non-agricultural labour force in developing countries. There are more women in manufacturing-women make up more than a third of the labour force in manufacturing in some countries and almost one-half in some Asian countries. Similarly, in Lattin America, the expansion of informal employment and the shift of employment from industry to the services sector have major gender dimension–women are over represented in the informal economy and in the services sector in Latin America. Women after take on production, working from home which saves them travel time, and offers them the possibility of adding to family income while still being engaged in their representative role. Women who were hitherto non-earning members of the household, or engaged in traditional activities on their own account, now take on new types of work an a sub-contracted basis. In the informal count of home workers in India at around 50 million.

Definition of Home Work

As "work carried out by a person: (i) in his or her home or in other premises of his or her own choice, other than the workplace of the employer (ii) for remuneration; (iii) which results in a product or service as specified by the employer, irrespective of who provides the equipment, materials or other inputs used (ILO. 1996).

Home workers in India represented 35.9 per cent of the employment in the non-agricultural informal sector in 1999. As such as 59 per cent of India's home workers are in manufacturing, 75 per cent are in rural areas (where 56.4 per cent of all home workers in all sectors are located).

Sub-Contracted Home Based Workers: Costs and Benefits

Home based work has a dual character. On the positive side, home based work offers several advantages to families. Above all, it offers employment and hence an opportunity to workers to enhance and diversify their income; it also saves workers travel time, allowing them to undertake other activities in addition to home based work. Home workers can gain specific skills in producing goods at home, increasing the human capital available at both the household and local levels. Sub-contracting is often beneficial to the local and national economy as well and offers prospects in principle, of strengthening inter industry linkages; enhancing the entrepreneurial skill of sub-contractors; taking industry to rural areas; increasing industrial competitiveness; spreading technology down to less skilled workers; and generating employment.

The exploitation of the home workers by local employers is just a first step in exploitation through the global value chain. The problem for home workers arises from their low market access and their lack of contact with the final consumers. The lack of unionisation can also be an important source of the vulnerability of home workers families children are often engaged in home based activities because of the low piece rate in many cases, and also in order to generate additional income for the household. This implies that many children do not go to school, while others, such as part time workers, register negative effects on educational attainment. Children are seen as a substitute for old age security. The combined effect of social security and health expenditures would cause a behaviour change comparable to the experienced by the now industralised countries in the 100 years between 1890 and 1950.

Sub-Contracting Phenomenon

High labour costs in Europe, Japan, USA have driven firms in industralised countries to outsource manufacturing of consumer non-durable to South -east and South Asia, as well as Latin America. Thus there is reason to believe that sub-contracting should have grown with export orientation and with it. Home based work. Historically, export oriented labour intensive manufacturing grew most rapidly first in the East Asia newly industrializing countries (NICs) Taiwan, Korea, Singapore, Hongkong. The same pattern of growth was rapidly emulated by the South East Asian economic–Malaysia, Thailand and Indonesia–from the late 1970s onwards. Thus like Indonesia and Philippines, the Thai government too adopted a policy of industrilisation for export with special emphasis on labour intensive industries during the fourth national development plan (1976-81). By 2000 years, those shares had risen to 67 per cent for Thailand, 39 per cent for Indonesia, and 56 per cent of the Philippines.

In India study it is clear that in the case of at least two of the products incense sticks and *Zardozi*–embroidered garments both have a large export market, this market has grown in the 1980s and 1990s the export market for *bidis* is shrinking. In Pakistan too carpets, incense and shrimps are three export products and it is most likely that their growth has led to greater sub-contracting. The competitive cost advantage of such sub-contracting comes partly from the ability of contractors and their principal firms avoiding the costs of formal social insurance.

Home Based Work in the Value Chain

There is a value chain in the production process where sub-contracting is involved. The value adding economic activities usually have different stages: Design, purchase of raw materials or inputs, production and distribution through wholesalers and retailing. None of the workers have written agreements with their sub-contractors. In India, almost none of the contractors are written. In Pakistan the share of verbal contracts is close to 90 per cent in Indonesia 93 per cent in Philippines 90 per cent. The sub-contractors are just above the home workers in the value chain.

It is in such way that a commodity costs Rs. 100 to consumers the home workers receives Rs. 15 in zardozi and Rs. 17 in bidi, but only Rs. 2.3 in incense sticks.

Home worker households in the clusters in South Asia live below the poverty time. Both sub-contracting have workers base in expanding. Home workers under conditions which were exploitative with workers obtaining a small share of the total price paid by the consumer of the products they produce. Girls can ply a key role in breaking the inter-generational transfer of poverty. Lower educational level of the home workers and health–related problems faced by them indicated need for intervention. Education and work experience have a positive influence on women's productivity in value. South Asia home workers were still in below the national poverty line.

Self Employed Women's Association (SEWA)

The aim of SEWA is to promote the protection and rights of home workers. It is a largest trade union of women workers

(5,31,000) in India. Indian home workers belong to the international alliance organisations, Homenet south East Asia. This network advocates for home workers rights and aims at influencing national policy and legislation in their favour.

Globalisation on Farm Sector

In 1990s Government aim was to attract foreign investment of all varieties and to bring reforms in fiscal and interest rates. Investments have to flow into agriculture and small scale industries, which provide largest employment and growth. Unfortunately after reforms the flow of Governments investments in agriculture were reduced. Agricultural production was fallen and diminished purchasing power of Below Poverty Line (BPL) group. No demand for PDS grains leads to starvation deaths. With the entry into the W.T.O. it is doubtful whether there will be any encouragement to ancillary industries. A large number of small scale units are being closed. The number of unemployed in 1997 (38 million job seekers) was more than the number employed in organised sector (31 million were employed). Because of global competition most of the comparies want to reduce costs and be competitive. Nationalised banks have introduced VRS for their staff and so far about 99,000 workers have taken advantage of such scheme. It is found that 8 lakhs workers have been lost jobs through VRS and retirement schemes. Now the Trade Related Aspects of Intellectual property Rights (TRIPS) agreement will not allow us to copy the designs of products.

U.S. is the major recipient of Indian migrants. In terms of numbers, nearly 30,000 Indians on an average have been migrating to the United States during 1986-1995 every year.

Jobs are being created only in very narrow fields such as information, communication and in certain informal sectors using low technology. Other areas of economic activities like traditional manufacturing agricultural and non farm activities are not experiencing any increase in jobs. Globalisation led growth cannot be described as a job led growth.

Conclusion

Globalisation represents the increasing integration of the world economy into a single market. Globalisation checks inflation and enhances consumer choices and consumer surplus. India had enough human resources to meet the competition.

Informalisation of labour Market is around 92 per cent in India. In South Asian economies women is preferring service sector employment. Home workers were dominated with 56 per cent in all sectors of economy. Lack of welfare amenities made them to suffer ever long. Sub-contracting became a common phenomenon. No value system and all are on below poverty line. In the wave of globalisation these fragil groups are needed social security measures both from private and public sectors level.

Notes and References

1. Peter Drucker (1999), Management Challenges for the 21st Century, Harper Business, New Delhi, p. 61.
2. Peter R. Drucker (1990), The New Realities, Mandrin London.
3. John D. Sullivan (2000), Preparing in the Global Economy, *Economic Reforms Today*, No. 1.
4. Kenchi Ohmae (1991), The Borderless World, Fontoma, London
5. Santosh Mehrotra (2003), Protecting Labour Locally Against Capital Investing Globally: Informalisation, Feminization and Sub-Contracted Home Work. *The Indian Journal Labour Economics*, pp. 422-442.
6. Ministry of Labour, GoI (2002), Report of the National Commission on Labour, pp. 610.

Appendix

SEWA Identified the Presence of Home Workers in Certain Major States

Rajasthan	:	Beedi, agarbathi, readymade garments, weaving shawls and durries, wool spinning, food preparing and packing, handicrafts and traditional crafts, black printing.
Delhi	:	Zari work, garments, Lifafa (Envelope) making
Madhya Pradesh	:	Beedi making, ready made garments stitching smocking, embroidery, making agarbathi, Pappad making, Zari work, Collection of tender leaves and Jadi booti and Jhadoo making.
Bihar	:	Lacquer work, weaving, Spinning, Bamboo work, Pappad rolling, Shawl weaving, beedi, Packing Cooked food, Tussar.
Maharastra	:	Beedi making, Leatherwork, rope making, Cashew garment making, Card board box making, Cleaning and sorting onion, Seafood, handicrafts, food products.
West Bengal	:	Handicrafts, lacquer work, Bamboo work, Spinning, Weaving Sea food, jute work, Carpet making, garment stitching, Sack making, leather work and footwear.
Tamil Nadu	:	Woollen carpet making, Shawl weaving, beedi rolling manufacture of scented betel nuts, garment stitching handloom weaving, ornament making, polishing gems making stencils, lacquer work, sea foods, footwear.
Karnataka	:	Beedi making, agarbatti, ready made garments, making pickles, cleaning and packing foods.
Uttar Pradesh	:	Beedi making, work on handlooms, ready made garments, Chikan work, food products, lacquer work, rope making, Zari work, Carpet weaving.

Source: Ministry of Labour, GoI, (2002), Report of the National Commission on Labour, Vol. I (Part – I) p. 610.

Section–II

Promotion of Industrialisation

6

SPECIAL ECONOMIC ZONES: A STEP FOR QUALITY INDUSTRIALIZATION

In a traditional society, any structural adjustment in a sector would bring much havoc chaos and confusion in earlier period. Slowly society understands the real benefit from it. SEZ is a new technique for expansion of both industrialization and employment.

An Overview

India was one of the first in Asia to recognize the effectiveness of the export processing zone (EPZ) model in promoting exports, with Asia's first EPZ set up in Kandla, Gujarat in 1965 with a view to overcome the shortcomings experienced on account of the multiplicity of controls and clearances; absence of world-class 'infrastructure, and an unstable fiscal regime and with to view a attract large foreign investments in India. The Special Economic zones (SEZs) policy was announced in April 2000. This policy intended to make SEZs an engine for economic growth supported by quality infrastructure complemented by an attractive fiscal package, both at the Centre and the State level, with the minimum possible regulations. SEZs in India functioned from Nov. 1, 2000 to Feb. 9, 2006 under the provisions of the foreign Trade policy and fiscal incentives were made effective through the provisions of relevant statutes.

The Special Economic zones Act, 2005 was passed by parliament in May, 2005 which received presidential assent on the 23rd of June 2005, came into effect on 10th Feb. 2006.

Objectives of the SEZ Act

They are:

(a) generation of additional economic activity,

(b) promotion of exports of goods and services,

(c) promotion of investment from domestic and foreign sources,

(d) creation of employment opportunities,

(e) development of infrastructural facilities.

This will trigger a large flow of foreign and domestic investment in SEZs. A single window SEZ approval mechanism has been provided through a 19 member inter-ministerial SEZ Board of Approval.

Incentives and Facilities Offered to the SEZs

The following incentives and facilities are providing to the SEZs.

(a) Duty free import/domestic procurement of goods for development, operation and maintenance of SEZ Units.

(b) 100% Income Tax exemption on export income for SEZ for the 1st five years, 50% for the next 5 years thereafter and 50% of the ploughed back export profit for next five years.

(c) Exemption from minimum alternate tax under Income tax Act.

(d) External commercial borrowing by SEZ units upto US$ 500 million in a year without any maturity restriction through recognized banking channels.

(e) Exemption from central sales tax.

(f) Exemption from service tax.

(g) Single window clearance for Central and State level approvals.

(h) Exemption from State sale tax and other levels as extended by the respective states governments.

Since February 10, 2006, 27 meetings of Board of Approvals have since been held. During these meetings, formal approval has been granted to 513 SEZ's approvals. There are 138 valid in principle approvals. Out of the 513 formal approvals, 250 SEZs have been notified.

Land Requirements for Approves SEZs

The total land requirement for the formal approvals granted till date is approximately 62,590 hectares, out of which about 107 approvals are for State Industrial Development Corporations/State Government ventures, which account over 20, 763 hectares.

Out of total land area of 29, 73, 190 sq. km in India, total agricultural land is of the order of 16,20,388 sq.kms (54.5%). It is interesting to note that out of this total land area, the land is possession of the 250 SEZs notified amounts to approximately over 293 Sq. Kms only. The formal approvals granted also works out to only around 625 sq. km.[1]

SEZs: Leading to Labour Intensive

Out of the 513 formal approvals given till date, 177 approvals are for sector specific and multi-product SEZs for manufacture of Textiles & Apparels, Leather footwear, Automobile components, Engineering etc., which would involve labour intensive manufacturing. SEZs are going to lead to creation of employment for large number of unemployed rural youth.

Nokia and Flextronics electronics hardware SEZs in Sriperumbudur are already providing employment to 13722 and 629 persons. Hyderabad Gems SEZ for Jewellery manufacturing in Hyderabad has already employed 1500 persons. Apache, Nellore, SEZ being set up in Andhra Pradesh will employee 30,000 persons to manufacture 10 lakh pair shoes every month, current employment in it is 5,325 persons.

Brandix Apparels, a Sri Lankan FDI project would provide employment to 60,000 workers over a period of 3 years. Even in service sector, 12.5 million sq. meters space is expected in the IT/ITES, SEZs which as per the NASSCOM standards translates into 12.5 lakh Jobs. It is, therefore, expected that establishment of SEZs would lead to fast growth of labour intensive manufacturing and services in the country.

Benefits from SEZs:

Net benefits derives from SEZs is evident from the investment, employment, exports and infrastructural developments additionally generated. The benefits derived from multiplier effect of the investments and additional economic activity in the SEZs and the employment generated thus will far outweigh the tax exemptions and the losses on account of land acquisition. Stability in fiscal concession is absolutely essential to ensure credibility of government intensions.

Table 1
Exports from the Functioning SEZs (During the last three years)

Year	*Value (Rs. Crores)*	*Growth rate (in per cent over previous year)*
2003-04	13,854	39
2004-05	18,314	32
2005-06	22,840	25
2006-07	34,615	52
2007-08	66,638	92

Source: Internet.

The Table 1 above as proved that growth rate was at the beginning itself it is one third and doubled within five years. In absolute terms also value has raised five times. It is really appreciable impact of SEZs in India.

Investment and Employment Prior to the SEZ Act 2005

At present, 1897 units are in operation in the SEZs. In the SEZs established prior to the Act coming into force, there are 1141 units providing direct employment to over 1.99 lakh persons, about 35% of whom are women. Private investment by entrepreneurs in these SEZs established prior to the SEZ Act is of the order of over Rs. 4043.28 core.

Current Investment and Employment:

Investment : Rs. 73,348 crores

Employment : 1,00,885 persons

Impact of the Seheme

The overwhelming response to the SEZ seheme is evident from the flow of investment and creation of additional employment in the country. The SEZ seheme has generated tremendous response amongst the investors, both in India and abroad, which is evident from the list of Developers who have set up SEZs.

1. Nokia SEZ in Tamilnadu
2. Quark City SEZ in Chandigrah
3. Flextronics SEZ in Tamilnadu
4. Mahindra worldcity inTamilnadu
5. Motorola, DELL and Foxconn
6. Apache SEZ (Adidas Group) in Nellore, Andhra Pradesh
7. Divvy's Laboratories in Andhra Pradesh
8. Rajiv Gandhi Technology Park, Chandigarh
9. ETL infrastructure IT SEZ, Chennai
10. Hyderabad Gems Ltd, Hyderabad.

By all means some Southern States have taken big initiative in establishing more SEZs. The following are the distribution of SEZs.

The Table 2 above has shown an impressive development of SEZs, especially Andhra Pradesh, Tamilnadu and Maharastra respectively, who are the leaders in establishment and operation. Out of 250, 156 are IT/ITE-SEZs only, that is above 60 per cent.

Table 2
Distribution of SEZs in India (as on August 11, 2008)

State	*Number*
Andhra Pradesh	56
Chandigarh	2
Goa	3
Delhi	1
Gujarat	22
Haryana	20
Jhakarkand	1
Karnataka	23
Kerala	8
Madhya Pradesh	4
Maharastra	35
Orissa	4
Punjab	2
Rajasthan	5
Tamilnadu	42
Uttar Pradesh	12
Uttar Khand	2
West Bengal	8
Total	250

Source: Internet.

SEZs in Kerala State

1. Electronics at Kalamassery, Ernakulam District 30 acres.
2. Food Processing Kakkanchery, Malappuram district 30 acres.
3. Animation and Gaming, Trivandrum District 25 acres.
4. Infopark, Ernakulam District.
5. Technopark, Trivandrum district 100 acres.
6. Health care products in Trivandrum District 100 acres.
7. Textiles, cherthala, Alappuzha district 250 acres.
8. Petrochemical Products Kasargod district 100 acres.

Future of SEZs

The Commerce Ministry Estimates SEZ projects to attract investments worth Rs. 2 laks crore by 2009 end.[2]

Controversy on Land Acquisition and Freedom

The controversy over the threatened withdrawal of Tata Motors from Singur in West Bengal has come not a day too soon. The Singur plant is not located in any designated special Economic zone (SEZ). The West Bengal Government extended all help to acquisition of land for Nano car manufacturing and also attracting investment to State. There was a trouble in Goa too where the SEZ developers are facing the wrath of the State Government despite a few SEZs having been notified by the Centre. In both the cases, the moot point is, how far the Central and State Governments to industry would renege on their commitments to industry, particularly when faced with political Choices for survival. In this case, the domestic investors who could ill-afford to squander their precious capital in endless litigation.[3]

Criticism

There is a big cry and criticism throughout country that land of farmers/livelihood of farmers was under great threat. In the name of Liberalization, Privatization Globalization (LPG), the fertile land of farmers was taken at cheaper prices and handing over to the Industrialists/foreign investors is not fair on the part of States and Centre. The labourer is also loosing his/her rights, security, provident found, leisure, health in these ventures. Certainly, opposition, left parties are crying that we are again going back to imperialism from developed countries and the spirit of Constitution is on verge of vapour. Governance with human face is another way of exploiting Agriculture and its households. The ruling party agenda is to facilitate to collect commissions and fixing contractors, alone, not welfare. We don't know where is "Be Indian, Buy Indian" spirit.[4]

Conclusion

To brings all relevant and identical industries to one place and facilitate to go for exports and imports, so that investment, and employment and economics can be generated. This is the experience of all developed countries and seven Tiger countries in Asia. In fact, State incentives are lesser than benefits gained by economy in long term. Initially, States have to bring awareness to that area, where industries are to be established. Centre and State have to acquire barren land as a priority than fertile irrigated land. Rehabilitation measures should be practiced so as to get continuous income to the land looser. A member of family by giving training is to be given an opportunity to get employment. Centre and state Governments have to give proper training to the opposition party members on it. Earlier, everybody will feel some apprehension latter it will go once fruits are reaching to bottom level poor and downtrodden. The capital and labour intensive industries may change the landscape of India. A strong political will is highly needed to over come the woes.

Notes and References

1. *http ://sezindia.nic.in*
2. Sunny Verma & Arun S. (2008), Subsidiaries Help SEZ Promoters Beat Land Caps, *The Financial Express*, Sept. 3, p. 2.
3. G. Srinivasan (2008), On SEZs and Land Acquisition, *The Hindu Business Line*, Sept. 2, p. 9.
4. S. Sudhakar (2007), For Whom Benefit by the, SEZs, *Veekshanam (Telugu)*, June 2007, p. 12-14.

7

WORLD TRADE ORGANISATION: LABOUR STANDARDS

An Overview

A healthy, educated and skilled workforce can contribute more significantly and effectively to economic development.

Labour standards are those that are applied to the way workers are treated. The term covers a wide range of things: from use of child labour and forced labor, to the right to organize trade unions and to strike, minimum wages, health and safety conditions, and working hours.

In the cause of labour market, earlier phase (1860-1914) saw much larger magnitude of movement of labour across borders. It is estimated that between 1860 and 1914 years about 60 million migrated from Europe alone to the new world. Between 1970 and 1990 years, the flow of new immigrants from developing countries to developed countries remained at the same rate of 1.5 new immigrants per thousand population. Following the Philadelphia Declaration of 1944, which stated that "labour is not a commodity". Increasing unemployment, as a consequence of globalisation, has been one of the major causes for concern all over the world.[2]

Earlier, Child labour used in the manufacture of exports from the developing countries is widely criticized by people in the developed countries. There is protest against this in the developing countries too. For example, carpet industry in India. Consumers are called upon to boycott such goods. A similar issue is the sweat labour. The argument is that goods manufactured by labour working in inhuman/ unhealthy working conditions not getting fair wages should be banned or boycotted. According to an International labour Organization (ILO) Report, it is a regrettable feature of many export processing zones that both male and female workers are trapped in low wage and low skill jobs and labour relations and human resource development remain two of the most problematic aspects of zone functioning.

Another important issue is "Trade Union" rights. Absence of trade union rights in some countries provides them a cost advantage. In fact, many multinational corporations are taking advantage of absence of trade union rights in some countries.

It is also valid that developed country firms which are adversely affected by the cheap imports blow up the issues to serve their vested interest.[3]

The core of the evaluation of the market driven growth of labour describes it as caustic terms as jobless, ruthless, voiceless, rootless and futureless. It drives home the fact that structural Adjustment programme (SAP) as part of globalization process is not in favour of either equality or redistributing either between or within the countries.

W.T.O. Labour Standards

The W.T.O points out that the debate an labour standards distinguishes between so called basic labour rights and less commonly accepted standards. Basic labour rights are part of the ILO conventions on human rights and labour standards and include the prohibition if forced labour, the freedom of association, right to organize and bargain collectively, the elimination of child labour exploitation and non-discrimination in employment. Other less common accepted standards include minimum wages, limits on the hours worked and occupational safety and health standards.

Trade could have adverse consequences on labour rights if individual countries disregard labour standards. Trade, it is argued, increases the demand for products produced with labour that does not enjoy adequate labour standards, and thereby encourages such practices. If poor working conditions are the main reason for a country's competitiveness, then international competition will induce companies to relocate to countries with weak, non- existent or unenforeced labour standards in a "race to the bottom". Value Judgments also play a role, when people argue that they are not willing to accept exchange of products which have been produced under morally unacceptable conditions. If trade has such adverse consequences on labor standards, critics argue, labour standards should become an integral part of the W.T.O framework. At Singapore meeting Ministers reconciled their differences through a statement which expressed their commitment to core labour standards.

Trade can contribute to more stringent labour standards and their enforcement. Trade promotes economic growth, which in turn increases people's demand for better working conditions. Growth and prosperity also provide the means to finance improvements in labour standards, and to send children to school instead of factories. International companies are reluctant to provide inhuman, working conditions or to use child labour for the fear of their reputation and boycotts. Finally, the production of exportable products today increasingly requires people with some skills, and safe and clean working conditions.

The empirical study proved that trade never undermines labour standards. There is a positive link between trade and labour standards and on income.

WTO Agreements

In general, these are 160 agreement in W.T.O. They not deal with labour standards as such. On the one hand, some countries would like to change this. WTO rules and disciplines, they argue, would provide a powerful incentive for member nations to improve workplace conditions and international coherence.

(The phase used to describe efforts to ensure policies move in the same direction).

On the other hand, many developing countries believe the issue has no place in the WTO framework. They argue that the campaign to bring labour issues into WTO is actually a bid by industrial nations to undermine the comparative advantage to lower wage trading partners, and could undermine their ability to raise standards through economic development, particularly if it hampers their ability to trade. They also argue that proposed standards can be too high for them to meet at their level of development. These nations argue that efforts to bring labour standards into the arena of multilateral trade negotiations are little more than a smoke screen for protectionism.

As a more complex legal level is the question of the relationship between the I.L.O's standards and the W.T.O agreements – for example, whether or how the ILOs standards can be applied in a way that is consistent with WTO rules.

Singapore Conference Level

In the 1996, Singapore conference, the members agreed that they were committed to recognize core labour standards, but these should not be used for protectionism. The economic advantage of low wage countries should not be questioned, but the WTO and ILO secretariats would continue their existing collaboration, the declaration said. The concluding remarks of the chairman, Singapore's Trade and Industry Minister, Mr. Yeo chrow Tong, added that the declaration does not but labour on the WTO's agenda. The 2001 Doha Ministerial conference reaffirmed the Singapore declaration on labour without any specific discussion.[5]

Singapore Declaration

(a) Members are committed to the observance of internationally recognized core labour standards, (b) these standards should be addressed in the ILO, whose work the members support, (c) standards are promoted by growth and development, fostered through trade liberalization, and (d) Members reject the use of labour standards for protectionist purposes, and agree that the comparative advantage of countries must in no way be put into question. Member of ILO recently agreed on a "declaration of fundamental principles and Rights at work," in which ILO member agreed to increase the scrutiny of adherence to core labour rights and reiterated the commitment in the Singapore declaration no to use labour standards for protectionist purposes.

Mobility of Labour

The migration of workers across international boundaries is one of the most striking aspects of the globalization of the world economy, with a major impact on well over 100 countries. It is currently estimated that at least 130 million people live outside their countries of origin. The large scale migration from one country to another, either permanently or for short durations, is essentially the manifestation of the large to search for better incomes and better working conditions. Political factors have also influenced people to leave their ancestral homes and seek refuge in other countries.

At the out set, it is important to highlight the basic characteristics of the labour flows from India to the industrialized countries in the period since independence. A large proportion of these migrants are persons with professional expertise, technical qualifications or other skills. For an overwhelming proporition of these migrants, the destinations have been the Untied States, Canada, and the United Kingdom, and in recent times some countries in Europe. It is called as "Brain drain".

Available evidence indicates that the United States is the major recipient of Indian migrants. In terms of members, nearly 30,000 Indians on an average have been migrating to the Unites States during 1986-1995 every year.

The oil price increases of 1973-74 and 1979 saw an enormous growth in the demand for foreign labour in the oil exporting States of the Gulf. The scale of labour movements into the Gulf was intimately linked to the escalation in oil revenues and the unprecedented rate of investment in domestic industry and infrastructure in the oil States. The period between 1974 and 1982 witnessed a large out flow of Indian labour to the Middle East labour markets.

Apart from providing a 'Safety valve' for the massive unemployment problems at home, migration to the Middle East would continue to be important source of foreign exchange for a country like India, which faced severe balance of payment problems as on before 1991 Economic Reforms. The migrant labour was 1.25 lakhs in 1987 year to 2.43 lakhs in 2000 year. The remittances to India were $ 233 crore in 1981-82 to $1229 crosses in 2000 year.

Human Rights Protection Standards

Non–Discrimination

Business partners do not discriminate in hiring and employment practices on grounds of race, colour, national origin, gender, religion or political or other opinion.

Working Hours/Overtime

Business partners who do not require more than 60 hours work per week on a regular scheduled basis except for approximately compensated overtime in compliance with local laws, and will favour business partners who use 48 hours work per week as their maximum normal requirement.

Forced or Compulsory Labour

Business partners do not force or other compulsory labour, including labour that is required as a means for political coercion or as a punishment for holding or for peacefully expressing political views, in the manufacture of its products. Do not purchase materials that were produced by forced prison or other compulsory labour and should terminate business relationships with any sources found to utilize such labour.

Fair Wages

The business partners who share our commitment to the betterment of wage and benefit levels that address the basic needs of workers and their families so far as possible and appropriate in light of national practices and conditions. The business partners should not pay less than the minimum wage required by local law or that pay less than prevailing local industry practices, whichever is higher.

Child Labour

The business partners should not use the child labour. The term "Child" generally refers to a person who is less than 14 years of age, or younger than the age for completing compulsory education if that age is higher than 14. In countries where the law defines "Child" to include individuals who are older than 14.

Freedom of Association

The business partners have to accept the right of employees to establish and join organizations of their own choosing. No employee is penalized because of his/her non-violent exercise of this right. It is recognized and respected the right of all employees to organize and bargain collectively.

Safe and Healthy Work Environment

The business partners that strive to assure employees a safe and healthy work place and that do not expose workers to hazardous conditions.

Conclusions

There is a big conceptual change on the labour word since inception of Industrial Revolution. The standards and laws are changed from time to time and country to country. Post Second World War period and starting of UNO branch of International labour organization, much research was taken place. Many safety and scientific measures were advocated. Since 1995, the W.T.O also following the guidelines of ILO for its member countries. Free trade had changed its impact on developed and developing countries performance on labour standards. No doubt, Developed countries improved labour standards, whereas developing countries are trying to improve it. Always cheap labour is a threat to developed countries. So that they are imposing standards like human rights and social clauses for improving appreciable standards.

Notes and Reference

1. Govt. of India (2008), Economic Survey 2007-08, p. 239.
2. D. Narasimha Reddy (2004), Economic Globalization and Labour Movement: The Challenge and Response ed., Better Expression on Globalization C. G. Krishnaswamy *et al.*, Bangalore University, p. 161.
3. Francis cherunilam (2004), "Global Economy and Business Environment, Himalaya Publishing House, Mumbai, p. 324.
4. Sheik Saleem (2006), Business Environment, Pearson Education Delhi, p. 506.
5. *http//www.org*

Appendix 1

International Labour Organization: established in 1919 as an autonomous part of the League of Nation, is an inter- governmental agency with a tripartite structure in which representatives of governments, employees and workers participate in 1969 the organization won the Nobel peace prize. It has 150 members. Its head office is at Geneva, Switzerland.

Appendix 2

Japan's work Culture: Japan is often described as the country with the best work culture. It is said that the Japanese worker does not need someone to supervise his work. Rather, if a superior is appointed, he/she often takes it as an insult. He/she does not like to take holidays.

8

MANAGING THE PROBLEMS OF MODERNISATION OF SMALL SCALE INDUSTRIES IN INDIA

Introduction

India at 60 is a nation of young People. To realize our true potential, we must invest in health and education of every child. We must create new employment opportunities for all, especially for the less privileged sections of Society, and for those living in rural areas. We must eliminate the rural urban divide in development indicators. We must also ensure that the process of industralisation generates enough jobs for our youth, in urban, semi-urban and rural areas. In the past 60 years, people moved to where work was available, in the next 60 years, work must move to where people live[1].

Planning Commission must ensure monitoring of the funds and schemes implemented for the disadvantaged groups that constitute an unbelievable 836 million people or 77 per cent of the population. For the remaining over 235 million, they are in position to take care of themselves. Interestingly, 79 per cent of the poor and vulnerable are in the un-organised sector and we describe them as the *aam aadmi*[2].

The discussion and debate an Small and Medium Enterprises (SME) is rather ritualistic and reality in India. In most discussions and development today, the key words are "enterprise development" and "entreprenuership". The SME sector is atomic in nature, that is, the large number of small and micro units make the sector what it is. Here lies their social significance under a democracy. Democracy is also characterized by it's atomic base. Hence, a correspondence of the two provides the logical foundations for public policy, which is specific to the context of SMEs.

The industry of the New Industrial Policy of deregulation, delicensing and disinvestment has opened a new environment in the country. A significant number of industries in the public sector are now thriving alongside many industries in the private sector. Often Foreign Direct Investors are setting new trends in a competitive playing field. The overall growth in the General index during 2002-03 has been 5.8 per cent.

Growth of Small and Medium Enterprises

As per the third All India Census of Small Scale Industries (SSIs) (registered and unregistered units) held for the year 2001-02, there were 105.21 lakh SSI units in the country, out of which 13.75 lakh (13%) were registered working units and 91.46 lakh (87%) un-registered units. Their contribution to production was Rs. 2,82,270 crore and to employment at 249.09 lakh persons. It is estimated that during 2004-05, the number of SSI units has increased to 118.59 lakh from 113.95 lakh is the previous year, registering a growth of 4.7 per cent. The value of production at current prices by the SSI units also increased by 13.95 per cent to Rs.4,07,630 crore from Rs.3,57,733 crore during 2003-04[3].

The following table gives a bird's eye view of performances of SSIs.

The Table 1 reveals that in post economic reforms, the number of SSIs have been raised, within a decade 69 per cent was the growth of production, 35 per cent at current prices, 48 per cent in constant prices, employment at 70 per cent and exports around 100 per cent. This shows reforms have given a positive boost up of SSIs.

SMEs are playing a crucial role in India's economic development. They have a 40% share in industrial output, producing over 8000 value added products. They contribute nearly 35% of direct exports and 45% of the overall exports from the country and are among the biggest employers after agriculture, providing employment to over 28 million people. The 3 million plus SME units that India has in various parts of the country, produce a diverse range of very basic to highly sophisticated products[4].

Table 1
Overall Performance of Small Scale Sector in India

		Production (Rs. Crore)			
Year	*Number of Units (in lakh)*	*(at current prices)*	*(at Constant prices)*	*Employment in lakh)*	*(Exports (Rs. crore)*
1994-1995	79.60	1,22,210	1,09,116	191.40	29,068
1996-1997	86.21	1,68,413	1,35,380	205.86	39,248
1999-2000	97.15	2,34,255	1,70,709	229.10	54,200
2003-2004	115.22	3,48,059	2,26,392	273.97	N.A.

Source: Ministry of SSI, Third All India Census on SSI, (Constant prices 1993-94).

Business Demography

Enterprises cannot be created simply through policy measures. The limited role of public policy is to make available the right incentives and market signals to private entrepreneurs. These incentives and signals will remain clear to the business community only if the business demography is properly documented and the changes therein are mentioned on a continuous basic. The key demographic indicators often used by analysts are:

Birth Rate: Real enterprise births of year 'n', as a percentage of the population of active enterprises of year 'n'.

Survival Rate: The percentage of all real enterprise births of year 'n' which are still active in year (n + x), currently, 2 year survivals are observed in the structural indicators; therefore, x = 2.

Death Rate: Real enterprise deaths of year 'n', as a percentage of the population of active enterprises of year 'n'.

Since 1992-93, there has been a progressive rise in the birth rate. This can be explained largely in terms of enhanced initiatives of the Government or through specific schemes like PMRY, and through training activities like entrepreneurship development programmes.

A satisfactory performance of the SSI sector would imply a significant inequality between birth and death rates. However, the two rate curves, birth and death rates, show a uniform pattern. Where a 43 per cent change in birth over a year corresponds with a 36 per cent death of units over that period, in essence, implies that the effective natality rate is only 7 per cent. This alarming situation demands that the thrust of any meaningful SSI policy should be to bring down the death rate rather than to enhance the birth rate. Two steps are needed to bring down the business death rate. *One* is to maintenance of a conducive policy environment for existing enterprises: this should include both supply side and demand side interventions. *Two* is to maintainance of enterprise health standards: this requires continuous monitoring of the demographic behaviour so that the circumstances under which a unit becomes sick is understood properly and corrective or precautionary steps are taken. Scientific models of enterprise development should form the basics of promoting starts up as also of nurturing growth[5].

Small Scale Industries: Lesser Help from Banks

Small Scale Industries (SSIs) continue to be an important segment of Indian Industry in terms of output and employment. Despite the general constraints of industrial growth, the specific constraints on the village and small enterprises (VSE) sector and increasing competition from domestic and foreign producers due to de-reservation and import liberalization, the SSI sector outstripped the overall industrial growth in the country. Employment also continued to grow in the sector during the first three years of the Tenth plan period. The vital blood is capital for industry. RBI has issued number of guidelines for lending to small enterprises. The setting up of specialized SSI branches in each district; dispensing with the collateral security requirement for loan up to Rs. 5 lakh and up to Rs. 25 lakh for units with a good track record. It has fixed a time limit of two weeks for loan upto Rs. 5 lakh for the disposal of loan applications and enhancement of the composite loan limit from Rs.50 lakh to Rs.1 crore. The banks have not adhered to[6].

Rising Bank Credit

Bank credit is a critical input for the growth of the SME sector. In recognition of the vast potential of SME sector credit flow to this sector has been steadily increasing. In fact, bank credit to SSIs has significantly increased in absolute terms to Rs. 76,100 crore in 2005 from Rs. 16,800 crore in March 1991, through as four times more of net bank credit.

The Government has asked the public sector banks to achieve a minimum 20 per cent year, on year growth in finding SMEs, which will lead to doubling of credit to the sector from Rs. 67,600 crore the 2004-05 to Rs. 1,35,200 crore by 2009-10.

The scope and viability of SME lending financial institutions need to: (1) tackle to enhance the problem of information asymmetry by educating the SMEs about the need for maintaining reliable financial data (2) to develop robust risk evaluation models (3) evolve relationship lending where lending is based on proprietary information about the entity; (4) imbibe flexibility in the lending policies; and (5) formulate credit guarantee schemes in line with the evolving financial scenario to support the flow of credit to enterprises[7].

II

Risk Assessment and Management

The credit flow to the SME sector can be raised substantially by reducing and managing the inherent risk associated with this sector. This realization has led to the inception and growth of SME rating agencies, which undertake comprehensive risk assessment of SMEs units to determine their credit worthiness. CRISIL and SME rating Agency of India limited (SAMERA) are the primary credit rating agencies active in the SME domain.

Institutions such as SIDBI, NSIC, CIBIL, D & B and CRISIL regularly introduce credit and assessment mechanisms, to aid commercial banks in: assessing SME credit proposals, reducing their transaction cost and taking more objective decisions while pricing risk for different segments. SMEs need to proactively avail themselves of credit rating schemes which help them get favourable credit terms by allowing banks to appropriately structure their interest rates based on the rating; expedite and streamline the credit delivery process and help attract equity participation. Credit rating should also be made a mandatory requirement for availing bank Financing. The growing presence of multinational banks in this sector has led to healthy competition in this space.

The Micro and Small Enterprise (MSE) sector constitutes an important building block of the economy. It contributes nearly 6 per cent GDP, 39 per cent of total industrial production, 34 per cent of exports and 60 per cent of employment. This sector forms the second largest source of employment, after agriculture[8].

Women Entrepreneurs' Empowerment

The participation of women in economic activities is necessary not only from a human resource point of view but is essential even for the objective of raising the status of women in society. The economic status of women is now accepted as an indicator of a society's stage of development. The women entrepreneurs are influenced by number of factors like economic independence, own identity, achievement of excellence, building confidence, developing risk taking ability, motivation, equal status in society and greater freedom and mobility.

In a study conducted in south East Asian Countries, women make up a significant part of those classified as employers and self employed. Average range from 23 per cent to 30 per cent of the total for Indonesia, Malaysia, Philippines and Thailand. In manufacturing, trading and community services in Indonesia, Malaysia, Philippines and Thailand, a substantial number of entrepreneurs are female.

In India, women constitute about 48 per cent of the population but their participation in economic activity is only 34 per cent. There is a continuing concentration of women in low paid and low status occupations, indicating that the women are marginalized in the labour force. Government of Andhra Pradesh, India is planning industrial estates exclusively for women entrepreneurs in every district[9].

Pandit Jawaharlal Nehru felt that when women move forward, the family moves and the nation moves. Employment gives economic status to women. Economic status gives way to social status and thereby empowerment[10].

Bugbear Faced by SSI

The entrepreneur of SSI would have been facing the problems. They are as such as obtaining adequate credit, marketing products, management expertise, difficult to meet the competition of imported goods, competition among local products and to identity appropriate technology. Further, the additional problems are bureaucratic red tape, consultancy, training skill, quality control, procurement of raw material, modernization, need of international technical and financial assistance and cooperation of developing countries.

The Union Ministry of Small Scale Industry has initiated quicker procedures to help the closure of SMEs that are not registered under the companies Act 1956. The World Bank considers 10 criteria to assess a country. These are–ease of starting business, getting a licence, getting a credit, protecting investors, paying taxes, cross border trade, enforcing contracts and closing business. Judged on these factors, countries like Singapore, Japan, Australia, U.S.A, Britain, Canada and some other European economies are rated at the top[11].

Opportunities of SSI

By its less capital intensive and high labour absorption nature, the SSI sector has made significant contributions to employment generation and also to rural industrialisation. This sector is ideally suited to build on the strengths of India's traditional skills and knowledge, by an infusion of technology, capital and innovative marketing practices. The diversity in production systems and demand structures will ensure long term co-existence of many layers of demand for consumer products/technologies/processes. There will be flourishing and well grounded markets for the same product/process, differentiated by quality, value addition and existence for various diverse types of units.

The process of liberalization coupled with government support will, therefore, attract the infusion of just these in the sector. The small industry sector has performed exceedingly well and enabled India to achieve a wide measure of industrial growth and diversification.

Sickness in SSI

RBI funded Kohli Committee defined sickness as incipient sickness was identified in terms of continuous decline in gross output. Sickness in the total SSI sector was the tune of one per cent, whereas in the registered and un-registered SSI sectors it was 3.38 per cent and 0.64 per cent respectively. The maximum number of sick units–about 59.33 per cent were located in West Bengal, Kerala, Maharastra, Karnataka and Andhra Pradesh. The States of Kerala, Tamilnadu, Adhra Pradesh, Karnataka and Maharastra had maximum number of sick/incipient sick SSI units. These five States together accounted for 54.28 per cent of the sick/incipient sick SSI units in the country. The measurement of sickness were used three yardsticks (a) delay in repayment of loan over one year (b) decline in net worth by 50 per cent and (c) decline in output in last three years. In registered units 13.98 per cent and un-registered Units 6.89 per cent were found in sickness. Lack of demand and shortage of working capital were the main reasons for sickness in both registered and un-registered. In Tamilnadu, Coimbatore is the forefront in Units next Chennai, Salem, Chengalput. Minimum units were in Perambular Tiruvarur, Theni, Namakkal, Karur, Thiruvallur. The standardisation and long term growth of SSI depends upon ethics of business.

Business Ethics

Ethics is a branch of philosophy. It's objective is to study both moral and immoral behaviour in order to make well-founded value judgements and to arrive at adequate recommendations. Business ethics evaluates and prescribes moral standards that match a specific sphere in modern society: the business environment. The very basis of business ethics refers to an idea of how business fits into modern society as a whole, a social philosophy business. Ethically valid performance is produced by preventing un-necessary harm and by the ability to build constructive and durable partnerships with employees, consumers and supplies. The unit management should set of rules as a part of wider ethical mission statement. This may involve staff training programme, a unit ethical committee or discussions with external stakeholders. Compliance with codes need enforcement, both positive and negative, in order to become effective, some system of sanctions must exist. Many units do not have severe sanctions against, for example, bribery.

In the rapidly changing business environment, Research and Development (R & D) is the pre-requisite for success and growth in SMEs. With motivation and support women entrepreneurs are now fast making a big and positive difference to the rapidly growing Indian economy. As the first ever women president of India rightly said in her inaugural address, "Empowerment of women is particularly important to me as I believe this leads to the empowerment of nation[12].

Government of India had taken number of measures for modernisation under Tenth plan review. They are technology upgradation and modernization scheme, adequate and timely credit, Growth Centre Scheme, Transport subsidy scheme, North-East Industrial Policy, Industrial Infrastructure upgradation scheme, Intellectual property Rights were taken up as a top priority in developing SSI in India.

Conclusion

The process and progress of industrialisation generates Jobs, production and exports. In democracy, every citizen is to be made our as entrepreneur. Public and private sectors are thriving significantly. After agriculture, the next the highest employment generation is founded in SSIs. Business demography can be changed unless State intervenes and supports them. Banks are not landing loans as expected by concerned States and Centre. Credit rating should be made as a mandatory for bank financing. Andhra Pradesh Government is planning Industrial Estates exclusively for women in each district, which is highly appreciable. The problem of sickness is not growing as an earlier decades. The economic reforms were made them to grow fast and competitively. To make them always profitable, there is a need for improving number of areas like improving managerial skills, upgradation of technology, upgradation of infrastructure facilities, emulation of business ethics, work for intellectual property rights, and competitiveness for exports with multi-national corporations. However, political will, empowerment of women, adoption of ethics, liberal finance by banks, continuous training and improving skills would go for sustainability of SSIs in India.

Notes and References

1. Manmohan Singh (2007), India @ 60, *The Economic Times,* 15 Aug. p. 2.
2. Arjun Sengupta (2007), The Approach to Planning Should Change, *The Hindu,* Sept. 5, p. 11.
3. Correspondent (2007), Manorama Year Book, p. 571.
4. Vikaskumar and Partha Gosh (2007), Small People, Big Achievements, *The Economic Times,* Aug. 15, p. 8.
5. P. M. Mathew (2006), Small Industry Promise of the New Package, *The Hindu Survey of Indian Industry,* p. 45.
6. Planning Commission (2005), Mid-Term Appraisal of 10th Five Year Plan (2002-2007) June, p. 402.
7. Subir Mehra (2007), SME Financing: Widening Options in Access, *The Hindu Survey of Indian Industry,* p. 68.
8. N. Balasubramanian (2007), SME Financing Expanding the Role of SIDBI, *The Hindu Survey of India Industry,* p. 70.

9. Correspondent (2007), Industrial Estates for Women in all Districts, *The Hindu*, Sept. 1, p. 4.

10. Poornima M. Charantinath (2006), Entrepreneurship Development Small Business Enterprises, Pearson Education, New Delhi, p. 110.

11. M. K.Venu (2007), Quicker Procedures for SMEs too, *The Economic Times*, August 27, p. 3.

12. Pooja Birai (2007), Empowered by Self Belief, *The Economic Times*, August 7, p. 9.

Appendix

1. *Entrepreneur:* is a person who creates an enterprise. The process of creation is called as "entrepreneurship". The word entrepreneur has been taken from French, where it was originally meant to designate an organizer of musical and other entertainment.

2. *Tiny Unit :* The investment limit in plant and machinery in respect of tiny enterprises is Rs. 25 lakh irrespective of the location of the Unit.

3. *Small scale Industrial Unit (SSI):* The investment in fixed assets in plants and machinery, whether held on ownership terms or on lease or by hire purchase, does not exceed Rs.100 lakh as on March 31, 2001 is to be treated as a small-scale industrial Unit.

4. *Ancillary Unit:* This is a sub-class of SSIs. An industrial undertaking which is engaged or is proposed to be engaged in (i) the manufacture of Parts, components, sub-assemblies, toolings or intermediates; or (ii) rendering services, or supplying or rendering not less than 50 per cent of its production or its total services, as the case may be, to other units for production of other articles and whose investment in fixed assets in plant and machinery, whether held on ownership terms or on lease or on hire purchase, does not exceed Rs. 1 crore as on March 31, 2001 is to be treated as an ancillary enterprise.

5. *Small Enterprise:* As per the Micro, small and medium Enterprises Development Act, 2006 in the manufacturing sector, an enterprise with investment in plant and machinery upto Rs.5 crore is termed as a small enterprise with investment upto Rs.10 crore is defined as a medium enterprise.

In the service sector, enterprises with investment in equipment upto Rs. 2 crore are classified as small enterprises and those with investment up to Rs. 5 crore are classified as medium enterprise.

6. *Small and Medium Enterprises Credit Rating Agency (SMERA):* which provides credit rating services to SMEs for affordable fees. Certain risk profiling studies have also been taken up. In due course, credit rating of clusters by SMERA will help not only the lenders but also the clusters by providing information of wider market opportunities for their products, strengthening them negotiating ability and help adopt improved business practices.

7. *Credit Guarantee Fund Trust:* The Government in association with SIDBI, has set up a Credit Guarantee Fund Trust for small Industries (CGTSI) to implement the credit guarantee scheme. The main objective of Trust is to facilitate hassle-free credit to SSI sector. SSI Loans upto Rs. 25 lakhs are covered under the scheme. At the end of November 2006, the Trust had extended guarantee for 56, 651 proposals from small entrepreneurs covering credit assistance of Rs.1441 crore.

8. *SME Technology Services LTD*: has bee assisting small enterprises in accessing the latest technologies to diverse industrial fields with limited success.

9. *SIDBI Foundation for Micro-Credit (SFMC):* a department SIDBI has been pioneering the spread of banking hitherto unbankable segments including weaker sections through Non-governmental Organizations. The SFMC is dealing with the huge task of developing on organized informal credit structure in an orderly fashion by providing capacity building support services.

10. *Export Oriented Unit (EOU):* An industrial Undertaking in which the investment is fixed assets in plant and machinery, where held on ownership terms, or on lease, or by hire purchase, does not exceed Rs. 100 lakhs and has an obligation to export 30 per cent of production.

11. *Women Entrepreneurs:* A small scale industrial unit/industry related service or business enterprise, managed by one or more women entrepreneurs in proprietary concerns, or in which she/ they individually or jointly have a share capital of not less than 51 per cent as Partners/shareholders/Directors of private limited company/members of cooperative society.

9

NEED FOR STRUCTURAL ADJUSTMENT OF INDUSTRIALISATION IN KERALA ECONOMY

Kerala is a God living place but found people learning place for livelihood in India and abroad. There is a general urge from all quarters for rapid industrialization of state. Regional disparities were formed adequately in Kerala Economy. There are two phases of industralisation in Kerala during the pre-independence period. The first phase was characterised by the pondering of small and cottage industries, which were dominated by agro-based units. The second phase started with certain policy initiatives of government of Travancore. The process of modern industralisation in the state started in the last quarter of the 19th century. The government of Travancore promoted small-scale units till the mid-1930s. The scale of operation changed to large and medium scale by the 1940s. Agro-based industries continued its domination, which accommodated more than 50 per cent of the number of companies and employment in Kerala in 1947. Formation of Kerala state was on Nov. 1, 1956. One of the ways of evaluating the structural change in the industrial system is to express the share of manufacturing in the regional economy. There was a gradual rise in the share of industrial sector in the net domestic product. Comparing the other states, Kerala has the lowest share compared Gujarat, Maharastra. In Kerala, the share of agriculture remains almost the same, while it declined at the national level during 1980-81 and 1997-98. According to the 2001 census, labour force participation in Kerala is one of the lowest (32%) in the country. Male participation is 50.36 per cent in 2001.

Level of Industralisation

There are several indicators of industralisatioin. One can consider five important variables as indicators of industralisation. They are gross value output (GVO), value added (VA), number of factories (NOF), Number of employees (NE) and fixed capital (FC). The following table analyses the variable impact on Kerala economy.

Table 1
The Rank of Kerala Industry

Year	*GVA*	*VA*	*NOF*	*NE*	*FC*	*WE*
1959	9	9	12	10	8	-
1970-71	11	10	11	10	14	10
1980-81	11	10	11	10	13	11
1985-86	13	12	11	12	14	11
1998-99	13	12	10	11	14	13
2000-01	12	13	10	9	15	-

Source: Annual Survey of industries.
* The rank is based on 14 major states in the country.

The Table 1 explains the positions of Kerala economy among 14 states of developing. The position of Kerala in the industrial map of the country gradually declined in terms of all indicators over time. The absolute positions in terms of GVO and VA slipped to 12 and 13 in 2000-01 from 9 each in 1959 respectively. A sharp decline occurred in terms of FC during the same period. There was a marginal improvement in terms of NOF but it did not help the state to enhance its ranking in value added. The rise in NOF is mainly attributed to the lopsidedness to SSI_S. It seems that the fall in fixed capital was a major contributory factor to the declined position of Kerala in industralisation. The fall in the share of capital is mainly contributed by its relatively slow growth compared to the growth in employment and input. While other southern Indian states improved or remained at the same level of industralisation, Kerala failed to catch up with them. Though Kerala has an impressive growth, its rank in terms of value added, employment and fixed capitàl was the lowest among the south Indian states.

Productivity Trends

Productivity represents the efficiency and source of growth. It can be represented by total factor productivity (TFP) and partial productivity (APL and APK). The overall growth of these variables along with input Gross value added (GVA) ratio and capital intensity is provided in Table 2.

Table 2
Annual Growth Rates of Manufacturing during 1960 to 1998-99

Item	*Simple Defilation*	*Double Deflation*
Total Factor productivity (TFP)	2.22	4.89
Average productivity of (APL)	4.13	6.29
Average productivity of Capital (APK)	4.74	6.89
Input/Gross value added (GVA)	0.08	-2.08
Capital/Labour	-0.06	-

Source: Annual Survey of Industries.

The Table 2 reveals that TFP, APL and APK grew in the same direction as the growth in GVA for the whole period of analysis. It has two implications: (a) the overall efficiency (TFP) increased over time and (b) rise in partial productivity's along with positive growth in employment (L) and capital (K). These implications show a healthy trend but is not evenly reflected in all decades. Another positive feature in the state industry was the insignificantly low (SD) or negative growth (DD) in the ratio of input and gross value added (GVA). It points to the fact that the industry had been using only less and less inputs over time. The negative growth in capita intensity (K/L) can be interpreted in two ways. Low capital intensity marks a low level of Technology. Public sector in the state employs a lot of employees, which can push down the K/L ratio the insignificantly low (SD) or negative growth (DD) in the ratio of input and gross value added (GVA). It points to the fact that the industry had been using only less and less inputs over time. The negative growth in capital intensity (K/L) can be interpreted in two ways. Low capital intensity marks a low level of Technology. Public sector in the state employs a lot of employees, which can push down the K./L ratio.

Decade wise Analysis

The overall performance of the industry for the few decades need not be uniformly displayed when each decade is taken separately. During the four decades, TFP growth changed with the direction of growth in GVA. Kerala registered positive trends in the process of industralisation during 1960 and 1980. This can be taken as the first stage of industralisation after formation of state in 1956. The growth receded in the third decade 1980s, in terms of GVA and TFP at DD. It further worsened in the early 1990s. This marked the second stage of growth of industry in Kerala. Any low, the industrial efficiency had been on the receding since 1980-81.

Labour and capital contributed positively to the growth in GVA in all decades. The growth in capital productivity was higher than the growth in APL in all decades except in the 1980s. The decline in the overall efficiency of the industry is a disturbing fact. The interesting feature is that capital intensity registered higher negative growth (1960 to 1990).

While discussing the growth of the industry, it is argued that the paradox of relatively high industrial growth and low level of industralisation in Kerala may be due to structure of the state's industry.

Structure of Industry

As industralisation progresses, food, drink and textiles were relatively less important in advanced countries compared to backward economies, while metals, metal products and chemicals were relatively more important in the former. One of the recent studies also points to similar structural change in the East Asian Countries.

Food Processing Industries

Kerala has a lopsided industrial structure in terms to Agro-based and small sized industries. The relatively large share of food processing industry (FPI) shows the industrial backwardness of the state. Kerala could have been called as an FPI economy as 54.41 and 27.81 per cent of employment and value added of the manufacturing sector accounted to this sector in 1965. The share of these two variables declined later but improved in VA in the 1990s. However, employment did not improve with VA, which moved with FC. They are low in the industrialised states like Tamilnadu and Maharastra.

Basic Chemicals and Products

Next to FPI, Basic Chemicals and Chemical Products (BCCP) is the major manufacturing sub-sector in the State. One does expect that this sub-sector can elevate the level of industrialisation in Kerala. Unfortunately, this does not take place here. Though this sub-sector shares more than 25 per cent of FC, the magnitude of VA is below 20 per cent on average. The relative employment generation is also higher among the industrialised states like Gujarat, Maharastra and Tamilnadu, than here. Thus Kerala state failed to generated VA and employment with the size of fixed capital in Basic Chemicals and Chemical Products (BCCP) industry. The rubber-petroleum, coal products and processing of nuclear fuels (RPPCN) industry has been gradually improving its position in Kerala since 1965. The increase in the share of fixed capital is explicitly reflected in value addition and not in employment. Though rubber and petroleum industry was prominent in Kerala, the State could not lessen the influence of FPI. As a result, Kerala continued at the lower end of the industrial ladder.

Metals and Alloys Industries

Basic Metals and Alloys Industries (BMAI) had a reasonable share in employment (7.5%) and VA (5.39%) in 1965. Though the share of FC improved in this industry, it could not arrest the fall in the share of employment and VA. This is another cause of concern as Kerala is not able to enhance the share of employment and VA in modern sector.

Machinery and Equipment Industry (MEI), Transport Equipment and Parts (TEP) had relatively better share in 1965, but declined in FC, employment and VA overtime. The industrial share analysis made that Kerala is dominated by traditional and small industries like FPI. Maharastra, Gujarat and Tamilnadu are at the top due to their diversification and modernisation.

Small Scale Industries

The role of Small Scale Industries (SSI) as compared to large scale units is relatively more in Kerala than at the all India level. Nineteen per cent of the value added in the factory (ASI) sector fell in the category of SSIs in Kerala, while it was only 16 per cent in the all India level in 1981. The ASI sector mainly consists of large and medium scale industries. The share in ASI and SSI sectors is 3.64 and 10.51 per cent respectively in 2001-02. Kerala had a stupendous growth of SSI Units to the extent of 397 per cent in the context of 145 per cent at the national level during 1987-88 and 2001-'01. Kerala claims 10.5 per cent of the total SSI Units in the country and rank third behind up (12%) and Gujarat (11.3%) in that variable. However, the magnitude of sick units is more in Kerala (34.6%), when the national picture is considered in Kerala (34.6%), when the national picture is considered (13.01%). Thus the ailing SSI units in Kerala is a scar.

The reasons for sickness of SSI units were insufficient demand, inadequacy of working capital, impoverisation in marketing, poor supply of power and problems in supply of raw materials.

Concentration in ETP area

Industrial scenario in Kerala is lack of spacial equity. Central part of Kerala has concentrated the industries. It is seen in the districts of Ernakulam, Thrissur and Palakkad (ETP). 57 per cent of large and medium scale units (LMIs) are located in these industries. Ernakulam shares more than 50 per cent of units in 2002-'03. More than one third of the State Public Sector Units (SPSUs) are established in the districts of Ernakulam and Trivandrum. Unlike in the context of the number of factories in ETP belt, employment is concentrated in Kollam (31.03%) in 2002. However, a limitation of this fact is that the lion share of employment take place in the cashew nut industry, which absorbs labour force seasonably.

Public Sector Industries

It has the largest number 110 of State Public Sector Units (SPSUs) in India. With 30 per cent of equity in the State. State owned capital is thinly distributed. The State is also noted for resisting the dis-investment process during the post-liberties period. Even though investment in the State PSUS is inefficiently distributed, they are able to meet one of the major social objectives of the State. It is evident from the fact that three per cent of the factories in the public sector are able to accommodate 25 per cent of the workers in the factory sector (Economic Review, 2004). PSUs confront with excess, less productive and high cost manpower lacking in professionalism. This adds fuel to the operational inefficiency and cost-disadvantage of State PSUs. The main reason for insensitive nature of SPSUs is the complex administrative system. Their administration is vested with 10 departments that create a crucial dilemma between autonomy, transparency and accountability. The trouble becomes deep rooted in the absence of professionalism and continuity of leadership.

Causes for Kerala Backwardness

There are so many explanations relating to backwardness of industry in Kerala. They may be grouped into regional specific and non-religion specific. The region specific argument mainly revolves around militant trade Unionism, low entrepreneurial skill, environmental lobby, power shortage and lack of certain strategic resources.

High and Dear Wages

The general notion is that Kerala labour is dear and thereby manufacturing has become less attractive. The load talk is that dear labour and strained atmosphere as the reasons for the flight of industries to neighbouring states have received wide popularity.

Under Utilisation of Capacity

In the tile industry, rubber and rubber wood, garments making, electrical machinery and handlooom industries raw material cost constitutes more than 50 percentage of the total cost. Interest burden is another major cost element both in private and public sector. Kerala has cost-disadvantage in a considerable part of modern manufacturing sector compared to the same at the national level. Psychic, personal and social factors along with economic calculations shape entrepreneurial decisions. In fact, industrial relations are better in Kerala. Generally high capacity utilisation increases the profitability. On an average, it is only just above 50 per cent in the case of public enterprises. Spinning mills, fruits and vegetable processing industry and industrial estates record more than 70 per cent capacity utilisation.

Sunrise Industries

Both forward and backward linkage effects are very weak in Kerala. Government itself is a poor buyer of commodities for the state enterprises. Technology enhances productivity and industrial growth. This is evident in the case of fishing industry. Government should follow an integrated approach for providing incentives and subsidies. The policy should emphasis the sunrise industries like information technology, tourism and industry related services. Till the 1990s Central government was a major investor at the regional level. After economic reforms, Centre has reduced the investment over state. The successful entrepreneurs strive to maintain balance among various aspects relating to cultural traits like activity, doing, thinking, environment etc.

Environment Lobby

The pressure tactics of the environmentalist lobby, lopsided structural growth, absence of marketing dynamism and absence an entrepreneurial culture are the major region specific supplementary factors contributing to industrial backwardness and also non-region specific factors such as rising capital-output ratio and declining credit–deposit ratio.

Conclusion

After formation of Kerala State 1956, industrialization was picked up rapidly. Among advancing States of fourteen Kerala was one. Upto 1990, State Public Sector Units were formed in impressive growth. Still, the state is dominant on food processing industry. This state had stupendous growth of the small scale units than the nation on or before 2001 year. Much of industries are concentrated in Ernakulam, Thrisssur, Palakkad belt and Thiruvananthapuram. Further, it had 110 Public Sector Units, leading state in India. Due to Complexity of administrative, location specific and non-location specific many industries are under sick and dying. It needs good governance, structural adjustment transparency and accountability for speedy development of industralisation with sustainability.

Notes and References

1. Pradeep Kumar Panda (2003), Poverty and young Women: Linkages in Kerala, *Economic and Political Weekly*, Sept. 20, p. 4034.
2. D. Rajasenan and Gerard de Groot (2005) Kerala Economy: Trajectories, Challenges and implications Department of Publication and Public Relations, CUST, Cochin.
3. S. Muraleedharan (2005), Industrial Growth in Kerala, edited by D. Rajasenan and Gerard de Groot, Kerala Economy, DPPR, CUST, Cochin.
4. Lathika (2002), Productivity of Coconut Cultivations Kerala (unpublished thesis) Kottayam.
5 K. N. Harilal, K. J. Joseph (2003), Stagnation and Revival of Kerala Economy: An Open Economy Perspective, *Economic and Political Weekly*, June 7, pp. 2286-2293.

10

ASIAN ECONOMIC INTEGRATION: LOOKING FOR SINGLE MARKET AND CURRENCY

International trade brings multi-dimensional merits to young and old economies of the Globe, provide they had interest in competitiveness. After successful experimentation of the European Union (E.U.) and North American Free Trade Agreement (N.A.F.T.A.), there is strong move for Asian Economic integration. Developing Asia accounted for 52 per cent of world population and 25 per cent of world income in PPP TERMS IN THE YEAR 2004.[1]

Trade–An Engine of Growth

The role of trade in economic development particularly in respect of developing countries, has been widely debated. While many economists view trade as a powerful engine of growth, there are many, including some very renowned economists, who highlight the deleterious effects of trade on developing countries. While economists like Haberler and Cairn Cross strongly argue that foreign trade can contribute substantially to the development of the developing countries. Gunnar Myrdal, Prebish Singer and several other maintain that the accrual of gains from trade is biased in favour of the advanced Industrial countries, that foreign trade has inhibited industrial development in the poor nations and that contrary to what would be expected from classical trade doctrine-free trade has in reality accentuated international inequality.

Trade, undoubtedly, has several benefits. It promotes growth and enhances economic welfare by stimulating more efficient utilization of factor endowments of different regions and by enabling people to obtain goods from efficient sources of supply. Trade also makes available to people goods which cannot be produced in their country due to various reasons. The role of trade in enhancing consumer choice is tremendous. The 'foreign trade multiplier' shows how an injection of income arising out of trade can lead to economic expansion.

Expansion of the export sector and acceleration of economic growth caused by export growth will benefit the economy in general. Experiences of South-East economies show the benefits of export led growth. The boom of India's IT exports has been generating large number of high paid jobs for the educated youth and it has trickle down effects.[2]

Global Vision and one Family

The reach of that global vision included, as Richard Cobden, the leading Manchester liberal, put it: "to change the face of the world, so as to introduce system of government entirely distinct from that which now prevails", where " the desire and motive for large and mighty empires and gigantic armies and great navies.......will die away....When man becomes one family and freely exchanges the fruits of his labour with his brother man. If that was a baby talk, it did move a huge lot of babies across the world.[3]

Integration of Trade

Forty five developing countries have fewer than 1.5 million people each. Their small local markets and small pools of workers limit domestic competition and diversity of economic activities. For them greater integration with international markets is crucial. It involves providing adequate infrastructure to facilitate trade and fostering regional cooperation. Regional integration enables firms to achieve economies of scale by expanding market size. It can reduce transaction costs and investment risk, also encouraging more investment.

The South Pacific Forum, a 16-member organization (including Australia and New Zealand) has adopted investment principles along the lines of those drawn up for the Asia Pacific Economic Cooperation (APEC) countries. Concerned about the high costs of transportation in the region, the Forum's main priority is shipping.[4]

Promotion of Regional Trade Agreements

India's exports are around 14 per cent of GDP and the trade–GDP ratio is almost 33 per cent. Around 30 per cent of India's global trade is under Regional Trade Agreements (RTAs). India is now using Regional Trade Agreements (RTAs) not just for trade in goods but also for trade in services, investment, and trade facilitation, especially customs procedures. RTAs help attract Foreign Direct Investment (FDI) from both members as well as non-members.

Special Economic zones (SEZs) are now an added alteration for FDI. RTAs would force a degree of harmonization in economic laws and regularly framework, thereby facilitating trade and capital flows that promise rapid economic growth.

As an illustration, India took initiative with Singapore for expanding trade. Nearly 2,600 Indian companies setup operations in Singapore in the last three years, while nine banks from India where also here now. The Singapore–India trade touched a record $20 billion mark in 2006.[6]

Singapore Pruned Procedures

Firms in developing countries often face long delays when importing and exporting goods. In recent years computerization has demonstrated the potential to dramatically speed up part of the process. One initiative uses software and procedures based on a program called Tradenet. Rather than submit multiple unique forms to multiple agencies, a trade can electronically submit a single document that contains all the information.

Singapore used these methods in 1989 to reduce processing time from two to four days to a few minutes, and the number of required documents from between 3 and 35 to a single document. Freight forwarders estimate that the program has reduced their cost of handling trade documentation by between 20 to 35 per cent.[7]

SAARC's Problems and Prospects

Unlike many other regional grouping across the world, South Asian Association for Regional Cooperation (SAARC) has been beset with problems which have hampered the transition to a regional trading arrangement. The asymmetry between India and the other countries stands out as a major hindrance. In spite of hurdles, India is doing trade with neighbours and their exports imports and ratio is given in the below.

Table 1
India's Exports, Imports and Exports/Imports Ratio with SAARC
($ Million)

Country	*Exports*	*1996-97 Imports*	*Exports/ Imports Ratio*	*Exports*	*2003-2004 Imports*	*Exports Imports Ratio*
Bangladesh	868.96	62.23	13.96	1740.75	77.63	22.42
Bhutan	21.98	33.78	0.65	89.49	52.37	1.71
Maldives	10.36	0.17	60.94	42.34	0.37	114.43
Nepal	165.72	64.07	2.59	609.36	286.04	2.34
Pakistan	157.22	36.16	4.35	286.94	57.65	4.98
Sri Lanka	477.41	42.84	11.14	1319.20	194.74	6.77
Total	1724.39	242.31	7.12	4293.55	709.32	6.05

Source: The Hindu Survey of Indian Industry 2007, pp. 31, 32.

The Table 1 reveals that during six years the export trade in between India and Bangladesh was doubled, with Nepal fourfold, with Pakistan doubled, thrice with Sri Lanka. Regarding imports, India is importing more from Nepal, Sri Lanka and Bangladesh, which are meager, comparing exports of India. Finally, we can say India had surplus trade with SAARC Countries. While India has the highest trade imbalance with the Maldives, Bangladesh and Pakistan, with Nepal and Bhutan; the trade imbalance is comparatively low.

India has not remained confined to South Asia in its quest for regionalism. A member of the Bay of Bengal initiative for

Multi-sectoral Technical and Economic Co-operation (BIMSTEC), Comprising Bangladesh, Bhutan, Mynamar, Nepal, Sri Lanka and Thailand. Another important initiative at the intra-regional level is the framework Agreement on comprehensive Economic Cooperation (CECA) with ASEAN signed in 2003, and with Thailand in 2003. The CECA between India and Singapore in effect from 2005 is structured as an integrated package of several agreements comprising a free trade agreement, trade in goods, trade in services, investments and economic cooperation, an improved double taxation avoidance agreement.

There are many other agreement on the anvil. CECA with Malaysia, a proposal for an agreement with Australia, an FTA with the EU, a trilateral FTA with the Southern Cone Common Market (MERCOSVR) and the South African Customs Union (SACV), the permutations and possibilities appear endless.[8]

Origin of Asian Crisis

Starting Thailand in the summer of 1997, the Asian Financial crisis swept through Indonesia, Malaysia and South Korea, turning the regions economic miracle into a debacle. Capital which had been flowing in flew out in huge amounts. Where these four economies and the Philippines had attracted in-flows of over $ 65 billion in 1996, the annual outflows during 1997 and 1998 were almost $ 20 billion, amounting to an annual resource crunch of over $ 85 billion–a staggering amount indeed, this caused currencies to collapse, stock prices to crash and economies to go into a tailspin.[9]

A Decade after the Asian Financial Crisis

Ten years ago, the Asian financial crisis of 1997-98 began to unfold. Few countries in the region were left untouched and the after effects reverberated across the globe. A decade later, Asia shines in the global economic landscape and its vitality stands out as a remarkable achievement. But what lies behind this success and what are the new challenges for a region that has become a dynamo for the world economy?

In retrospect, the Asian financial crises proved to be a temporary setback, despite its enormous economic and social costs. Today, Asia is among the star performers in the global economy. The region found strength in no small part by turning crisis into opportunity. Regional policy forums have taken on renewed importance. India–regional trade has grown rapidly, with the development of complex supply chains entered on China.

What lies behind their success? The key to today's dynamism has been nimbler macro-economic policy frameworks and comprehensive reforms in the financial and Corporate sectors. More flexible exchange rate régimes have cushioned external shocks and an impressive War chest of official reserves has been built up; Inflation targeting has provided a monetary anchor in many cases, and fiscal policies have taken on a longer term perspective to safeguard debt sustainability. As for structural reforms, measures to deal with the immediate strains in the financial system have been complemented by steps to address the under-lying weaknesses. Mechanisms to facilitate financial restructuring are now in place, regulatory and prudential frameworks have been upgraded, and corporate governance has been strengthened. China and India have made further strides as regional power houses, the Philippines has weathered bouts of turbulence and gained considerable resilience.

The Next 10 Years?

What is ahead for Asia? Much will depend on whether it can tackle a number of issues over the medium term. While priorities differ across countries, a common theme stands out–coping with globalization and harnessing the tremendous upside it could deliver.

Over the past decade, inequality has risen steadily across the region. For example China displays now a more skewed income distribution than the United States or Russia. Even Japan, once the poster child of a fairly equalitarian society, is today more unequal than the average industrial country. Besides ethical or social implications, worsening inequality is a concern for economic policymakers. Growing income inequality and potentially erratic capital flows are but two examples of the challenges that globalization presents to Asia?[10]

East Asia: Domestic Integration is Lagging

East Asia integrated first with global trade markets, and its success with global integration growing. Emerging East Asia (which excludes Japan) has increased its export market share to 20 per cent, double its share, and total merchandise trade has reached the same size as total GDP.

Despite successful integration and increasing regional integration, many East Asia countries are falling behind in domestic integration. Growing inequality is pressuring East Asia's social cohesion. Inequality in income levels, schooling, and access to basic services in much of the region has risen. Consumption is severely sanctioned and opportunities for corruption are curbed by a rule based government.[11]

The India–ASEAN FTA has been facing Choppy waters right from the time talks started on the pact. The negotiations had come to halt following ASEAN'S rejection of India's offer to reduce tariffs on four agricultural products–palm oil, Pepper, Tea and Coffee–to 50 per cent. ASEAN wants duties on the products brought down to atleast 40 per cent. India now seems to be prepared to compromise further and lower duties to about 45 per cent.[12]

Hunger Index: India Scores Low

India ranks way down at 96 among 119 developing countries included in the Global Hunger Index (GHI). This rank is well below all its neighbours, barring Bangladesh, and falls in the category in which the hunger situation is deemed "alarming". Even Nepal is four notches higher than India at number 92 and Pakistan eight points above India at number 88.

Even neighbouring countries facing continuous domestic strife, such as Myanmar and Sri Lanka are ranked markedly above India, being placed at number 68 and 69 respectively. Mauritius is among the top 20 countries where the problem of hunger is the least. China, though ranked at number 47 falls in a category where the hunger is the least. China, through ranked at number 47 falls in a category where the hunger is "not a serious" issue.[13]

Further, the International Labour organization's 2008 Global Employment Trends report shows an "impressive" poverty reduction in South Asia (Largely dominated by India). Extreme working poverty (income of less than $ 1 per day) fell by 20 per cent in a decade from 53 per cent in 1997 to 33 per cent in 2007, the greatest decrease in any region of the world. Between 1997 and 2007, labour productivity in South Asia rose 3.6 per cent annually. In comparison in East Asia, it rose at almost double the pace at 6.4 per cent and in developed economies and the EU it increased by 1.6 per cent. But South Asia has a lot to catch upon especially on the issue of women workers. Women's participation in workforce in South Asia is the among the worst the employment to population ratio for women stands at 34.1 per cent against 65.2 per cent is East Asia.[14]

The Political Economy of Electricity Populist Measure in India

Indian electricity utilities generally provide unsatisfactory service to their customers, whether firms a households. In recent budget document the central government noted that electricity shortages routinely lead to outages and voltage fluctuations that disrupt all aspects of economic life and require substantial investments in voltage stabilizers generators and new motors.

Most electricity is generated and supplied by State owned electricity boards, which are experiencing severe financial difficulties and draining State budgets. Before privating its electricity utility in 2002, for example, the Delhi government provided it with implicit subsidies of $ 200 to $ 300million a year, in loans unlikely to be repaid. Even so, the company still face financial problems and provided poor service; power cuts were common in summer and winter.

Under pressure from well organized groups of voters, governments have kept average price below average costs, allowing politically influential customers to pay especially low prices. Farmers often receive electricity for pumps at prices well below costs. The subsidies became popular in the late 1970. in Andhra Pradesh the government offered flat-rate or no tariffs to farmers as an election promise. Soon after, in Tamilnadu demonstrations by the Agriculturists Association led to the provision of free electricity to some farmers. Other states then followed with their own agricultural subsidy programmes. Many of the recipients are fairly well-off land owning farmers. Farmers are not only beneficiaries: many customers steal their electricity, costing suppliers an estimated $ 4 billion a year. According to one report, utility employees who conspire in the theft of electricity can receive many times their annual salary in bribes.

Although some farmers, employees and politicians benefit, low prices discourage both the conservation of power and further investment in increasing supply and improving its reliability. That is why other users, including many firms, have to pay more.[15] Populist measures like free lunches, subsidies always bring financial problems to the trade promotion for India

Look East Policy

The bilateral trade between India and ASEAN countries had increased five fold since early nineties following the "Look East Policy". The bilateral trade which was around $ 5 billion between India and ASEAN 14 years ago went up to $ 27 billion in 2005. The policy had a visible impact on trade and civil aviation sectors. There were more flights now and the connectively between India and South East Asian nations had increased, leading to more travel by businessmen and tourists.[16]

India would end 2007-08 with export target in the range of $150-155 billion but achieved $ 125 billions.[17]

Impact of International Oil Prices on South Asia

Renewed increases in international oil prices area a major source of uncertainty for the region, potentially affecting current accounts, fiscal positions and inflation. Several countries suffer from internal conflicts which also add to uncertainty. As in the past, countries are prone to natural disasters (Like Tsunami 2004) and poor weather conditions can adversely affect the agriculture sector. Escalation in political tensions during an election year, as is the case in Bangladesh and Pakistan in 2007, could also present a drag on economic growth.

Growth is the newly industralised economies (NIEs) is also forecast to slow in 2007, as the global electronic cycle continues to weaken and export growth decelerates. While domestic demand in the Republic of Korea is slowly recovering from its slump of the two previous years, domestic demand in the other NIEs is expected to compensate as unemployment decreases and private consumption is expected to rise. In contrast, growth in Indonesia, Malaysia, the Philippines and Thailand "Association of Southeast Asian Nations. (ASEAN-4) is expected to accelerate or remain stable in 2007, supported by a rebound in private consumption in Indonesia as monetary policy is loosened, and by continued healthy domestic consumption growth in the other countries. In Thailand, 2007 could bring some renewed consumer and investor confidence after a year of political uncertainty and policy stagnation in 2006, depending on the performance of the interim government.[18]

Conclusion

International trade is considered as an engine of economic growth. By using natural resources, economic welfare can be multiplied. Export growth will benefit both economy and people. RTAs would harmomise the laws and development. Within short period, on 2006 year, as a miracle Singapore touched $20 billion trade with India. All procedural delays in trade were cut shorted from 35 document into a single document. India, as leader/big brother has to play friendly role in boosting up of SAARC trade, inspite of hindrances raised by Pakistan. The Asian Crisis 1997, was a reminiscence of 1930s depression, was overcomed by adjustment of macro-economic policies and financial reforms. The significant feature of Asian economy was growing inequalities in income levels of those people. The social menace of corruption is also eating away the vitals of these economies, which is to be curbed through political will and action, India is facing internal problems like bitter poverty, more subsidies like power, which become strong hurdle for speedy trade in Asia. India has to solve the internal issues first, then can win heart of Asian economies trade. Even a single Asian Currency and market are highly preferable within short period.

Note: The global hunger index has been complied by the Washington based International Food Policy Research Institute (IFPRI) and formerly released globally on Tuesday last as part of the report entitled "The Worlds Most Deprived: Characteristics and Causes of Extreme Poverty and Hunger".

The index is designed to capture three dimensions of hunger: lack of economic access to food, shortfalls in the nutritional status of children and child mortality which is, to a large extent, attributable to malnutrition.

Notes and References

1. Manoj Panda (2008), Macro-economic Overview, *India Development Report,* p. 33.
2. Francis Cherunilam (2006), International Economics, Tata McGraw-Hill Publishing Co., Ltd., New Delhi, p. 204.
3. Amartya Sen (2007), Lead Essay: India in the World, *The Hindu,* Independent India at 60, August 15, p. 2.
4. The World Bank (2005), International Integration is Especially Important for Small States, World Development Report, p. 65.
5. Prashant Goyal (2008), Are RTAs the Right Strategy? *The Economic Times,* Jan. 31, p. 22.
6. P. S. Suryanarayana (2007, Singapore can be a Bridge between India and Growing Economies: Nathan, *The Hindu,* October, 22, p. 14.
7. The World Bank (2005), World Development Report, p. 114.
8. Moana Bhagabati (2007), Regionalism: India's Relentless Quest, *The Hindu Survey of Indian Industry,* pp. 32-33.
9. Jagadish Bhagwati (2007), in Defense of Globalization, OUP, p. 199.

10. David Burton and Alessandro Zanello (2007), Asia Ten Years after *Finance and Development,* June, pp. 22-25.
11. Indermit S. Gill and Homi Kharas, (2007), Back in the Fast Lane, *Financial and Development,* March, p. 40-41.
12. Amiti Sen (2008), India, ASEAN Cook FTA Away from Limelight, *The Economic Times,* Jan. 9, p. 16.
13. Surinder Sud (2007), India Scores low in Hunger Index, *Business Standard,* Kochi November 12, p. 1.
14. Our Bureau (2008), Extreme Poverty in South Asia Dips, *The Economic Times,* Jan. 25, p. 22.
15. Agarwal *et al* (2005), India-Ministry of Finance (2003), *World Development Report,* p. 125.
16. Special Correspondent (2008), "Look East" Policy Pays off, *The Hindu,* January 11, p. 5.
17. News Item (2008), Export May Miss Target, *The Hindu,* February 5, p. 16.
18. United Nations (2007), *World Economic Situation and Prospects,* p. 109.

Section–III

University Education

11

UNIVERSITY SYSTEM ON PREGNANCY PAINS: LOOKING FOR DELIVERY OF INTELLECTUALS

The healthy growth of any nation requires educated citizens with skills and expertise in all disciplines in all subjects both at basic and professional levels with equal emphasis and importance. The objective of higher education is to contribute to the initiation and strengthening the process of development with the equity, justice, solidarity and liberty as the key elements. The core mission of higher education is to educate, to train, to undertake research and to provide services to the community-must be preserved and re-inforced and further expanded. This requires that higher education should enjoy autonomy and freedom exercised with responsibility.

The scenario of higher education has been changing in 21st century, as India entered into World Trade Organisation (WTO) and its affiliate, General Agreement on Trade in services (GATs). To meet the world class demand the system has to change to suite future needs of generations, ever change in quality, continuous development research, linking with business and industry, encourage new information and communication technologies, Management of finance and export of higher education and seeking international cooperation. How is it that lowering standards to make an extra buck? Making allowances for bright through socially deprived pupils become social engineering[1].

To gear up the University system performance radars for different universities are being developed for ranking the University, while overseas education is an attractive and increasingly viable option for many Indian students.[2]

Almost all the institutions of government in the United States, Japan, Singapore, Korea and the countries in the European Union have effective performance appraisal systems for review and rewards.[3]

Origin and Development of Universities

At the time of independence, in 1947, there were 20 Universities and 500 Colleges in the country. The number of students and teachers in higher education system was also very small. But, after independence, there has been an exponential increase in all these numbers. It has been regarded a fifteen-fold increase in the number of Universities and thirty fold increase in the number of colleges while student enrolment has gone up by nearly thirty-four times[4]. The University Colleges with affiliated colleges increased from 10,678 in 1997-98 to 15,343 in 2002-03 year, registered 46 per cent. Regarding student enrollment was 52.65 lakhs in 1991-92 year raised to 92.28 lakhs i.e. increased 75 per cent . In the year 2002-2003, faculty wise student enrolment was 45 per cent in Arts, 20 per cent in Science and 18 per cent in Commerce/management. In faculty wise 11,899 number of doctorate degrees were awarded in 2001-2002, out of which 38 per cent in Arts, 34 per cent in Science and 7 per cent from agriculture.

Management of Higher Education

To make efficient, effective and responsive Higher Education and to bring socio-economic changes, University Grants Commission (UGC) is implementing the following programme in Tenth plan.

Resources Mobilisation by Universities

- to encourage Universities to mobilise resources by participation/contribution of society in their development.

- to evolve a process for participation of society in University development.
- to encourage and enhance the flow of resources coming from the society for university development.
- to encourage Universities to provide consultancy on payment basis not only to the industries but to the government, and other bodies and society at large on vital issues of national importance and
- to provide incentives to the Universities which involve society in their development activities.

Universities may mobilise external resources through participation/contribution/consultancy from individual Indians or non-resident Indians-Alumni Associations, Public and Family Trusts, Industrial/Business houses, Cooperatives, Professional Associations, Unions/Association of employees, Municipalities/Panchayats, M.P/M.L.A/Counsellor's funds for encouraging their internal resources. The contribution of the UGC will be upto the extent of 25 per cent of the contribution received by the University, subject to a maximum of Rs. 25 lakhs *per annum*.

During the 2002-03 year, an amount of Rs. 63.17 lakhs was given as UGC share to 4 State Universities. In addition to this an amount of Rs. 23.79 lakhs was sanctioned to the Indian Institute of Technology, Roorkee (Non-University Institution).

In money terms, International students brought over 13 billion to the US economy in money spent on tuition, living expenses and related costs-placing Higher education among the top 10 largest service sector exports for the U.S.[5]

Quality in Higher Education

GATs has opened the eyes and ears of Higher education system, that education is a service, which is to be given like as high quality durable good to the society. U.K, U.S.A. Australia, Canada have been constantly maintaining the quality, due to assessment and accreditation of institutions. Many Indian students are moving for those countries, the reason is high quality of education. UGC introduced National Assessment and Accreditation Council (NAAC) in September 16, 1994 at Bangalore. The objective of NAAC is to promote the development of quality higher education infrastructure in the Country. To develop criteria for assessment and accreditation, periodically review the criteria, publicise widely, devise and establish mechanisms for assessment, encourage self-evaluation and initiate research on the process of assessment and accreditation. The target group of NAAC are the Universities and colleges in India. It has completed the process of accreditation of 94 Universities and 409 colleges during the past eight years. It is proposed that approximately 1000 colleges would be reviewed per year for the next five years. To promote quality, NAAC has popularized the concept by conducting seminars, conferences, workshops, manuals, NAAC News. *Indian Higher education caters to only 7% of the 17-23 age group. In any developed country this group is between 50-80%.* Even in China 17% of college age student find place in Universities.[6]

Inter-University Resources for Promotion of Quality

The main objectives for establishing these Centres are to provide common advanced centralised facilities/services for universities, to offering the best expertise in each field to teachers and researchers, excellent library facilities. The UGC is instrumental in producing more than a thousand educational films or programmes. The first "Country Wide Classroom Programme" was telecast on the network of Dooradarshan on August 15th, 1984. On an average, 300 to 400 programmes have been packaged every year at consortium of Educational communication for telecast on Dooradarshan, Gyandarshan and other Educational channels for dissemination of Higher Education beyond the classrooms. In the field of Humanities and Social Sciences, Indo-American Centre for International studies, Hyderabad would provide dynamic and vibrant platform for academicians from India, SAARC region, South-East, Central Asian and other countries. The main objective of the Centre would be to address contemporary development issues with multi-disciplinary approach, such as Education, Commerce and Economics of development of above countries along with interface with the developed countries; World trade GATs, IPR, financial management for international understanding; conflict management, diplomacy, development and peace initiatives between various countries; Human rights, Human values, life skills and learning to live together and Art, literature and other allied areas.

Table 1
Inter-University Centres and their Objectives: 2002-2003

Name	*Year of establishment*	*Objectives*
Nuclear Science Centre, New Delhi	1984	Nuclear Science Research
Inter-University entre for Astronomy and Astrophysics, Pune	1988	State of the Art Instrumentation for Research in Astronomy
Inter-University Consortium for DAE facilities, Indore	1989	Use of Facilities of Department of Atomic Energy
Information and Library Network (INFLIBNET) Ahmedabad	1991	Networking of University Libraries through electronic media
Consortium of Educational Communication, New Delhi television	1993	To disseminate Country Wide Classroom Programme through
National Assessment and Accreditation, council Bangalore	1994	To assess and accredit public and private institutions of higher learning.

Source: UGC (2003), Annual Report 2002-03, p. 157.

Promotion and Preservation of Indian Culture Heritage and Values

India has a heritage of great thinkers and social leaders whose revolutionary and path breaking thoughts and actions have left a lasting impact not only in India but also on the whole world. To acquaint teachers and students in Universities with their thoughts and actions and to involve them on studies and research, the UGC has been providing assistance to the Universities on selective basis, for selling up and running the Centres of Gandhian, Buddist, Nehru, Ambedkar, Swami Vivekananda, Dr.Rabindranath Tagore, Dr. Zakkir Hussain, Pt. Madanmohan Malviya, Dr. S. Radhakrishnan and Sardar Vallabai Patel Studies.

To promote values education in Universities/ Colleges is essential for student and society. It is ingrained in various regular courses and programmes. Further, Human Rights and Duties Education is promoting in various Universities and colleges.

Development of Universities award of P.G. Scholarships State/Deemed Universities, Management, Computer and Women Universities are emerging to meet the World Challenges and opportunities.

Eradication of illiteracy from the country, various programmes in Higher Education system were introduced such as National Adult Education programme (NAEP 1978-1983), Adult Continuing Education programme (ACEP-1983-1990), Area Based Approach programme (ABAP-1989 to 1992) Total Literacy Campaign Programme (TLCP-1992-1997) Continuing Education, Extension and Field outreach (ACEE & FO 1997 to 2002) by involving the Centres/Departments/ Universities and Institutions. These institutions, in turn involving the Centres/Department/Universities and Institutions. These institutions, in turn involving students and teachers, have organised programmes such as literacy, post literacy, continuing Education, Science for the People Environment education, legal literacy and technology transfer

Facilities for Scheduled Castes and Tribes

The Scheduled Castes and Scheduled Tribes have been identified as most depressed/oppressed groups of Indian Society which constitute about 15 per cent and 7.5 per cent respectively to the total Indian population. To safeguard their interests specific provisions have been made by providing reservation in various services under Central and State Governments. SC/ST Cells are started in 113 universities to ensure effective implementation and monitoring of the reservation policy of SC/STs and Programmes of the Government. In 1994, a special scheme namely Remedial Coaching for the benefit of the Under Graduate and Post Graduate students belonging to SC/STs. The other programme in 1994 for minorities/weaker sections among educationally backward communities was implemented to enable them to compete in various competitive examinations. In 1999-2000 year, Teachers Preparation in Special Education (TEPSE) and Higher Education for Persons with Special Needs (HEPSN) were introduced to develop courses for special teachers and counselors and also to provide facilities in various forms for the differently abled persons. If possible open more Dalit an Tribal Universities in the country, where the population is sizable and concentration.

Role of Women in Higher Education

Sam pitroda's recommendations of recommending 1500 Universities is highly laudable and implementable. Further add specialized subjects wise Universities like Mathematics and interrelated subjects as one University etc.

In Ninth plan, to reduce gender imbalances technological courses for women in Women Universities for providing financial assistance was given. In Tenth plan, technical courses for Women Universities have been extended. To migrate women, pursue higher education and with safe environment, construction of Women's Hostels were promoted. Since 1986 year, Studies on Women were promoted and arranged facilities to undertake research, development, extension work, economic self reliance of women, girls education, population issues, human rights and exploitation. There are 34 Women Studies Centres are functioning in Universities. For combating violence and sexual harassment in Universities, Cells were started in 45 Universities. The unemployed Ph.D degree women scholars for pursing research in any course, 100 slots per year are opened and available. Day Care Centres are started in Universities to provide facilities on payment basis for children around three months to six years, whose parents are working for pursing their academic career.

Promotion Physical Education and Sports

The Ministry of Human Resource Development has introduced the Scheme of creation of Sports infrastructure in Universities and Colleges. The National Adventure Foundation (NAF) was implementing the programme for promotion of Adventure Sports in Universities and Colleges. The Scheme of three year Degree Centre in Physical Edcuation, Health Education and Sports was introduced. The courses like Forest trekking, Mountaineering, Skating, Cycle Safari, Rock climbing, Water rafting, Hill Climbing, Jurdle trail watch and Bird watch expedition.

Since 1993 Yoga education and practice Centres were promoted in the Universities. At present, 64 Universities are running Yoga Centres. Further 10 Universities are established department of Human Consciousness and Yogic Sciences.

International Cooperation

In India, with 51 countries bilateral Exchange programmes are established under University Sector. Foreign language teachers are encouraged in Universities, whoever interested. Fellowships and Scholarships, Social Scientists Exchange Programmes, Higher Education Link Programme, SAARC Fellowships, Common Wealth Academic Staff Fellowships, Shastri Indo-Canadian Programmes, UNESCO Programmes, Travel Grant to Teachers to visit foreign countries were liberally promoted.

Development of Human Resources for Teaching and Research

The UGC conducts a national level test to determine eligibility for lectureship (1989) and Junior Research Fellowships (1984) to ensure minimum standards for the entrants in the teaching profession and research in Humanities, Social Sciences, Computer, Electronic Science, Forensic Science and Environmental Sciences. The test for other Science subjects is conducted by the CSIR jointly with UGC. The tests are conducted twice a year generally in the months of June and December. For candidates who desire to pursue research, Junior Research Fellowship is available for four years. The subject of Defence and Strategic studies was introduced from June, 2002 NET Exam, thus making the total number of subjects in which NET is held as seventy six. Presently, NET Examination is being conducted in 76 subjects at 65 Centres spread across the country and six Centres abroad for Indian nationals.

In response to the proposal of some States to conduct their own examination for eligibility for lectureship, the UGC has so far granted accreditation to conduct State Level Eligibility Test (SLET) for Lectureship only. At present, 19 States are using this SLET, which is reviewed periodically by UGC, SLET became a failure scheme. The reason is Universities are not giving employment to the passed candidates. Universities and Colleges are giving employment by their own advertisements.

Research keeps the process of inquiry vibrant and alive. The Universities are major training ground of researchers. The UGC inputs provide the base to the teachers for attracting very large research funds from other funding agencies. The financial assistance is provided to permanent, regular, working/retired teachers in the Universities and Colleges. Priority is given to inter-disciplinary research and inter-institutional collaborative research. The scheme of award of Research Scientists was originally initiated in 1983 to check the brain drain and also to attract the meritorious scientists of Indian Origin, who may be working abroad, with a view to promote high quality research in Science, Engineering, Technology, Humanities and Social Science and to build a cadre of Research Scientists in Indian Universities by providing opportunities to persons with outstanding merit. Under this scheme, 200 awards were made available at any given time. The Research awards scheme, Emeritus fellowships visiting professor/fellowship, National Lectureship were promoted liberally.

Studies in Emerging and Inter-disciplinary Areas

To implement emerging areas and innovative programmes, identified various disciplines with respect to educational, national and global priorities. They are Environment, Biotechnology, Electronics, Atmosphere Science, Remote Sensing, Super Conductivity, Innovative and Computer application. Further, *"Area Study Centres"* identified for undertaking studies relating to Social, Economic, Political and Cultural affairs of a given area and for developing inter-disciplinary research and teaching with a comparative framework. They are on SAARC, Nepal, South and South East Asian Studies, Chinese and Japan Studies, Canadian Studies, Latin and American Studies, Indian Diaspora, Federal Studies, Russian, Central Asian, East European, West Asian and African Studies, Manipuri, African, Central Eurasian, Indian Ocean, Himalayan, Indo-China studies etc.

Vocationalisation of Education

Vocationalisation of Education at undergraduate level is being implemented since 1994-95. The programme has been designed to ensure that the graduate who pass-out after completing these courses, would have knowledge, skills and aptitude for gainful employment in wage sector in general and self employment in particular. 35 vocational courses were identified with detailed syllabi. Subsequently, seven subjects were not in demand, were dropped and fourteen other subjects were included to cater to the needs of students from rural, hilly and tribal. The revised list of 42 vocational subjects is as follows.

Table 2
Vocational Subjects

Discipline/Area	*Subjects*
Arts, Humanities and Social Sciences	1. Functional Hindi
	2. Functional Sanskrit
	3. Functional English
	4. Archaeology and Museology
	5. Rural Handicrafts
	6. Early Childhood Care and Education
	7. Fashion Designing
	8. Gemology and Jewellery Designing
	9. Cosmetology
Commerce, Economics and Management	10. Principles and Practices of Insurance
	11. Office Management and Secretarial Practices
	12. Tax Procedures and Practices
	13. Foreign Trade Practices and Procedures
	14. Tourism and Travel Management
	15. Advertising, Sales Promotion and Sales Management
	16. Computer Applications
Sciences	17. Industrial Chemistry (Seven Streams)

Contd...

Discipline/Area	*Subjects*
	18. Food Science and Quality Control
	19. Clinical Nutrition and Dietetics
	20. Industrial Microbiology
	21. Bio-technology
	22. Biological Techniques and Specimen Preparation
	23. Sericulture
	24. Seed Technology
	25. Information Technology
Engineering and Technology	26. Industrial Fish and Fishery
	27. Instrumentation
	28. Geo-exploration and Drilling Technology
	29. Mass Communication and Video Production
	30. Still Photography and Audio Production
	31. Electronic Equipment Maintenance
	32. Computer Maintenance
	33. Electrical Equipment Maintenance
	34. Environment and Water Management
Subjects-Relevant to Rural, Hilly and Tribal Areas	35. Agro-Services
	36. Domestic Animal Farming
	37. Forestry and Wildlife Management
	38. Social Conservation and Water Management
	39. Hill Agriculture
	40. Non Conventional Energy Sources
	41. Dry land Agriculture
	42. Silvipasture

Source: UGC (2003), Annual Report 2002-'03 p. 117.

Since inception of the scheme in 1994-95, 2186 colleges and 32 universities have been selected for support for the introduction of different vocational subjects.

II

Impact of Foreign and Private Universities

Indians heading to the US for further studies are seeing a strange sight these days. Their American counterparts packing their suitcases, to do a stint in Indian Universities. Slowly, but surely American students are finding there way into Indian campuses as well. In 2002-03, 703 Americans received credits from their US institutes for study they spent in India. That is a rise of over 12% from 627 reported in 2001-02[7]. Higher education in India has become a global market for investment by Foreign Universities, NRIs, industrialists, Politicians. All this can be paid for the easy installments by interest accruing an deposits of high fee structures paid by end users. The number of International Students in higher education across the world is estimated 1.8 million (50 per cent of these go to U.K and U.S.A). This mobile population of international students has created an interesting situation as source of revenue, creative ideas that can be translated into wealth in various sectors ranging from health, engineering, medicine, agro-veterinary sciences to IT etc. China has the largest population and it also contributes maximally to the fraternity of mobile international students followed by South Korea, India, Japan and Greece. Creamy layer of students from IITs, IIMs, Central Universities and other are leaving country for bright prospects. Only 17 per cent of youth is able to get into professional courses leaving behind 83 per cent in general education.

Merit is Dead in Indian Universities

Poor syllabi, low teaching standards, lack of inter-disciplinary courses, very low dedicated teachers, dilapidated buildings, dysfunctional libraries, rank indiscipline amongst faculty, politically polarised unions of students, faculty and non-teaching staff; administrative mismanagement, corruption at every level, malpractices in recruitment, political and caste based Vice-chancellors are the few symptoms, which are very difficult to remove. State apparatus has failed to run higher education. Universities were turned as State Public understandings. The coterie of politicians in nexus with subservient civil servants, sycophants and pseudo- intellectuals has created an atmosphere where any intelligent and independent view is branded as opposition. Merit is moved to information technology sector and abroad assignments. At present, University system is on pains, which has to deliver intellectuals and make Universities on par Cambridge, Oxford and Horward, which are to sustainable for centuries together.

Need of an 'U' turn

One would welcome establishment of Foreign and Private Universities with adequate safeguards, monitoring and auditing system. One has to be alive to the possibilities of indoctrination of our youth by ideologies that may be in conflict with our heritage, culture, moral values, traditions and practices. Caution must also be exercised to ensure that they do not become centres of espionage, brainwashing etc.

The impact of foreign universities and private universities should be taken as a catalyst of change in our 300 plus Universities and over 15,000 colleges. They should gear up to develop their curriculae, teaching, research, management on the basis of national priorities and global interests. The aim should be to compete for not only stemming the westward mobility of 'Creamy layer' of our youth by providing them with state of the art facilities and training but also develop programmes which bring students from China, Japan, Korea, USA, UK, Australia and Canada for Indian Colleges and Universities. Our Universities can survive only when they can compete positively. It is not a revolutionary suggestion that the government should gradually phase out from areas of higher education in terms of financial, administrative and academic control. Higher education need free from politics and government interference. Pressures for drastic changes are mounting[8]. State should play as a facilitator than provider and producer.

Conclusions

Under the GATs, University education system is continuously changing its scenario, to meet world class demand. Exporting of educational, became an important item not only in developed nations but also in developing nations like India. Performance appraisal is taken as a yardstick for measuring it in all countries. Earlier, State initiated the university system, at present, it is better to withdraw from this scenario. Mobilisation of resources, quality, inter-university promotion, preservation of heritage and values, placement of women, facilities to SCs and STs, Development of Human resources,

Inter-disciplinary areas and Vocationalisation of education were observed changing to suite international competition. Foreign and Private Universities are to be nurtured to keep positive competition among traditional Indian Universities. So that developed countries children have to come for learning in India. Time is riped to keep politics and government intervention far away to University system, so that a healthy and prosperous development can be seen forth -with by introducing Regulatory Authority.

Notes and References

1. Hasan Suroor (2004), Who is Afraid of Social Engineering, *The Hindu,* November 5.
2. Karan Gupta (2004), Put to the Test, *The Economic, Times,* November 22.
3. Ashoke, K. Mitra (2004), Babudom's Measure for Measure, *The Economic Times,* September 20.
4. UGC (2003), Annual Report, 2002-2003, p. 44.
5. Ishami Duttagupta and Condice Zachariahs (2004), Great Indian Escape, *The Economic Times,* November, 15.
6. Candice Zachariahs (2004) , Private Varsities is No Man's Land, *The Economic Times,* November 5.
7. Candice Zachariahs (2004), Indian Varsities Beckon Yankees, *The Economic Times,* November 15.
8. S. B. Lall (2005), Unassessed Impact of Foreign and Private Universities on Higher Education in India, *University Today,* February 1, p. 8.

12

NEEDED GLOBAL PEACE UNIVERSITIES FOR SUSTAINABLE CIVILIZED GANDHISM

Since the very dawn of human civilization, the Hindu mind has reflected on the true nature of universe and man and their interrelationship. The depth and profundity of their enquiry in this regard is revealed in various schools of philosophy developed in India. The quintessence of the *Upanishadic* thought is that Brahman alone exists without a second. *Atma* itself is Brahman. All this is Brahman, I am Brahman, so art thou, and that which is in microcosm is also in the macrocosm Brahman is all pervading, it is subtler than the subtlest and larger than the largest.

All objects and events in the physical world are interdependent and inseparable 'parts' of the "cosmic whole". The whole and its 'parts' are constantly and mutually interacting. Consciousness is the essential aspect of the universe. The holistic approach prohibits the domination or torture of nature, since man and his environment are inseparable. Humankind must learn to live in peace and harmony with nature.

Levels of Globalization

Globalization is defined as free cross-border flow of goods, services, capital, labour, information, ideas and intellectual property.

Joseph Stiglitz, winner of Nobel prize for Economics-2001, has argued that globalization is not at fault but the way it has been managed is faulty. Single economic model does not suit whole world, he said. Part of the problem lies with the international economic institutions, with the IMF, World Bank and W.T.O., which help to set the rules of the game. They have done so in ways, that all too often, have served the interests of the more advanced industrialized countries and particular interests within those countries–rather than those of the developing world. But it is not that they have served those interests, too often, they have approached globalization from particular narrow mind-sets, shaped by a particular vision of the economy and society[1].

It can be easily recognized that the affluence of western world was the result of a techno-economic system based on Cartesian-Newtonian reductionist approach or the mechanistic world view. This system was capital and energy intensive, and in order to survive in competition required cheaper labour and raw materials and also huge markets. The basic concept that it was possible to have unlimited growth on a limited planet was itself unsustainable. Therefore, it is not the mismanagement of globalization but the world-view behind it which is responsible for the discontents.

Disparities in Global Development

Under the globalization, the disparities are growing very fastly in 21st century. In the globalized world 20 per cent of the world's richest people account for 86 per cent of the total private consumption expenditure, the poorest 20 per cent consumes 1.3 per cent. The richest fifth consumes 45 per cent of all meat and fish, the poorest fifth, 5 per cent, the energy consumption the richest fifth have a lions share of 58 per cent, the poorest fifth are left with less than 4 per cent. The gap between the rich and the poor is glowing at a fast rate, in 1970 the ratio was 30:1 today it is 74:1 or more. The moot question is can the present model of international economic order provide any solution to the world complex problems? Paul Samuelson, Nobel Prize winner, felt that inequality among nations is not an accident but a built in characteristic of the system. The "Global village" phenomenon is obviously an integral part of globalization. Marshall Mc Luthan coined this term "Global village" in 1960s to express his belief that electronic communication world unite the world by bringing together diverse cultures and distant people of the world. Therefore, global village does not really represent the "shrinking of the world" but widening of the electronic instantaneous communication network for bringing people into togetherness.[2]

Torturing Global Nature

The foundation of capitalist economic system rested upon Cartesian-Newtorian mechanistic world-view. A world-view which was basically emanated from Francis Bacon's advocacy of "torturing nature to reveal her secrets". Obviously this attitude gave a philosophical justification to the indiscriminate exploitation of natural resources. Any Socio-economic system based on this concept would tend to be exploitative and oppressive[3].

Globalization and Pitfalls

Globalization is certainly not free of pitfalls. Over the last decade the world has seen greater exchange of information and ideas between nations. At the same time, it has also seen alarming rise in the volume of narcotics trade, flesh trade, cyber crimes, proliferation of the AIDs, viruses and terrorism. Another undesirable consequence of globalization has been the marginalization of several local, ethnic cultures as a result of greater dominance of advanced nation cultures in the international media[4].

In spite of certain initial lacunae, globalization also appears to be having number of apparent Gandhian values such as:

(a) Global unity and integration

(b) Fast growing antipathy to mass-violence, especially in the aftermath of the terrorist attack on New York WTC, on Sept. 11, 2001.

(c) In evidently receding trend in ideological clashes among nations.

(d) Globally expanding mosaic of acceptance of the Gandhian principle of non-violence among nations and their leaders (India response and patience to terrorist violence and attacks and

(e) End of or doing away with "war as an instrument of national policy" at least among countries of the European union.

Globalization is certainly giving solutions to number challenges like population, pollution, poverty, proliferation of armaments and peace of the world. Globalization is a continuous process toward a new and just world order.

Globalization and Education

In earlier civilization, there were no four walled compuses of universities, but these were created in garden was the university, where he discovered law of gravitation, the laws of floating bodies, and for James Watt, Kitchen was the university where he discovered the theory of steam engine and for Nehru, the first Prime Minister of India, Prison was the best of universities (as told by him in his letter dated 7th April 1932, from Bareily District Jail adressing jointly to his sisters who were both in Lucknow District Jail). Prison itself he made a university by his creative use of nine years that he spent in detention during the struggle of India's freedom and morals and the whole philosophy of life[5].

These examples bring situation, which provokes the persons for these learning and creation. Nehru also did not mean that the students of Universities should be kept in prisons or universities should be converted into prisons for the study of politics, sociology and philosophy. The main thrust of his was to law to use the leisure creatively by being conscientised.

Perfect Human Being: A Search

Awareness towards total situations–social, political and economic–enables individuals to encounter with them non-violently which made them true men. In this connection, we reveal a story of a Greek philosopher who was walking in a broad day light with a lantern in his hand. Every body was surprised and asked why he was carrying a lantern in his hand. He said "I am searching a man and I could not find in that a lantern". All of them said, "we are all men". He replied, I am sorry, I am looking for a man who is full of love for everybody in the world, who is full of scholarship, who is full of compassion and who is real human being. All of them know that they could not satisfy his conditions. No doubt, Jesus, Buddha, Mahavir, Socrates, Confucius, Saint Kabir, Comenius, Johan Huss, Saint Francis of Assisi, Galilio and many more were found as fall human beings.

True Spirit of University

The Greek philosopher's ideas, principles, theories, laws, formulas, preaching and practices, for which they were humiliated, tortured, killed are the real foundations of University curriculum. Their statements are the true spirit of university. About the University spirit, here we would like to give the example of the great Johan Huss, who was one of the early Rectors of Prague University. In him we had seen the true symbol of the university. Faggots were piled up to his neck and the magistrate was there saying, if you withdraw your statements, you will be let off. Otherwise I will light the fires. His answer was "light the faggots". And the last word, which he altered, was one that crosses frontiers of race and nation. He stood for universal humanity when he said". I prefer a good German to a bad Czech".

Kyung Hee university, Seoul Republic of Korea (1949-99) is also the real symbol of true university spirit. Because its main function is to restore humanity and mortality for the creation of a global society on the principles of United Nations. Its purpose is "The creation of a civilized world". Its philosophy is democratization of school, ideas and living. Since 1949, this international peace university has been educating the young men to create a better living for mankind. The Global University was found by great world peace educator professor (Dr.) Young Seek Choue, who was himself a living symbol of university spirit. Kyung Hee University has been extending its knowledge beyond the campus through "the creation of new civilized work" serving national and global society through sharing its knowledge with 161 universities of the world. These universities should share the common mission of building peace for the new millennium.

Let the university education be free for all the children of rich and poor parents both to feel themselves obliged and indebted towards all mankinds. University education should not be considered as non-merit good and services, and it should not be compared equally with electricity, diesel and fertilizer with respect to subsidies. University education is highly merit good. Hence, expenditure on higher education is not expenditure, but it is an investment–investment in human resource development, and in long run, not only the particular society, but all societies of the world will get heavy returns for centuries while the cost of ignorance can be very high for every society. Therefore, university education is not only necessary for all, but also essential for the same and peaceful growth and development of any society. According to some estimates, upto 35 million people–90 per cent civilians have been killed in 170 wars since IInd world war. Thirty wars are now taking place, most inside national boundaries. And a billion people are hungry and malnourished in the world due to poverty.

Role of IAEWP in University Education

International Association of Educators for World Peace (IAEWP) was affiliated with five specialized agencies of United Nations, Viz. UNESCOSOC, UNDPI, UNICEF, UNCED, UNESCO. They are promoting University education throughout the world through more than 100 chapters by encouraging development of Colleges and Universities for peace research. Support of UN-efforts in this regard, and of developing the kind of education, will contribute to the formation of characters capable of delaying aggression. So that conflict situations may be solved in positive manner.

In 1998, IAEWP was sponsored for the establishment of the Global Open University for world peace in Italy. The purpose of making university education is to reach all to be enlightened, for being helpful in building a non-exploitative, nonviolent and peaceful democratic society.

Some Genuine Proposal for Peace University Education

1. Pursue the truth, might turn pacifists in all free universities, re-planned to build peace.
2. University education should be free for all rich and poor. Merit should be criteria, not money.
3. Seek funds from donors like rich persons, industrialists, philanthropists, alumni-alumnae.
4. Abolish armies and destroy arms and ammunition; divert this money for peace University education.
5. Impartial selection of meritorious teachers and non-teaching staff in the university.
6. Better service conditions are to be provided to teachers and non-teaching staff.
7. A National Directory of unemployed highly qualified persons holding Ph.D. or D.litt. or D.Sc. in different disciplines. A reasonable pay and appointments are given.
8. Professional education must be de-linked from the university, for example medical, engineering and agriculture education must be attached with hospitals, industries and farms respectively.
9. The Peace University must be autonomous with national character, should extend whole world.
10. The university should train men and women to think themselves and ultimately to the whole world.
11. In universities, at least, feeling of love and brotherhood among all communities should be fostered.
12. The students of a university should be trained to struggle against ignorance, injustice, oppression and fear of all men of whole world, and for international understanding and peace.

13. The University should create attitude favourable to the values necessary for a peaceful progressive and democratic governments in different parts of world.
14. The University must render support to the United Nations.
15. The University must teach peace, disarmament, human rights and about NGOs, United Nations, UNESCO, and other agencies of UN.
16. The university should be a sanctuary of international awakening and peace, and a lighthouse of perpetual learning.
17. The University should produce save leaders for mankind.
18. The Universities must be looked after by a Ministry of Peace in the Nation for smooth running of national universities to serve the cause of Peace.
19. There must be a University for Peace in each nation having affiliation with the United Nations.
20. Last but not the least, the university must develop a global common society an oughtopia–a society which would be spiritually beautiful, materially affluent and humanly rewarding.

Thus the role of university should be preserve to develop and to create a culture of peace and ultimately its mission would be to build peace for the new millennium.

UN's Peace Building Commission

Kofi Annan, Secretary General UNO at World Summit 2005 proposed to establish a new body of peace commission. A round 50 per cent of the conflict of the past 20 years have recurred within five years of peace agreements. The commission will act only by consensus, proposing integrated strategies for stabilizing economic recovery and development and improving co-ordination. 31 members committee was formed to make a detail action programme [6].

Gandhi and Creativity

Martin Luther King used to say that Mahatma Gandhis was probably the first person in the history to lift the love ethic c

Jesus above mere interaction between individuals to a powerful and effective social force on a larger scale. Gandhi preached and practiced that love that suffered was more powerful than the force that inflicted pain and suffering. For him non-violent insistence on truth was in fact a "moral equivalent of war". Those who are genuinely creative are the people who enjoy soemd metal health and face personal, inter-personal and other kinds of problems with poise and equanimity. They are not cunning but are altruist. Using Gandhi's words we can say that the freedom of the sky is better than the shelter of the cocoon. The ways of invention and discovery also follow the course of freely accepted discipline and intellectual standards. Struggles is the nucleus of human life. Struggle creates tension and tension at times makes man behave in an aggressive and violent manner. So, to conceive a society which is completely free from violence will amount to asking for the noon. However, we can aim to create a society which is completely free from violence will amount to asking for the moon. However, we can aim to create a society in which aggressive tendencies of man and women are utilized for constructive and creative purposes. The scope for their indulging in violent and destructive behaviour is reduced to the minimum possible limit by ensuring on open climate in the institution and organization.[7]

Sarvodaya conveys that the good of all is served by promoting the good of the poorest–the lowest and the lost[8].

Gandhi and Globalism

Gandhi has a holistic approach to human problems in which reform or reconstruction should concentrate, more or less at the same time, at all levels of human existence and activity, i.e. individual, local, national and international levels. Globalization is an ever accelerating trend of modern "civilization". Gandhi was gone beyond civilization. Real globalization for Gandhi is possible only through *Pancha Yama* of *Pathajali* i.e. *non-violence, non-steading, truth, non-possession and chastity.* Global though sectored reformation programme for regeneration of every individual is needed for balancing the negative effects of the process of globalization. It was Gandhi's conviction that individuals–of whom the nations and global communities are constituted–must have priority in any scheme of reform or reconstruction.

The cultivation's of non-violence by the individual and the establishment of non-exploitative economy at different levels will lead eventually to the emergence of what he calls non-violent nationalism. Ultimately, these non-violent Nations will functions under a world federation on the basis of economic independence. Voluntary efforts, development within, equality for all, decentralization on all spheres, general disarmament, common good of all, amicable settlements of disputes, impartial media and mutual sense of service are must for creating a happy peaceful society.

Gandhi is one with Thoureau's principle that "Government is best which governs the least". To quote Gandhi: "I look upon an increase in the power of the state with the greatest fear because ... it does the greatest harm to mankind by destroying individuality which lies at the root of all progress. In order to curb emergence of authoritarianism, Gandhi looks forward to the emergence of a world where "no state has his military".

Socio-economic decentralization is yet another corrective measure to curb undemocratic tendencies. Gandhi's global vision moves upward from the individual and a federation of village republics to an international federation of nations in a society marked by voluntary cooperation and decentralization, which certainly leads to effective global village.

Conclusion

Developed countries applied intensive technology, generated mass production and high mass of consumption of nature; whereas developing countries applied labour intensive technology for subsistence level of living standards. Globalization created inequality and unjust societies. Gandhi practiced *Pancha Yama* of *Pathajali.* He struggled and fought for peace, which creates creativity and universal brotherhood in the globe. He was not against industrialization and staunchly worked for "welfare of all" in the globe. Gandhi's, Peace, and

Non-violence are like tail and head of same coin. He will be ever remembered as father of peace in globe, provided peace universities are spread through out globe. Time has come to destroy the Armies, Arms, Ammunition and spend that investment on welfare of low income groups of world to bring eternal peace on this good earth.

Notes and Reference

1. Joseph Stiglitz (2002), Globalization and its discontents, Penguin Books, New Delhi.
2. Anurag Gangal (2004), Impact and Prospect of Globalization: A Gandhian Perspective *Anasakti*, Vol. 2, No. 1, Jan-June.
3. Murali Manohar Joshi (2003), Globalization and its Discontents, *University News*, March 24-30, pp. 17-21.
4. Yashwant Sinha (2001), Responsibilities in a Globalized World, *University News*, December, 10-16, pp. 15-16.
5. Surya Nath Prasad and Suman Shukla (2006), Peace as the Role and Mission of University, *University News*, Feb. 19, p. 13.
6. UN News (2006), UN Establishes Peace Building Commission, January, Vol. 61, No. 1.
7. Umrao Singh Chandari (1998), Creativity and Non-violence, *University News*, October, 12, p. 2.
8. P. K. Chaubey (1993), Gandhian Social Welfare Functions: An Attempt in Characterization, *The Indian Economic Journal*, Vol. 40, No. 4, April-June, p. 70.

13

INTELLECTUAL PROPERTY RIGHTS: GEAR UP INDIA TO MEET THE CHALLENGES AND OPPORTUNITIES

One of the most controversial outcomes of the Uruguay Round (UR) is the Agreement on Trade Related Intellectual Property Rights (TRIPRs). IPRs along with TRIMs and services were called the new issues negotiated in the UR.

Protection of Intellectual Property Rights has become a thorny issue of wide and serious debate, with the formation of the General Agreement on TRIPRs under World Trade Organisation. It is feared that IPRs regime is largely against indigenous communities in developing countries and would escalate bio-piracy in the name of Science and Development. Indian Government wants a balanced view on IPR, adding that phenomenal technological advancement was a double edged weapon which posed serious challenges along with opportunity[1]. IPRs agreement put numerous burdens on the developing countries-raising cost consumer products such as medicines and hindering innovation and technology upgrading[2].

Definition

IPRs may be defined as "information with commercial value". IPRs have been characterised as a composite of "ideas, inventions and creative expression" plus the public willingness to bestow the status of property. IPRs are nine categories: patent, trademarks, copy rights, geographic indications, undisclosed information (such as trade secrets) industrial designs, industrial designs, integrated circuits, micro-organism and plant variety protection[3]. Special (*Sui generis*) forms of protection have also emerged to address specific needs of knowledge, products in the case of plant breeder's rights and the protection of layout designs of integrated circuits.

Objectives

The following are main objectives:

(a) *To Encourage and Reward Creative Work:* Protection of copy right and related rights is to encourage and reward creative work.

(b) *To Encourage Innovation:* They are designed to provide protection for the results of investment in the development of new technology.

(c) *To Promote Fair Competition:* To protect distinctive signs and other IPRs aims to stimulate and ensure fair competition among producers.

(d) *To Help Consumer Protection:* To protect distinctive signs and other IPRs aims to stimulate and ensure fair competition among producers.

(e) *To facilitate Transfer of Technology:* To facilitate foreign technology in the form of FDI, joint ventures and licensing. There should be a balance in between legitimate interests of right holders and of users.

Benefits

Stronger IPRs protection may encourage investment, both foreign and domestic. Stranger implementation of IPRs could be expected to give a boost to R & D in countries like India, whose intellectual capital potential may be expected to grow in great width and depth. IPR system provides a great opportunity to developing countries to benefit from protection of indigenous property rights and traditional knowledge.

Developing countries hold approximately 90 per cent of world biological resources, which are particularly important in the development of new pharmaceuticals. Mechanisms of sharing the proceeds from commercialising genetic resources can be written into the IPR law[4].

Disadvantages

The developing countries are very poor and are ill equipped for significant R & D. Industrial countries are the major producers of technology and developing countries heavily depend on imports of technology. Probably, IPRs turn out to be generally, more beneficial to industrial countries than to developing countries. Developed countries enormously benefit from the benefits of higher prices resulting from the market power provided by IPRs, at the expense of developing countries. Industrial countries gain huge amounts of net transfers from TRIPRs, developing countries including India, are expected to experience net outwards transfers on account of TRIPRs. A strong IPRs regime without adequate safeguards to protect interests of weaker sections can cerate very serious problems in developing countries. Exorbitant prices will make patented essential drugs beyond the reach of common man.

Developing countries don't have adequate institutional mechanism and resources to properly administer IPRs regime. For example, a proper competition law (make in India) and its efficient enforcement are required to combat the potential anti-competitive abuse of IPRs. While in many industrial countries such abuses are dealt with by general Competition Law.

Unless developing countries rapidly establish adequate competition frame works and regulatory institutions that also address monopoly abuse of IPRs, it is possible that increasing IPR protection could result in welfare losses from monopoly behaviour. This country preserves 6 per cent of world's flowering plant species, 14 per cent of worlds birds, one third of the world's identified plant species numbering over 45,000 and over 5 per cent of the 81,000 species of wild animals (The World Bank 1996). Biological resources immensely contribute to agriculture; at least 166 species of crop plants and 320 species of wild relatives of cultivated crops originate in India. 90 per cent of medicinal plants are harvested. Under IPRs it may endanger species as forest authorities are not allowing people.

Experiences and Practices

Studies have shown that a realistically designed IPRs system becomes beneficial after a country has attained a certain level of technological development and R & D capability. It is observed that although ensuring a core level of IPR protection may increase developing country access to foreign technologies by safeguarding returns for foreign technology producers, excessively strong IPRs can inhibit the diffusion of knowledge. In developing countries, knowledge is built more through access, imitation and diffusion of foreign technologies rather than only local research. Japan introduced patents in the early 20th century after reviewing IPR systems in Europe and the United States. Malaysia and Koreas', growth in industrial sectors took place under weak IPR regimes, and later periods governments emphasised incentives for innovation in IPRs as sophisticated local technology sectors developed.

Developing countries can avoid patenting life forms and can apply special provisions under TRIPRs to exempt public goods from IPR protection. They can expand IPR scope to protect genetic resources, traditional knowledge and folklore, as is promoted by the World Intellectual Property Organisation. Free trade in IPR protected goods ensures competition in product markets, reduces prices, and enhances consumer access to new technologies. But trade in IPR protected products may restrict access to new technologies for developing countries. TRIPRs neither endorses nor prohibits parallel imports.

Patents

A patent is a legal protection granted for an invention that is new, non-obvious and useful. The patent grants the patent holder the exclusive right to make use or sell the patented products or process. The main purpose of the patent is to benefit the society patents, by providing an opportunity to recoup the cost of invention and to make profit out of the invention, encourage research and development and thereby contribute to the well being of the society. An invention, to be patentable, must satisfy three conditions–it is new, it is useful to the society, it is non-obvious to a person possessed of average skill in the art. Exclusion of an invention from patentability for commercial exploitation is permitted if it is necessary to protect public order or morality, including to protect human, animal or plant life or health or to avoid serious prejudice to the environment.

Indian Patent Law

East India Co., was introduced patent law in 18th century. Formal patent protection was enacted as patent Act, 1911. The patents Act, 1970 amended and consolidated the law. Being a member in World Trade Organisation, India was accepted to follow it with effect from January 1, 2005. The Indian patents Act 1970, as amended and effective from Jan 1, 2005 as follows–eligibility, procedures and conditions for grant of patents, inventions and other subjects not patentable, Rights and Obligations of patentee, grounds for revocation of patents, matters related to working of the patent and compulsory licensing and Rights of government regarding patented products. The amendment expanded the scope of patentability to all fields of Technology including food, drugs and pharmaceutical and agri-chemicals[5].

Items Not Patent

Inventions which are frivolous or contrary to public interest; method of agriculture or horticulture; any process of treatment of human beings or animals; plants and animals; a mathematical or business method or a computer program *per se* or algorithms; the mere discovery of a scientific principles or the formulation of an abstract theory or discovery of any living thing or non-living substance occurring in nature; a mere scheme or rule or method of performing mental act or method of playing game; a presentation of information; topography of integrated circuits; an invention which, in effect, is traditional knowledge or which is an aggregation or duplication of known properties of traditionally known components.

Patent Product and Period

The amended Act provides for grant of product patent. Previously, for food, pharmaceutical and chemical products only process patent was granted in India. This meant that any body was free to manufacture the same or similar product by a process different from the patent one. For Food, Pharmaceutical and Chemical products, previously the patent period was 14 years. Now patents are granted for all products for a period of 20 years from the date of application. Patents are granted merely to enable patentee to enjoy a monopoly but to encourage inventions and to secure that the inventions are worked in India on a commercial scale. The benefit of patent invention would be available at affordable price to the public.

The critics fear that adoption of product patent will enable the multi-national drug firms to exploit the Indian consumers. The patent protection period of 20 years is too long a period. Five to seven years may be reasonable period.

By participating in the international system of IPR protection, India, with its vast pool of scientific and technical personnel, and well-established expertise in medical treatment and health care, has unlocked vast opportunities in both exports and outsourcing and has the potential to become a global hub in the area of Research and Development based on clinical research.

Biodiversity and Traditional Knowledge

The Doha Ministerial declaration emphasized the importance of traditional knowledge (TK). It instructed the Council for Trade-Related Aspects of Intellectual Property Rights (TRIPRs) "to examine, *inter alia,* the relationship between the TRIPRs Agreement and the Convention on Biological Diversity, the protection of traditional knowledge and folklore, and other relevant new developments raised by members Traditional knowledge is essential to the food security and health of millions of people in the developing world. In many countries, traditional medicines provide the only affordable treatment available to poor people. Moreover in developing countries upto 80 per cent of the population depend on traditional medicines to help and meet their healthcare needs. However, it is only recently that the international community has started giving recognition to traditional knowledge.

Some of the patents are even based on Geographical Indications (GIs) from developing countries; for instance, patent on Basmati rice from India and jasmine rice from Thailand. After a patent on Basmati rice lines and grains granted by USPTO to M/s Rice Tee Inc., USA on September 2nd, 1997, India contested this patent. In a long litigation of almost five years, ultimately the title of the patent was changed in the year 2002. The products list could include goods such as Indian saris. Oriental carpets specialty Teas such as Darjeeling (India), Cheeses such as parmigiano Reggiano (Italy), Jamon de Huelva (Spanish Ham), art paper (China), porcelain from Limoges (France)[6].

Geographical Indications

Geographical Indication (GI) is defined as an indication which identifies a good as originating in the territory of a member country of the WTO or a region or locality in that territory where a given quality, reputation or other characteristics of a product is essentiality attributable to geographical origin. Often it was an indication of source of the product, like Swiss Watches, German Lens, Florida Oranges, and was the "appellation of origin"[7].

A GI certificate will mean that only the rice grown in India will quality to be called as "thus conferring legal protection to the product and safeguarding its un-anthorised use by other countries or producers besides eliminating unfair competition for the benefit of genuine producers and consumers. Basmati is a major export earner for India with exports touching 11,20,000 tones in 2005, registering a growth of about 45 per cent over the previous years. In value terms, exports rose to $596 million in 2005 from $432 million the previous year.

The application filed with geographical Indications Registry in August 2004 by Heritage Foundation, a trust based in Karnal, Haryana for registering basmati as a GI is found to be flawed in terms of representation of basmati growers/ farmers on the trust[8]. Europe Union alone has granted so far more than 5,000 different GI's.

India's ancient use of Haldi (Turmeric) was sought to be patented under the American law in 1995. Luckily for India, Dr. R. A. Mashelkar, Director General, Council of Scientific and Industrial Research Challenged it. The U. S. patent office acknowledged its mistake and cancelled the patent on "Haldi". An American Company has been granted a patient right for Neem as a pesticide.

IPRs on Indian Economy

India felt IPRs had disastrous effects especially more on two vital areas i.e., pharmaceuticals and agriculture. Both theses areas affect the well being of the people. A dangerous provision has been introduced in patent protection and this relates to changing the philosophy of the patent regime whereby products imported or locally produced, will be covered under patent protection without any discrimination. This implies that the patent regime not only tries to establish import monopoly.

Pranab Mukerjee, former Minister for Commerce stated that India does not recognize patents in the field of drugs, food products and chemicals, has been allowed a transition period of 10 years for establishing a product patent regime for such items. Government retains the right to institute price control on drugs. Many intellectuals may not accept it. India is plagued by mass poverty and high unemployment, which is needed life saving drugs and other basic medicines should be available at affordable and low price. This can be achieved by control over drugs of prices at global level. The government has to continue with the drug price control and keep medical treatment at lower level, reach to the poor. Already, the situation has been changing in this direction with the growing trend of privatization in health. Stronger IPRs can increase the price of input and consequently denial of life saving medicines to the poor[9].

The Government of India has been under constant attack that the Sui generis (plant Breeder Rights) system is against the interest of the farmers and would act as an impediment to the development of new plant varieties.

IP on Seeds and Monopolisation of Life

The inherent right of the farmers to save and exchange seeds is under threat. The proposed plant variety protection act fails to protect the rights of the small and marginal farmers. The patents (second) Amendment Act 1999 provides for patenting on life and promotes biopiracy of our indigenous knowledge and resources.

The plant variety, protection act is being amended to allow corporate IPRs on farmers varieties. This made the farmers were become custodians and steward of biodiversity and its knowledge IPRs on biodiversity as evidenced in Canada, the US and other countries where they are in place, increase the cost of seed for the farmers leading them deeper into debt.

The Biodiversitiy act is better as a Biopiracy Act, as it takes away the rights of our communities and indigenous healers to use biological resources for their livelihood and survival. The importance of IPRs to agri-chemical and agri-business corporations revolves round the fundamental issue of control. Seed is the first link in the food chain. Whoever controls the seed, controls the food supply. Therefore Monsanto spent over $8.5 billion acquiring seed and bio-tech companies Dupont spent over $ 9.4 billion to acquire pioneer Hi-Bred, the worlds largest seed company and Dow chemical brought Cargill seeds north America in Mid September 2000. Today, the farmers saved seed and state run seed programmes are worth around $22 billion which is almost equal to the $123 billion total commercial seed market worldwide. Thus the Gene Giants are developing new mechanisms such as the genetic Engineering technology to enforce their corporate monopolies. Biological control by corporate lead to enslavement's of agriculture. In 1999, at least 43 patents were issued relating to genetic trait control technology. Patent and IRPs regime as system of monopoly control will further aggravate the severe crisis the farmers facing. The TRIPRs regime of W.T.O. will therefore create conditions for a deepening of the economic crisis for the farming community in India. Therefore, Indian Government and Multinationals have to share equally the responsibilities and liabilities to balance the production of seed and distribution, we must develop our indigenous *Sui generis* system to protect farmers seed sovereignty.

Traditional rights of the farmers to freely conserve, develop use share, exchange their seeds are fundamental rights, which can not be alienated by any IPR law. To defend the rights of the small farmers and for the food security of people there should be a call for exclusion of seeds, life and life forms from TRIPRs/W.T.O. In fact, farmers representatives should be adequately represented in the commission on Agriculture on commodities and prices[10].

Biopioracy from India

Large number of patents were grounded over genetic resources without the consent of the indigenous people, who possess Indigenous Environment Knowledge (IEK) over the resources in India. Aswaganda traditional aurvedic system of medicine of India has been patented to Reliv International Inc. for Dietary supplement for nutritionally promoting healthy joint function. Karela, Jamun and Bringal have already been patented to non resident Indians. Patent has also been granted to cromark research Inc. US on Karela, Jamun and Gumar for herbal diabetic properties to reduce sugar. India's herbal products like Amla, Vasab, Saptrangi and baelbel have been granted patent by the US patent and trade marks office for their derivatives. Pepper, ginger, mustard, bitter gourd, soapnut, gooseberry black berry, cumin–India's traditional herbs, plants and fruits have all been Patented. In this economic hijack, the corporations were gained people and nature loose.

The use of bio-resources including turmeric, Neem, basmati has been inscribed in an Ancient Sanskrit Text and it has been the long standing art and common knowledge and practiced for thousands of years by India's indigenous community. Some of the popular/journals like *Down to Earth and Honey Bee* are also exposing the apathy of local communities usage of bio-resources in their respective regions[11].

Maintenance of biodiversity register at the national level comprising documented indigenous knowledge is the need of the hour. The future economic development making use of a variety of diversity resources such as genes and plant varieties etc is impossible without prior consent of the holders of IPRs on such resources. It is difficult to sustain the balanced and equitable multi-lateral trade based on the principle of shared access. Finally, patent regime would put farmers to depend upon multinational corporations for seeds to food and health of a nation.

Conclusion

Introduction of Intellectual property rights by World Trade Organization in Indian Agriculture would bring many reforms both advantages and disadvantages. New knowledge is patented is good, but developing countries have not produced it. They have to depend on developed countries. Transfer of technology can change the developing countries economies, but developing countries also be ready to change their mindset for exporting it. With robust optimism developing countries should facilitate to modernise their "knowledge centres" to generate innovations and inventions in order to copy foreign technology. Our indigenous flora and fauna are to be protected and sustained and keep multinationals as competitive and complementary. Under IPRs regime, many products prices many rise, but state has to take firm steps to produce and keep them affordable to the poorest of the poor. Nonetheless, India has to gear up it's economy to face challenges and took it as an opportunity to make India as a developed country in 2020 through IPRs.

Notes and References

1. Correspondent (2004), Govt. for New Norms to Protect IPRs, *Hindustan Times,* October, 15.

2. Martin Khor (2006), Impasse at the WTO: A Development Prospective, *Economic and Political Weekly*, November 11, p. 4659.
3. Shaik Saleem (2006), Business Environment, Pearson Education, New Delhi, p. 502.
4. Francis Cherunilam (2006), International Economics, Tata McGraw-Hill Publishing Co. Ltd., New Delhi, p. 598.
5. Planning Commission (2005), Mid-Term Appraisal of 10th Five Year Plan (2002-07) p. 396.
6. Research and Information System (2003), World Trade and Development Report 2003 Cancum and Beyond, Academic Foundation, New Delhi, p. 94.
7. Dr. S. Nagaraj (2006), Several Policy Initiatives in Place, *The Hindu Survey of Indian Agriculture*, p. 49.
8. P. Manoj (2006), Bid for Patent for Basmati Rice Hits a Hurdle, *The Hindu*, November 5, p. 10.
9. Joseph Stiglitz (2002), Globalization and its Discontents, Penguin Books, New Delhi, p. 245.
10. Vandana Shiva and Kunwar Jalees (2006), Seeds of Suicide, Navdanya, New Delhi, pp. 252-259.
11. C. Nanjundaiah and S. Rajendran (2004), Intellectual Property Rights and Protection of Indigenous Environmental Knowledge of Indigenous Community *National Seminar on Institutional Policy Options for Sustainable Agricultural Development, Pre Conference Volume*, April 10-11, Dept. of Economics, Osmania University, p. 419.

14

DECLINE OF ETHICS A THREAT TO GLOBE AND ENVIRONMENT: NEED FOR A SHIFT IN PARADIGM

Ethics are based on social life and *'Artha'*. Ethics are good guidelines for every generation.[1]

The objectives of ethics are to study human behaviours and make evaluative assessments about them as moral or immoral, and establish moral standards and norms of behaviour. Values that guide us how we ought to behave are considered moral values for example such as respect, honest, fairness and responsibility[2-]. Since vedic and epic period, India was a home of a few ethical philosophers and practitioners in every aspect of life.

Conceptual Development

"Ethics means a set of principles or morals, science of morals, moral principles, rules of conduct and the whole field of moral science. The development of moral principles and codes of conduct is a process which is directly linked with the development of a society. There is a school of thought which holds that the entire issue of morals is situational. Thiruvalluvar said that telling falsehood may be justified. Yudhistra has to face the issue of *narova Kanjarova*".[3]

In the Bhagavad Gita, Lord Krishna describes spiritually that rhythmic play of creation in the following words. "At the end of the night of time all things return to my nature; and when the new day of time begins I bring them again into light.[4] Development could then be defined as a qualitative as well as quantitative process, which raises living standards in a manner which does not sacrifice the social and ecological balance achieved over centuries. It is inadequate to address ecological and social problems by relying entirely on pragmatic utilitarian moral attitudes in combination with a scientific understanding of natural systems. Some form of "environmental reverence" is also required which requires a metaphysical grounding. Cultural heritage may be a starting point for the task of generating "environmental reverence". Most of the world's main religions have prescriptions concerning individual and social behaviour towards the social and natural environment and a foundation might be thought to exist for encouraging the re-adoption of traditional ethics in modern life. A strong theme in environmental philosophy holds that a society's behaviour towards the environment depends on the relationship between humanity and nature propounded by its cultural and religious traditions.[5]

Origin of Society

Human Society has evolved over thousands of years. At a time when the primitive life was "harsh, brutish and short" having an eye for an eye or tooth for a tooth and each unto himself might have prevailed, as the guiding principle. But as people came to live together as hunter, gatherer societies, the functions got divided between men and women and rules of conduct evolved. Basically these rules were such that they contributed to the public good. The Ten Commandments for example are required to have a peaceful and orderly society. Moral principles like prohibition of stealing or condemning adultery or encouraging the telling of truth are all designed to ensure that human beings are able to evolve into smooth healthy happy societies. A society in which there are high ethical standards is bound to be a happy society.

Historical Growth

Koutilya found corrupt bureaucrats were fish in water, one never knows whether fish is drinkingwater. In Indian History, we think of the Gupta period as the period when perhaps the best moral standards were maintained. In 20th century, when giants like M.K. Gandhi, Sardar Patel dominated Politics we found that there has been a distinct fall in moral or ethical standards. The question is how to improve the system. Owing to strong moral fabric only India produced a great leader like M.K. Gandhi, who introduced "peace and non-violence" After Gandhi, today independent India rated as 9th most corrupt country in the world. The change of the mindset can be brought about by intelligent use of the media and public opinion. Few are thinking that a certain degree of corruption is necessary. A businessman is a practical person and if he has to get things done, he may not mind so long as his work is done. The late Baburao Patel is supposed to have said that can eliminate corruption in our country by making one verbal change. We can all corruption can simply be called "Service Charges".

Organisational Values

Corruption probably helps to make the choice. But, Kleptocracy in the long run does into help. Values not only enhance the quality of life of the individuals of society, but also, they make the society and thereby the world, a better place to live. Various social institutions like family, school, other extra-curricular bodies like sports, club, debating, painting, singing, religions, society, community play an important role of inculcating values in individuals. Some common–personal/organizational values include following: Honesty, truth, Respect, self-fulfillment, sense-accomplishment, at social responsibility, security/stability courage, generosity creativity, patience, Humility, Loyalty and Simplicity. A person with all these values has equanimity. Such a person can mobilize his own and others energy and can help accomplish wonders.

Benefits of Ethics

It cultivates moral cause, strong team work and productivity, supports growth, helps policies, avoids criminal acts, quality managements, strong public image improves trust legitimizes actions, strengthens coherence, enterprises values enhances, ethical value dimension and vision. Ethics give rise to an efficient economy. *It is not the government or law which will protect society; ethics alone.*

Globalization and Ethics

Globalisation involves movement of four elements of the economy across borders. These are physical capital in terms of plant and machinery, financial capital, labour and technology. While the movement of physical capital, labour and technology has been going on for thousands of years, the movement of financial capital is a recent phenomenon of less than three decades. This became possible because of the integration of the global market and the world becoming a global village. Today at the touch of a computer key or a click with the mouse, billions of dollars can be sent across borders. The mobility of the capital is because there is always a search for better returns. South East Asian nations become more attractive areas of investment. Capital flow should not be speculative in nature. Economic growth can be linked to corruption is an illusion. In the long run, real economic development can come only if there is a better disciplined financial sector which means better business ethics.

"Honesty is the best policy" is not only merely an adage, but also, an operational reality on very day, If you improve ethics in business, industry and public life; we should adopt a pragmatic approach. Suppose, 10 per cent of them are Harichandras, Mahatmas. Certainly, people think they are crooks. However, slowly 90 per cent of people slowly decide to move towards model ethical behaviour of 10 per cent.

Corruption and Ethics

Third world countries were considered as highly corrupt, especially India also. The system encourages corruption by these conditions. They are (a) scarcity of goods and services (b) lack of transparency in decision making (c) delay and *red tape* attracting speed money (d) cushions of safety which have been created for the corrupt by our legal and administration system on the very healthy principle that every body is innocent till proved guilty. The procedures evolved and the delays that take place in bringing the gently to book are so long and time consuming that many a time the corrupt escape, (e) sense of tribalism, casteism or *biradri*, by which corrupt officials defend and protect each other.

If we want to improve the level of ethics in administration, business, industry and public life, we must tackle these factors of our systems. One sectors ethics, certainly influences other sectors also and finally it has a close linkages with the public life of political democratic system. Lack of ethics, can deal with individual cases of corruption and punish the corrupt like dealing with individual victims of malaria. A much better solution is to see that the mosquitoes do not breed and therefore there is no malaria.

Need of Sunset Principle

United States have a sunset principle behind every rule and act, they enact. No rule or act should be in perpetuity. It should have a life time of say five years or ten years at the end of which it will lapse, unless it is reviewed and decision consciously taken to extend it or modify the rules. We must, when we design systems, think of putting everything on autopilot. The whole system must be able to correct itself. In fact, when Harshad Mehta Scam took place, the replay of the government was that it was because of systemic failure. What people conveniently forgot was that the system is not God given, it is man made. What about those who were responsible for designing the system? What action have to be taken to change the system? Simplifying procedures and making procedures for example fix time limits for reducing delay are methods by which improvements can come, like 30 days maximum.

The corrupt tend to flourish are able to protect each other of the financial clout they enjoy. After all even if a corrupt man is found out and punished, he still continues to keep his ill-gotten wealth. Corruption flourishes because it is a low risk high profit business. If we are able to increase the risk, then it should be possible to reduce the corruption in the system. In this model a law drafted called the Corrupt Public Servants (forfeiture of property) Act 1999.

Make Politician as a Clean Character

Forthnately, we are in the biggest democratic Country, in the world. Politicians, are also found taller in corruption. Luckily, the JMM judgment of the Supreme Court has said that the Ministers and MPs are also public servants. Hence they came within the purview of the prevention of corrupt Act. Our objective should be to focus action against the people at the highest levels because unless the people at the highest levels are brought to book, the common man in this country and the public at large are likely to take the view that our whole system is like spiders web. The small and weak insects and flies may be caught but a real big bumble bee can just burst through the web. We do not want that to happen it we want to improve the levels of ethics in our society. Initiatives have to be taken and system changes have to be brought in a number of areas if we have to succeed. Of course, we should follow *Ragvedic* dictum that we should keep our minds open for all ideas. Let noble thoughts come to us from all sides. Let us come together, let us enjoy together, let us strengths come together, let our intellect shine, let there be no misunderstanding or hatred.[6]

II

Environment in Peril

Environmentalists have long thought of economic globalization a threat to the environment. Western tradition has felt that nature is sub-ordinate to man, whereas Japanese have always viewed themselves in harmony with nature, rather than exploiting it. The environmentalists tend to value environment over income, where as trade economists conventionally tend to value income over the environment. This difference lies at the heart of their conflict in recent years. Adam Smith, Father of Economics, discovered trade as Central to economic thinking and markets. Environmentalists are typically dealing with situations, where markets do not exist–as when pollutants are dumped into lakes, rivers and Oceans and into the sky above, so that State has to regulate it through "Pollution Pay" principle.

Herman Daly (American environmentalist) and Edward Goldsmith (British environmentalist) recalled that free trade was blamed for environmental problems and other ills in the world. The examples of agriculture and car imports were favourable to free trade; the Coastal shrimp example was not. Environmentalists are right to argue that growth rates must be adjusted for environmental damage. Keeping this in mind, the Yale University economists William Nordhans and James Tobin (Nobel laureate) have long proposed a new measure of national income and its growth that subtracts for environmental degradation. Reduced estimates of growth rates, so adjusted, have been made by Herman Daly.

Environmental Valuation

Environmental valuation has indeed risen in the last three decades as the environmental movement has come into its own. Intensity of environmental preference is characterized by a U-shaped curve. If you plot intensity of preference on the vertical axis and age on horizontal axis, the plotted curve comes down and then moves up in a U-shape, since the preference is high among the young and the old. Increasing incomes can reduce rather than increase pollution. Many empirical studies proved that a bell shaped curve. Pollution levels first rise with income but then fall with it. Environmental activism has stimulated new regulations that have in turn produced environmental friendly improvements. All of this has made development and environmental improvement frequent bed fellows.[7]

Earth Ethics for Sustainable Living

Earth ethics involves a respect for all living and for the processes that sustain it. Such respect implies limits on our actions: There are things we should not do, not because they can not be done, but because doing them shows disrespect for life. There is nothing wrong with humans exploiting their environment; every living thing must get resources from its environment to survive. The problem is knowing how far we should go. The ethical guidelines are that we should not degrade earth's physical, chemical and biological capital; cooperate with the nature as we belong to the earth; people has to work with the rest of the nature for sustainable ecological integrity; to alter nature to meet our needs; before altering the nature to meet our needs or wants, do least possible harm and carry out Environmental Impact Analysis and Grand child Impact Analysis.

The man has to protect every species, strive not to cause the premature extinction of any wild species, protect ecosystem and no human culture should become extinct because of our actions.

True earth Citizens are the people who respect all life, learn all you can about how nature works, learn from nature and children, evaluate your life styles day, today, people are most influenced by what we do, simple living, Think globally and act locally, target the big polluters and earth-degraders, work with others to help sustain and heal the earth, don't try to do every thing' love one another not threaten one another and have fun and make time to enjoy life.

Since human survival is at stake, gospel of value education has a major role to play at Schools, Colleges, Universities and Non-Governmental organizations.[8]

A Threat to India's Biodiversity: Tiger Population

High population explosion, too much urbanization, fast deforestation, high standard of living were found the unfriendly factors for flora and fauna development. The latest National Tiger conservation Authority 2005 report on the Tiger revealed only 1411 (except sunderbans in the grip of Naxales insurgency in Chittishgarh, Andhra Pradesh and Parts of Jharkhand). The reasons are direct poaching, subsistence killing of prey by humans and habitat degradation and loss off Forest Rights Act made the Advivases not to move from forest became another hurdle. The Centre and State Governments rift on laws and relocations. Rehabilitation and Resettlement of tribal is very costly under Forest Rights Act. With an alarming dip in the number of Tigers in the wild, will human beings succeed in eliminating them altogether? There is still a fighting chance of their survival provided we control our greed.[9] It is a small indicator that how India's invaluable biodiversity is on decline. If present poor are become rich and practicing same habits, survival human species is quite doubtful in very nearest future. Empowered poor have to follow ethics and' save the nature. Ethical empowerment alone can protect Global life and flora and fauna in future.

Conclusions

Cultural heritage may be the starting point for the assignment of generating environmental reverence. All religions are in favour of social human behaviour towards sustainable nature. There is a need of fusion between basic utilitarianism and *rightarianism*, is called *Dharmanomics* (Ethiconomics).[10] Culture and religion pays the best efforts to protect nature. In a society where are high ethical standards are there, they are bound to be a happy society. Gandhi, Patel contributed for high ethical standards. In India, post independence days encouraged corruption which is considered as an unethical norm, India got the highest position at Global level on corruption index. Ethics, certainly, brings high efficient and productivity in the economy. One sectors ethics, certainly influences other sectors also and finally it has a close linkages with the public life of political democratic system. Politician in India, has to show his/ her ethical life more transparent and accountable to every citizen. Earth is to be protected and respected by every citizen of this globe. At present, human survival is at stake, gospel of value education has to pay major role in transforming mind-sets of people, especially political will.

Notes and Reference

1. T. Y. Ramesh (2007), Ethics of Chanikya, Sahini Publications, Delhi, p. 18.
2. Shaikh Saleem (2006), Business Environment, Pearson Education, Delhi, p. 269.
3. N. Vittal (1999), Ethics in Business, Industry and Public life, Forum for Free Enterprise, Mumbai, p. 3.
4. N.A. Palkhivala (1994). India's Priceless Heritage, Bharathiya Vidya Bhavan, p. 22.
5. Nirmal Chandra Sahu and Amit Kumari Choudhary (2005), Dimensions of Environmental and Ecological Economics; Economics and Environment; A Case of Ethical Neglect by T.N. Jenkins, Universities Press, Hyderabad, p. 83.
6. N. Vittal (1999), *Op. Cited.*
7. Jagadish Bhagwati (2007), In Defense of Globalization, OUP, New Delhi, pp. 135-145.
8. Y. Anjaneyulu (2004), Introduction to Environmental Science, B.S. Publications, Hyderabad pp. 509-511.
9. Anand Sankar (2008), Predator on the Prowl, *Business Standard, Weekend,* Feb. 23/24, p.I.
10. P. R. Brahmananda (1994), Ethics, Utilitarian and Kantian and Economics, *The Indian Economic Journal*, April-June, pp. 142-171.

Appendix

World Economy: A birds Eye View

The wealth of a country depends on its industrial strength, natural resources, population size and political stability. Trade creates wealth and jobs by encouraging Countries to produce goods that can be sold abroad. However, many poor countries have to borrow money from richer countries to finance their industries.

Item	*Country / Good*	*Amount in US$ Millions*
Highest foreign debt	I[st] Country USA	Millions 862 ,000
Foreign Aid	Japan	Donor 9,100
Main recipients of Aid	Indonesia	Aid received 43,000
International trade	USA	Exports 716,000
Export goods	Automobiles	$ 220 (billion)
Worlds largest stock Market	USA	New York (wall Street)
Richest Country	Luxembourg	33,609 PCI in USA)
Poorest Country	Sierra Leone	478 (US $)

Source: Illustrated Family Encyclopedia (2007) World Economy, p. 933.

Ethics

A branch of philosophy concerned with the nature of ultimate value and the standards by which human actions can be judged right or wrong.

Ethics is traditionally subdivided into normative ethics, meta ethics and applied ethics, Normative ethics seeks to establish norms or standards of conduct such as" Don't tell a lie". Metaethics is concerned with the nature of ethical judgments and theories. Since 20th century, much work is focused on moral language, like naturalism, intuitionism emotivism and prescriptivism. Applied ethics consists of the application of normative bioethics, business ethics, legal ethics and medical ethics (Source: Britannica (2005) Ready Reference Encyclopedia, New Delhi vol.3, P.273)

Classification of Environmental Ethics

Ethical principles are needed to guide human behaviour with respect to nature. They are classified into three.

Anthropocentric: Anthropocentric environmental ethics is based on the world view that man's welfare is the determinant of the use of nature. The protection and conservation of nature is important because it is in the interest of man. Man is the supreme to take action. Nature provides the means of livelihood, man should use nature judiciously.

Bio centre: The anthropocentric approach extended and expanded to include the whole eco-sphere called Bio centric. Nature should be protected not only because it is the interest of man; it should be protected because it is in the interest of all living things. It provides sustenance, maintains bio-diversity, eco-balance and carrying capacity of the nature.

Gaia–Centre: This approach calls for an earth centered ethics i.e. ecological, Community–centered ethics. In Indian cultural tradition, the whole world is one family and the earth is the home (*Vasudhaiva Kutumbakam*). It considers the living as well as non- living (organic and inorganic) elements of the earth as interdependent and difficult to separate. It rejects the superiority of man and confirms biospheric egalitarianism.

(*Source:* R. S. Misra (1996), Environmental Ethics and Jurisdiction Relationships and Interdependence, from "Ethics in public life" edited by T.N. Chaturvedi, 11PA, New Delhi, p. 296.)

Ethics and law

Legislation and Ethics cannot stand alone for desired public conduct.

Ethic	*Law*
It is self regulatory	It is prohibitory
It is duty centred	It is rights centred
It is informal	It is formal
It is Unwritten	It is written
It is behavioural	It is contractual
It is wisdom based	It is knowledge based.
It is voluntary	It is obligatory
It is related to heart	It is related to head
It is created by the people	It is created by society
It is spiritual in orientation	It is scientific in orientation
It evolves slowly	It can be enacted as and when needed.

Source: R. S. Misra (1996) *op. cited.*

Section–IV

Environment Protection

15

IMPACT OF ENVIRONMENTAL DEGRADATION: A THREAT TO TWO REGIONS OF ANDHRA PRADESH DEVELOPMENT

Introduction

In economics the environment is viewed as a composite asset that provides a variety of services. Environment is defined broadly, the relationship between the environment and economic system can be considered a closed or interlocked system. For example, the standing forest is a stock of trees, while the harvest of timber considered as flow. "There is a widespread agreement that development is critically linked with the State of environment and vice versa. Environment degradation, in most of the developing countries, is becoming a major constraint on future growth and development. The real costs of environmental degradation are increasingly felt in terms of health costs, declining productivities of natural resources like land, water, grass land etc."[1] The impacts are widespread and conspicuous in land hunger agrarian economies like India, in general and Andhra Pradesh, in particular. In fact, it is observed that environmental degradation is reaching irreversible levels (desertification) in some regions of Andhra Pradesh like Anantapur District.

Environment is a multi-disciplinary subject involving subjects like biodiversity, atmosphere, water, land and soil and human settlements. "Long back, Aristotle observed that plants exist for the sake of animals, and brute beasts for the sake of man-domestic animals for his use and food, wild ones for food and other accessories of life, such as clothing and various tools. Since nature makes nothing purposeless or in vain, it is undeniably true that she has made all animals for the sake of man."[2] Former Prime Minister, Indira Gandhi remarked that it is hard to lift oneself up by ones bootstraps, when one is too poor to be wearing boots.[3] That is, poverty fellow can't do sustainability neither in person or nor nature. Poverty, greediness are the-basic ingredients for nature degradation. If we want ever-green civilizations, certainly sustainable development of economy is necessary. "The concept of sustainable development defined as meeting the needs of the present generation without compromising the needs of the future generations" covers the resource utilization and development bringing into focuses the risks of depletion of nature resources. A world in which poverty is endemic will always be prone to ecological and other catastrophes".[4]

Methodology

To study the levels of degradation in three diversified geographical regions of Andhra Pradesh, we availed Government of Andhra Pradesh's Compendium of Environment Statistics as a main source to satisfy the above indicators. Few like forest cover, drought affected areas, pesticides use, concentration of slums, solid waste management were taken for this study.

Composition of Bio-sphere

The biosphere/eco-system of living organisms or biological processes lying at the interface between the atmosphere, lithosphere and hydrosphere. The distinguishing feature of the biosphere is that it supports life. It is estimated that the biosphere contains more than, 3,50,000 species of plants including algae, fungi, mosses and higher form of plants, and

11 million animal species ranging from uni-cellular pratozoa to man. The biosphere supplies the essential requisites of life all these species, namely light, heat, water, food and living space or habitats. India has lost over 50 per cent of its forest cover, 40 per cent of its mangroves, and a significant part of its wetlands in the past couple of centuries.

The loss to biological diversity and the decrease of natural habitats cannot be recovered as a result of growing urbanization and industrialization. The ecological balance of *flora, fauna* and forest is disturbed by the rapid increase of population. Out of the total twelve biodiversity hot spots in the world, India has two, one is at the North East Region and other at western ghats.[5]

Forest Growth: Lung Spaces of People

The National forest Policy of India 1952 prescribed a target for bringing 33 per cent of the countries total geographical area under forests in the best method of land use and to protect the environment. The forest area of Andhra Pradesh is 63,814 sq. kms, which constitutes 23.20 per cent of the total geographical area of Andhra Pradesh . The per capita availability forest area in Andhra Pradesh is of 0.0842 hectares in 2005-06. Due to increase of population, industrialization, urbanization, Housing and deforestation the forest area is shrinking year after year.

Forest play an important role in moderating the soil mantle, improving soil fertility, purifying the air, arrest soil erosion and in regulating the flow of water in rivers and streams. Forest Development activities commenced on a really big scale in Andhra Pradesh with the commencement of 3rd Five year plan. Forest programmes and quick growing species, large areas of mixed deciduous forests of poor quality were cleared and planted with teak, eucalyptus and Bamboo and more recently high yield varieties of cash are being planted on a large scale. Now in the year 2006, over 46,389 hectares of area has been afforested and 88,809 hects., agricultural land was treated with various soil bunding, bench terracing, gully plugging, stabilization of river banks etc.

The State has three well developed zoological parks at Hyderabad, Visakapatnam and Tirupati and also four National parks out of which one at Hyderabad two in Ranga Reddy district and one at Tirupati. There are 13 deer parks and 22 wild life sanctuaries are existing in the State.

The following table explains about forest degradation.

Table 1
Forest cover and Inventory Results in Andhra Pradesh, 2003-04.

District	*Forest cover Area (Dense, Open, Mangroves)*	*Degraded Forests (in Hectares)*	*Percentage of Forest to Total geographical area*
Coastal Andhra			
Srikakulam	46,567	60,224	11.76
Vizianagaram	99,617	86,895	18.24
Visakapatnam	4,53,809	4,46,979	39.53
East Godavari	2,53,862	1,52,389	29.91
West Godavari	54,553	40,903	10.48
Krishna	21,477	34,693	7.61
Guntur	1,03,026	1,39,725	14.22
Prakasma	2,53,632	3,42,958	25.10
Nellore	93,553	1,35,839	19.27
	13,80,101 (36.0)	14,40,605 (32.0)	176.13
Mean of a District	1,53,345.00	1,60,067	
Rayalaseema			
Chittoor	2,34,163	3,66,314	29.83
Kadapa	2,26,539	2,64,753	32.57
Anantapur	64,314	1,88,306	10.30
Kurnool	2,12,201	2,88,147	19.91
	7,37,217 (18.0)	11,07,520 (25.0)	92.61
Mean of a District	1,84,304	2,76,880	
Telangana			
Mahabub Nagar	1,70,355	2,64,066	16.45
Ranga Reddy	33,644	56,594	9.48
Hyderabad	-0-	-0-	-0-
Medak	47,919	73,284	9.34
Nizamabad	1,03,950	1,04,187	22.78
Adilabad	4,94,253	4,63,076	44.84
Karimnagar	1,43,705	1,61,485	21.52
Warangal	2,56,318	2,28,200	28.88
Khammam	5,53,749	4,91,276	52.64
Nalgonda	31,701	69,377	5.88
	18,35,594 (46 0)	19,11,545 (43.0)	211.81
Mean of a District	1,83,559.0	19,11,54.0	
Total	39,52,912 (100.00)	44,59,670	23.20

Source: Compendium of Environment Statistics Andhra Pradesh, 2006, p. 24, 26, 27.

The Table 1 denotes that except Khammam, Adilabad, all districts are found in below 33 per cent of forest area in Andhra Pradesh. Hyderabad, Medak, Ranga Reddy Districts in Telangana, Anantapur in Rayalaseema, Krishna, West Godavari, Srikakulam were observed as the lowest forest area districts.

Unfortunately, degradation of forests are higher than original forest area in each District such as Srikakulam, Krishna, Guntur, Prakasam, Nellore (5) in Coastal Andhra; Chittoor, Kadapa, Kurnool, Anantapur in Rayalaseema (4) and Mahabub Nagar, Ranga Reddy, Medak, Nizamabad, Karimnagar and Nalgonda (6) that is, 15 districts are under the highest degradation. More the intensity of degradation of forests leads to drought in that areas.

Management of Drought

The Government of India started the Drought prone Area Programme (DPAP) in Fifth Five year plan on a massive scale with an idea of optimizing use of available resources and improving the living conditions of the rural poor. Efforts were made to overcome drought through water harvesting and conservation, alternate crop planning and other compensatory programmes on watershed basis, Dryland farming practices are adopted in the State to mitigate the drought. The following table gives a bird's eye view of droughts in A.P.

The Table 2 explains the frequently high degree of droughts occurred years and Mandals. 1986-87 is the 1980s biggest drought and 1997-98 got another. In first decade of 21st century 2002-2003, 2003-2004 years also considered as the biggest drought recurrent years. The table proves that droughts are concentrated more in Rayalaseema and Telangana Districts.

In twenty years, drought is concentrated very much in Prakasam, Srikakulam, Vizianagaram, Visakapatnam in Coastal Andhra; Kurnool, Anantapur, Chittoor, Kadapa districts of Rayalaseema and Mahabub Nagar, Nalgonda, Ranga Reddy Districts in Telangana. In the overall State, Anantapur District is worst affected by arid to dry semi-arid and suffers from high land degradation due to intense biotic pressure, mono-cropping and over exploitation of ground water. Resources conservation, proper cropping and land use and participatory irrigation management are needed for sustainable development of Anantapur district.[6]

Table 2
District-wise Mandals Declared as Drought affected areas in A.P.

District	*Total Mandals*	*1986-97*	*1994-95*	*1997-98*	*2004-05*	*2006-07*
Coastal Andhra						
Srikakulam	38	37	0	37	8	0
Vizianagaram	34	34	4	34	6	0
Visakapatnam	43	39	0	41	7	0
East Godavari	60	0	0	17	20	0
West Godavari	46	24	0	10	25	0
Krishna	50	22	0	20	21	0
Guntur	57	0	0	37	24	0
Nellore	46	14	0	36	40	0
Prakasam	56	56	0	56	53	-32
Sub Total	430	226	4	288	204	32
		(56.0)	(1.0)	(31.0)	(24.0)	(11.0)
Rayalaseema						
Kurnool	54	8	53	54	46	30
Kadapa	51	50	31	50	49	33
Anantapur	63	0	53	63	53	63
Chittoor	66	0	32	32	62	37
Sub-Total	234	58	169	199	210	163
		(14.0)	(44.0)	(22.0)	(25.0)	(55.0)
Telangana						
Mahabub Nagar	64	62	60	64	64	56
Karimnagar	57	0	32	56	56	0
Nizamabad	36	0	24	36	32	0
Nalgonda	59	21	32	53	55	32
Ranga Reddy	37	26	28	35	34	5
Khammam	46	12	0	41	5	0
Adilabad	52	0	0	52	51	0
Medak	46	0	0	45	46	10
Warangal	51	0	20	51	40	0
Hyderabad	16	0	14	0	16	0
Sub-Total	464	121	210	433	399	103
		(30.0)	(55.0)	(47.0)	(51.0)	(34.0)
Total	1128	405	383	920	853	298
		(100.0)	(100.0)	(100.0)	(100.0)	(100.0)

Source: GOAP (2006) compendium of Environment Statistics A.P., p. 104-05.

Pesticide Use

Andhra Pradesh is agriculture dominant and rivers state. In agriculture, the highly poisoned medicine to plant is pesticide to remove disease, which State used abundantly. By adopting Integrated Pest Management, it has reduced. Rachel Carson's "Silent Spring"–a bosok that awakened about pesticides finding their way into the food chain and causing havoc with wild birds. Lead is considered as a serious health effects on Urban poor children.[7] The district wise consumption of pesticides are given below.

The table 3 informs the use of pesticides in different regions of Andhra Pradesh. In general, Guntur in Coastal, Kurnool in Rayalaseema, Khammam in Telangana were used more doses of pesticides both in the 1999-02 and 2005-06. In an average, Rayalaseema district had dominated 203 MTs in 1999-2000 year and also 77.25 MTs lesser in 2005-06 among other regions. Of course, Coastal Andhra was used lesser pesticides than other two regions.

As agriculture is not giving adequate income, employment, so that land less and low landed people moved front rural to urban areas, where they are fallen in the trap of slums. Slowly slum population has raised around drainages, river beds, bunds, hillocks, road sides. Recent estimates by UN-Habitat suggest that there are 900 million slum dwellers in the developing world, accounting for 43 per cent of the Urban Population.[8]

Slum Population Growth

Urbanisation has led to congestion leading to complete environment problems and poor health due to non-availability of safe drinking water and sanitation. The growing urban population and urban agglomeration lead to a large number of slums which is a real unit having 25 or more *kachcha* structures of temporary of nature. Percentage of the identified estimated slum population for the years 1981, 1991 and 2001 is 22.9, 24.1 and 24.1 respectively as against the urban population. The following table explains a sample slums.

Table 3
District-wise Consumption of Pesticides, 1999-00-2005-06

(Qty. in tones)

District	*1999-2000*	*2005-2006*
Coastal Andhra		
Srikakulam	23	7
Viziznagaram	57	21
Visakapatnam	2	38
East Godavari	167	64
West Godavari	124	96
Krishna	65	85
Guntur	683	236
Nellore	80	85
Prakasam	210	113
	1411 (35.0)	745 (39.0)
Rayalaseema		
Kurnool	483	212
Kadapa	63	31
Anantapur	202	35
Chittoor	65	31
	813 (20.0)	309 (16.0)
Telangana		
Ranga Reddy	98	108
Nizamabad	70	59
Medak	108	48
Mahabub Nagar	118	105
Nalgonda	106	83
Warangal	246	115
Khammam	812	222
Karimnagar	190	94
Adilabad	82	29
Sub-Total	1830 (45.0)	863 (45.0)
	4054 (100.00)	1917 (100.00)

Source: Directorate of Economics and Statistics (2006) compendium of Environment Statistics Andhra Pradesh p. 95.

The Table 4 finds that in Coastal Andhra, Eluru; in Rayalaseema Kurnool; in Telangana, Nizamabad were found the biggest slum population Districts in these regions. The lowest slum population was identified in Visakapatnam, Kadapa and Kukatpally (Ranga Reddy). By all means, in urban Agglamerations only more slum population had been living in Andhra Pradesh, which needs relief and rehabilitation.

Table 4
Slum Population of the Biggest Municipality in A.P., 2001census

Name of the Municipality	*Total Population*	*Slum Population*	*Percentage of Slum population*
Coastal Andhra			
Srikakulam (U.A)	1,17,066	48,632	41.54
Vizianagaram (U.A)	1,95,562	67,525	34.53
Visakapatnam (U.A)	13,45,776	1,71,211	12.72
East Godavari (U.A) Kakinada	4,13,349	1,12,003	27.1
West Godavari (U.A) Eluru	2,15,462	1,04,716	48.0
Krishna (U.A) Vijayawada	10,33,562	2,63,973	25.54
Guntur (M.C)	5,11,993	1,70,772	33.35
Prakasma (U.A) Chirala	1,65,838	84,482	50.94
Nellore (U.A)	4,04,624	1,56,346	38.64
Rayalaseema			
Chittoor (U.A) Tirupati	3,02,678	75,528	24.95
Kadapa (U.A)	2,60,962	33,994	13.03
Anantapur (U.A)	2,43,359	67,545	27.76
Kurnool (U.A)	3,42,628	1,20,387	35.14
Telangana			
Mahabub Nagar (U.A)	1,39,534	51,481	36.89
Ranga Reddy (M) Kukatpally	2,91,202	19,585	6.73
Hyderabad (U.A)	57,51,780	11,70,424	20.35
Medak (M) Siddipet	61,650	33,924	55.15
Nizamabad (M)	2,86,956	1,64,001	57.15
Adilabad (U.A)	1,29,041	63,913	49.53
Karimnagar(U.A) Ramagundam	2,47,751	94,868	38.29
Warangal (U.A)	5,77,968	230190	39.83
Khammam (U.A)	1,98,665	64,062	32.25
Nalgonda (U.A)	1,11,745	14,296	12.79

Note: U.A: Urban Agglomeration
M.C: Municipal Corporation
M: Municipality

Source: Govt. of A.P. (2006) Compendium of Environment Statistics A.P. pp.175.178.

Urbanisation has generated another the biggest environmental problem is waste products, like solid, liquid, gases, which spreads number of diseases like Malaria, Asthma, Diarrhoea, Diabetes.

Solid Waste Management

Due to rapid growth of Urbanization, there is a substantial generation of solid waste and hazardous waste. Andhra Pradesh Pollution Controlled Board (APPCB) has identified 1582 hazardous waste generating/handling industries in Andhra Pradesh. The total quantity of hazardous generation from the State is estimated around 5,07,046 Tonnes *per annum* (TPA), out of which the disposal waste is 2,30,109 (TPA), incinerable waste is 12,597 (TPA) and recycling waste is 2,64,341 (TPA).

If the solid waste is not collected and disposed of efficiently and effectively, it attracts rodents and flies, which spread diseases. It also pollutes and degrades land and water sources. If these wastes are left untreated, they would ferment slowly and produce bio-gas contains 65-70 per cent methane gas, which is a *"green house gas"* have a global warming potential 34 limes more than that of carbon dioxide. APPCB was instrumental for establishment of common treatment storage and disposal facility located at Dundigal Village in Ranga Reddy District with the assistance of Government of Australia.

Human development is adversely affected by the environment degradation. Polluted air and unhygienic conditions in human settlements, contribute to reduction in life expectancy and increase in infant mortality.

The fallowing table analyses the impact of solid waste management in the biggest Municipalities of each District in Andhra Pradesh.

The Table 5 reveals that in Coastal districts Visakaptnam, in Rayalaseema, Chittoor and in Telangana, Ranga Reddy Districts generated more solid waste. Of course, Hyderabad - the capital is the leading in generation of heavy solid waste. It is found that Hyderabad Municipal Corporation generates more than 21 big Municipalities in Andhra Pradesh.

The collection and efficiency of solid waste are found around 90 per cent. In practice physically, they are not taking place everyday. Infact all municipalities are found in murkier and murkier, leading to all chronic diseases.

Table 5
Total Amount of Solid Waste Collected and Collection Effectively in Biggest cities of A.P. 2005

(Qty. in Tonnes)

District/ Name of the biggest Municipality	*Population as per the 2001 census*	*Solid waste (tones) generated*	*Collected*	*Collection efficiency in per cent*
Coastal Andhra				
Srikakulam, Srikakuam	1,09,905	120	118	98
Vizianagaram, Vizianagaram,	1,74,651	110	105	95
Visakapatnam, Gajuwaka	2,59,180	140	135	96
East Godavari, Samalkot	53,602	29	28	96
West Godavari, Bhimavaram	1,37,409	70	70	100
Krishna, Machilipatnam	1,79,353	54	50	92
Guntur, Tenali	1,53,756	100	100	100
Prakasam, Ongole	1,50,471	100	95	95
Nellore, Kavali	79,682	55	50	90
Sub-Total	12,98,009	778	751	96.0
Rayalaseema				
Anantapur, Hindupur	1,25,074	70	64	91
Kurnool, Adoni	1,57,305	80	70	87
Kadapa, Proddutur	1,50,309	80	80	100
Chittoor, Chittoor	1,52,654	105	102	97
Sub-Total	5,85,342	335	316	94.0
Telangana				
Warangal, Janagaon	43,935	22	19	86
Karim Nagar, Ramagundam	2,36,600	120	114	95
Adilabad, Adilabad	1,09,529	60	57	95
Ranga Reddy, Kukatpally	2,92,289	146	127	87
Nalgonda, Nalgonda	1,10,286	56	54	96
Medak, Sangareddy	57,113	28	22	79
Mahaboob Nagar, Mahboobnagar	1,30,986	58	53	91
Nizambad, Bodhan	71,520	35	32	91
Sub-Total	10,52,258	525	481	90
Municipal corporation, Hyderabad	36,12,427	22,00	2200	100
Total	65,48,036	3838	3748	95.0

Source: Compendium of Environment Statistics Andhra Pradesh 2006, pp.183-187.

Positive Developments for revival

Forest cover is to be given top priority in extending 33 per cent of its geographical area. Further, forest cover brings wild life, biodiversity, herbal, *flora fauna* will be strengthened. Of course, water bodies can improve through springs. Human beings are to be taught not to destroy *flora* and *fauna* indiscriminately. Too much urbanization, high population explosion, high mass of consumption, high poverty and greediness, technology for destruction, are to be checked in rationally. What Mahatma Gandhi had said that nature can give for every one the needy but not greedy one.

Conclusion

Andhra Pradesh State has been facing a big threat from environmental degradation. Except Khammam, Adilabad, degradation of Forest is more than forest cover. Drought are concentrated more in the districts of Rayalaseema and Telangana Districts. In Agriculture, highly poisonous pesticides were used to cure pests of crops, which finally destroyed soil quality and productivity. Rayalaseema farmers were used more pesticides follows Telangana. More slum population was found in Eluru city of Coastal Andhra, Kurnool in Raalaseema and Nizamabad in Telangana. In production of Solid waste, Visakapatnam in Coastal Andhra, Chittoor in Rayalaseema and Ranga Reddy District in Telangana District were found as dubious leaders.

In overall, relatively, Rayalaseema and Telangana district were found as high levels of environmental degradation than Coastal Andhra, which is a big threat to entire development of Andhra Pradesh State.

Notes and References

1. V. Ratna Reddy and Bhagirath Behera (2003), Andhra Pradesh Development, Centre for Economic and Social Studies, Hyderabad.

2. Peter Singer (2000), Environmental Values, Reprinted in Writings on an Ethical Life (New York: ECCO) p. 88.

3. Jagadish Bhagawathi (2007), In Defense of Globalisation, Oxford University Press, New Delhi.
4. World Commission on Environment (1987), Our Common Future, OUP, New Delhi.
5. Directorate of Economics and Statistics (2006), Compendium of Environment Statistics Andhra Pradesh, p. 23.
6. S.N. Jadhav and K. Biswar (2006), Community Participation in Protection and Development of Forest in Anantapur District, Regional workshops on Deserts and Desertification by AMR-A.P. Academy of Rural Development, Hyderabad, p. 68.
7. Charles D. Kolstad (2004), Environmental Economics, OUP, New Delhi.
8. S. Chandrasekar, TesfayiGebreselassie (2008), Exploring Intra Urban Differences in Economic well-being in India, India Development Report 2008, Oxford, New Delhi.

16

IMPACT OF ECO-TOURISM IN INDIA

Tourists as individuals who are rude, arrogant and insensitive to the reality of their impact. The new generations of travellers who are 'money rich and time poor' are increasingly looking for unique experiences. Agriculture and industry are location specific, whereas tourism can be promoted and developed any where. It is an ideal tool for decentralised regional development. It provides infinite product possibilities-anything under the Sun if properly packaged and marketed-such as culture, heritage, nature, sun and beach, cruises, business, spirituality, adventure, sports, ethnicity and so forth. The benefits are more spread out and not centred around urban areas as in the case of most industries. The multiplier effect of Tourism is very high[1].

Introduction

King George-III (1738-1820) was probably the first "tourist", taking regular holidays to the sea side town of Weymouth. In the 18th century educated and wealthy British noblemen travelled to Rome, Tuscany, Alps as part of their education. Leisure travel in its present form began in Britain as the Industrial Society was the first to offer time for leisure. Initially it was restricted to the owners of the machinery of production, the economic oligarchy, traders and the new middle class. In

20th Century, manual workers got paid holidays and jumped on the tourism Bandwagon. The era of mass tourism in the mountains of industrialised countries began soon after the second world war, the result of many factors including increase in urban populations, income, vacation time and mobility. For aspiring middle class, the conspicuous consumption of leisure became an important status maker. A cynic says "tourism simply puts a hedonistic face on neo-colonialism".

According to Ministry of Tourism for every million rupees invested at 1985-86 prices, the comparative employment generation in some of the sectors were as follows-Agriculture 44.7, manufacturing, 12.6, mining and quarrying 2.6, railways 0.9, other transport 13.8, tourism 47.5, and hotel and restaurants 89.0. Another survey by the Ministry shows that the impact of tourism on local level employment-about 96 per cent of the total income of artisan households in Kerala and 90 per cent in Rajasthan comes from tourism related income. The study also indicates that tourism plays a vital role in enhancing the standard of living of the artisan families. As regards folk artists, their average per capita income during the peak season is nearly four times that in the lean season. Share of female employment is the highest in the lower income segment of the artisan households. By 2020, the Asia Pacific region will be the second largest tourist generating market in the World. The World Tourism projection shows that by 2020, this region will generate 405 million of the total 1561 million tourists.

Concept of Eco-tourism

Ecotourism is that (a) provides for conservation measures, (b) includes meaningful community participation and (c) is profitable and can sustain itself.

Earlier said than done. In 1984, Maxican conservationist Ceballos-Lascurian helped set up a travel agency 'Ecotours' to give tourists a quality education experience and boost the local economy. Eco-tourism became a buzz word after that and soon came to encompass any form of tourism that was related to nature or made token murmurs towards sustainable development. The ability of a region to absorb tourist without destroying the balance of nature. Open sites will suffer from wear and tear of countless feet, particularly in fragile ecosystems ass and dunes. The ecological balance of a region can also be affected by souvenir-collecting by visitors.

In Malaysia, lands were cleared and locals displaced for a huge dam project just to provide eco-travelers with electricity in Malaysia. Another is a Casino in Laos being described as a eco-tourism because it was sited in un-touched countryside.

Eco-tourists are no different from other tourists and consume non-renewable resources to arrive at their destinations; perhaps even more since the areas they target are often the most remote and pristine.

Ecotourists, who pursuit of reefs, rain forests and ruins, they did not reflect on the environmental impact of the construction of hotels, the use of airlines, the manufacture of diving equipment, the consumption of imported goods or even something as visible as taking a motorboat out to the reef, which polluted the water. The Ecologists said that "Ecotourism's perceived lack of widespread benefits for local peoples is substantiated in a recent UNCTAD study, which shows that, despite efforts of governments to develop suitable policies dealing with tourism, their efforts are often undetermined by external forces beyond their control. Even the World Bank, a champion of eco-tourism development for a decade, has suggested that few eco-tourism projects have actually generated substantial income for the parks they are intended to protect, much less the local people living near them.

Ecotourism is increasingly introduced in third World countries in the form of a development package, involving capital, expertise, technology and management systems, and is, thus, becoming something like a new green revolution.

Ecologists has added that just as the green revolution initially led to high yields, and soon gave away in many places to darker stories of soil degradation, loss of indigenous plant species and knowledge and dependence on monocrops, so the picture of eco-tourism's environment record is revealing a darker side.

Growth and Development

Ecotourism has been called ego-tourism. World Trade Organisation claims tourism is World's largest service industry. The economic impact is second only to weapons industry. It's revenues are in excess of $ 3 trillion. In industrialised nations, tourism is the third largest household expenditure after food and housing. International tourism accounts for 36 per cent of trade in commercial services in advanced economies and 66 per cent in developing economies. Tourism is one of the top five exports for 83 per cent of counties and the main source of foreign currency. International tourists arrivals in 2002 was 702.6 million. India's share in global tourism was dismal and stood at 0.4 per cent[2]. Tourism demand in India is growing at 10.1 per cent per annum and most of the over 3.7 million foreign travellers visiting India are in search of adventure and wild life experience[3].

India's New Tourism Policy, 2002

It is implemented in Tenth Plan, will generate awareness about the benefits of tourism for the host population. It will mobilise State Governments to use tourism as a means for achieving their socio-economic objectives, encourage the private sector to enhance investment in tourism and provide legislative and regulatory support for sustainable tourism and to protect the interests of the industry and the consumer. India's tourism performance has failed to match its potential even as countries not blessed with natural and cultural endowments have taken the lead in reaping the benefits of tourism development. The interaction between tourism and environmental pollution requires sensitive handling. There is complimentarity, not conflict, between the high quality environmental, requirements of tourism and the imperatives of maintaining the ecological balance. The September 11, 2001 event brought global recession. The World Travel and Tourism Council estimates 4.5 per cent per annum increase in the total amount of travel and tourism economic activity between 2002-2012. The earnings from tourism have made it one of the World's largest industries and fastest growing sectors of global trade accounting for 10.7 per cent of global gross domestic product. Only 3.5 per cent of the World population travels internationally. The demand for eco-tourism and nature based holidays is expected to double and even triple in the next 20 years. India's has a vast array of protected monuments with 22 World heritage sides, 16 of which are monuments. The tourisms are focussed on beach and coastal tourism, variety of cuisine, village tourism, wild life sanctuaries and national parks, adventure tourism, international and domestic trade and commerce, holistic healing, fairs and festivals, village hats and Delhi-cultural capital of India. The need of physical infrastructure for tourism ranges from ports of entry to modes of transport to destinations to urban infrastructure. This underscores the need for inter-sectoral convergence of infrastructural schemes and programmes that could support tourist destinations. The road communication is arduous and time consuming. Air communication has of late improved, but is not yet tuned to tourism requirements. The availability of trained manpower is essential to achieve excellence in the tourism sector. The internet has a great impact on the marketing of travel and tourism. The Tenth Plan target of the creation of 18 million jobs through tourism requires a substantial investment of Rs. 38,800/- crores at the rate of 47 jobs per one million rupees of investment, both from the public and the private sector[4].

Uneven Economy

Since tourism was merely a leisure activity, it neither respected the environment nor indigenous groups. While initially ecological impact was brushed aside, it was argued that locals benefitted the most from tourism. But that has not been the case. Tourism's financial gains are highly un-evenly distributed. Most of the money ends up in the hands of international or local elites - hotel owners, package tour operators and airlines. Tourism was assumed to be neutral option for development of developing countries because, it relied largely on natural resources already in place-e.g., sand, sun, friendly people, but it has also ended up causing a collective humiliation of people at tourism sites. International tourism accounts for 3-10 per cent of GDP in advanced economies, but upto 40 per cent in developing economies.

Till all the inequities are addressed at the local, national and international level, tourism can be less harm than good. And of course, there is also the issue of ensuring that environment stays protected.

Ladakh has changed more in the past seven years than in the past seven centuries, once it became accessible to tourists (Christian Adler in Tourists Cannibals of culture). As more and more shining middle class Indians head off to their favourite destinations for shopping and entertainment this summer, we need to stop and reflect on how travels impact this world. Need we be the great Indian ugly tourists?

Every year in the Himalayas, 2,50,000 pilgrims, 25,000 trekkers, 75 mountaineering expeditions climb to the Gangothri Glacier. They deplete forests for firewood, trample riparian vegetation and strew litter. Cruise ships in the Caribbean produce more than 70,000 tonnes of waste a year. Fresh water used for 10 big hotels in Phuket equals the water used by the whole local population of Phuket. Some trails in the Peruvian Andes and in Nepal frequently visited by the tourists have been nicknamed -Coca-Cola trail and toilet paper trail.

Tourist sites require reconstruction of the landscape and increased use of Petroleum products and toxics such as chemicals, fertilisers and pesticides. These cluster sites greatly disturb natural human patterns of living, are at odds with wildlife and natural world. Tourists, on the other hand, also have a huge ecological foot prints, bringing with them their consumption - driven city life style, with little regard to the habitat, eco-system or locals that they happen to visit. So that it is a double whammy for the environment.

In *bhakti* tourism, Tirumala can be cited, where every day 50,000 devotees are touching for *darshan*, in an average. Population pressure has brought scarcity of water, destruction of forests, wild life disturbed, alarming rise of prices, spreading epidemic diseases like AIDS, more suicides, etc., which are to be addressed carefully.

Eco-tourism on Whale Shark

The Shark does not consider fisher folk to be a threat. It is easily caught. Hundreds of Whale sharks are being killed along the Western Coast of India each year. These beasts are the largest of all shark species and are found mostly in warm tropical and sub-tropical waters. Many weigh upto 70 tonnes and can be 20 metres long, though most of them measure about 12 to 15 metres. A living whale shark is worth between Rs. 20,000-Rs. 30,000. This includes Rs. 5,000-7,000 from the sale of Shark meat at the rate of Rs. one per kg and the sale of shark liver oil at the rate of around Rs. 10-20 per litre.

If eco-tourism is promoted, only one sighting of a Whale shark can bring in as much as Rs. 50,000-75,000. But rules need to be amended if the Whale shark is to be protected. This would also help people earn a livelihood that is not coloured in blood. The issue here is not just the protection of the animal. An alternative livelihood for the local communities of fisher folk is as necessary. In fact, finding a solution to the latter can automatically lead to a safe Suarashtra coast for Whale Sharks[5].

Eco-friendly Mountaineering

Around 60 per cent of the country's mountaineering expeditions are undertaken in Uttaranchal. Uttaranchal government formulated a new policy to regulate mountaineering activities and make them more eco-friendly. The aim of new law is to stop haphazard mountaineering. The State will provide better facilities, including guides, porters and rescue services to the climbers. Only two expeditions will be allowed per peak in a month. Since mountaineering season in the State last for six months. This would work out to only 12 expeditions per peak in a season. The maximum number of climbers for an expedition has been fixed at 10, including a doctor. Each expedition will also have to deposit Rs.10,000 as security littering the mountain. Bachendri Pal, the first Indian women to scale Mt.Everest, suggests: such a policy can become a bench mark for other states. Local people should be involved and conducted orientation course for its staff[6].

Acceptable Tourism

Tourism must have some ground rules, that is, it must be acceptable to the host community. It is an imposition-a form of oppression in which rich and powerful interests manipulated the people in the interest of their profit. A reasonable share of the profits derived from tourism must return to the people. Numerous studies have reinforced the view that the real economic beneficiaries of tourism in the third World have been foreign Corporations and local elites. It must be based on sound environmental and ecological principles, be sensitive to local, cultural and religious traditions and should not place any members of the host community in a position of inferiority. The number of tourists visiting any area should not be such that they overwhelm the local population and deny the possibility of genuine human encounter. While tourism offers the hope of wealth, it is also threat to many counties who are fearful of the threat it poses to the social structure. A country like Bhutan is so offended by the impact of tourism on neighbouring Nepal that it has closed its borders to almost all tourists[7]. The employment multiplier to tourism is defined as the number of jobs or fraction thereof directly and indirectly generated or induced per unit of tourist spending[8]. In some cases, the number of jobs created per unit of tourist will be low, but in rural areas even a few jobs can make a big difference. Still, ecotourism benefits should not be oversold, or there may be backlash as reality fails to live up to expectations[9].

Inherent Dangers

World Tourism Organisation had listed the middle East crisis. Recessionary trends in the U.K., U.S.A., higher fuel costs and air fares, weakness of the U.S. dollar. Pleasures are concentrated and distributed to tourists and pains and problems are for local touts and beggars. Diseases like AIDS, cultural destruction of nature and emergence of dependents would be the future; provided people are not joined in right spirit.

Conclusion

Eco-tourism has emerged as an agent for change of economic, cultural, social aspects of society without harming flora and fauna. Local people have to gain from tourism. India has taken in right direction for boosting up of tourism of different styles. Of course, India's share in World Tourism is 0.4 per cent. Traditionally, much of Indians are nature killers, which today want to change their habits for sustainable development. Negative effects are to be removed and positive developments are to be promoted, for sustainable eco-tourism.

Notes and References

1. M. P. Bezbaruah (2005), Prospects of Tourism, *Seminar,* 550, p. 32.
2. *The Hindu* (2005), CII Moots Monsoon Tourism to Boost Sector, July 4.
3. *The Times of India* (2005), Country Club (I) Ltd., Ventures into World Life and Adventure Tourism, May, 4.
4. Planning Commission (2002), Tenth Five Year Plan: 2002-2007, Vol. II, pp. 817-828.
5. Kushal P. S. Yadav (2000), Blood on the Beach, *Down to Earth,* October 15, pp. 28-29.
6. Raju Gusain (2004), Summit Watch, *Down to Earth,* Sept. 20, p. 19.
7. Ron O'Grady (1993), Tourism-Boom or Bane, Logos, Vol. 32, March.
8. Shirley B. Seward and Bernard K. Spinard A.D. (1982), Tourism in the Carribbean: The Economic Impact, p. 83.
9. Kreg Lindberg (1996), The Economic Impact of Ecotourism, Charles Stuart University, Internet, November 3.

17

CLIMATE CHANGE: A THREAT TO HUMANITY

Introduction

Environmentalist have long thought of economic globalization as a threat to the environment.[1] Climate change will be recognized as the most crucial problem that facing America and world.[2] Climate change is the most important global environmental challenge facing humanity with implications for food production, natural eco-systems, fresh water supply and health. The earth's climate system has demonstrably changed on both global and regional scales since the pre-industrial era. The unequivocal warming of the climate system is now evident from observation of increases in global average air and ocean temperatures, widespread melting of snow and ice, and rising global average sea level.[3] The atmosphere may be broadly divided into four regions–troposphere, stratosphere, mesosphere and thermosphere. The troposphere contains 70 per cent of the mass of the atmosphere. The stratosphere is a calm layer having a positive lapse rate.

In the last quarter of the 20th century the average atmosphere temperature rose by about 1 degree Fahrenheit. By 2000, that increase was responsible of the annual loss of about 1,60,000 lives and the loss of 5.5 million years of healthy life, according to estimates by the World Health Organization.

The toll is expected to double to about 3,00,000 lives and 11 millions years of healthy life by 2020.[4]

Global Air Circulation and Biomass

Two important factors determining the climate of an area are temperature and precipitation. The temperature and precipitation patterns that lead to different climates are caused mostly by the way air circulates over Earth's surface. A slight change in solar planetary axis wobbles and result in long term variations in solar radiation received by the earth. As air is heated earth surface will be heated. As Earth's annual revolution is tilted various regions are tipped away. Due to CORIOLIS effect earth rotates on its axis it prevents air currents from moving from north and south. The principal driving forces for the horizontal movement of the wind in the atmosphere, are uneven heating of the earths surface modified by the effect of the earth's rotation and the frictional resistance offered by the ground and the sea. Averaged over the year, the solar heat flow to the earths surface at the equator is 2.4 times than at the poles. An 18th century meteorologists, George Hadley, postulated that the air would continue to the poles before descending. In actuality it descends at a latitude of about 30°C and then returns to the equator, forming what are known as a Hadley cell. Heat and moisture are distributed over Earth's surface by vertical convection currents that form into six large convection cells (Called Hadley cells) at different latitudes. The uneven distribution of heat and moisture over the planets surface leads to the forest, grasslands and deserts that make up biomes.

Kyoto Protocol

The problem of 'Climate Change' is becoming a growing concern of the world community. Under Kyoto protocol, developed countries would have to take definite commitment for reducing emission of GHG's during the first phase of the five years 2008-2012. Developing countries are not required to take any commitment during this phase, however, under the protocol all countries have to reduce emission of GHGs by making mitigation efforts like improving efficiency of energy conversion and utilization, afforestation, stabilizing population growth, limiting methane emissions through proper waste management and phasing out subsidies on power utilization.[5]

Nature is, evidently, not an objective thing-in-itself. It is an idea specific to a society and so, to that extent, determined by its inimitable social relations and the singular hierarchy of human needed the foster. The primary task before and ecological politics now would be transform the undemocratic socio-economic relations that currently prevail through popular mobilization at both the global and local levels. That would render society more equitable and participatory by accordingly reconfiguring its hierarchy of needs. Till that happens, nature and its preservation will continue to be an un-democratic and dysfunctional–an unfettered prerogative for some and a destructive burden for the others.[6]

EL NINO Phenomenon

It is a Spanish word meaning the 'Christ child' known as the December phenomenon in the EL NINO phenomenon. Normally, the water of Eastern Pacific off equator Peru and Northern Chile are cold, 10°C Cooler than the waters of western Pacific rich in fish due to high nutrients.

During EL NINO years, a large pool of warm water in the western pacific causes convection currents that result in a stable tropical low pressure cell and heavy rain in Indonesia and southeast Asia. Subsiding air in the eastern pacific brings dry weather to the West Coast of South America. Trade winds flowing back toward the low pressure cell push warm surface water westward, allowing upwelling of cold, nutrient rich deep waters that support Vast Schools of fish and flocks of seabirds along the Coast of Peru. In EL Nino years, the warm water shifts back eastward, reversing the wind flow and ocean surface currents, bringing torrential rains to South America and droughts to Australia and South East Asia. This oscillating pattern is called the EL Nino Southern Oscillation (ENSO). A strong ENSO can trigger extreme weather changes over atleast two thirds of the globe, especially in lands along the pacific and Indian Oceans. When ENSO lasts 12 months or longer, it severely disrupts populations of plankton, fish and sea birds in upwelling areas and can trigger extreme weather changes over much of globe.

More significant effects were observed in Dec., 1982 resulting global impact on India food production dropped by 4 per cent, China grain yield dropped by 4 per cent, Indonesia starvation deaths, Bolivia, Peru-floods South Pacific Commission which coordinates and keeps tract of ocean levels, temperature, salinity levels, wind patterns observed connections between Green house effect and EL NINO effect.

Green House Gases and Global Warming

The Green House Effect is caused by gases such as carbon dioxide, water vapour, trace amounts of Ozone, methane, nitrous oxide, chloroflurocarbons and other gases that trap infrared waves that radiate from the Earth's surface. Collectively these gases known as green house gases act some what like the glass planes of a green house. They allow light, infrared radiation and some ultraviolet radiation from the sun to pass through the troposphere. Earth surface absorbs much of this solar energy and degrades it to longer wave, infrared radiation – that is heat – which then rises into the troposphere. Some of this heat escapes into space; some absorbed by molecules of green house gases, warming the air and some radiated back towards earth's surface. This natural trapping of heat in the troposphere is called the green house effect.

As a result of human activity such as the consumption of fossil fuels, the carbon dioxide level has risen more than 20 per cent in the past century. Fossil fuel consumption alone is responsible for the annual release of 5 billion metric tons of carbon into the air, or roughtly 1 metric ton for each person on earth CO_2 is the major contributor–over a 100 year horizon, it contributes 70 per cent of the total green house gas radiative forcing.

An International Committee of Scientists Commissioned by different World Governments to provide a definitive verdict on what is happening to the weather around the globe in the past decade. The report states that the world has been warming up since the 1980s. The world has already warmed up by about 0.5°C. It is expected to get 4°C warmer by the year 2030. According to present information, the over all average temperature is rising by 0.5°C for each increase in the carbon dioxide content by 18 per cent with a net increase of 1°C by the end of 2005.

Forests are the areas where a great deal of photosynthesis occurs through which they act as sinks for CO_2. Moreover they maintain vast reservoirs of fixed but readily oxidizable carbon in the form of wood and humus. The overall result is that they serve to maintain a balance in the atmospheric CO_2 level. The major sink for CO_2 is the ocean which contains the bulk of dissolved carbon dioxide as bicarbonate. Covering some 70 per cent of the planet, the oceans act as gigantic fly-wheel in the Earth's machinery. Another important sink is the biomass, Eg. Living green plants, in which the photosynthesis rate is known to accelerate with increase in the carbon dioxide level.

Emissions of Carbon from Fossil Fuels

88th per cent of world energy needs are supplied by fossil fuels while the balance coming from hydro-electric generation and nuclear power plants. Nearly 75 per cent carbon is released per unit of energy when coal is burnt instead of natural gas while the synthetic oil or gas made from coal or shale oil, produces about 80 per cent carbon than coal.

Carbon dioxide is not the only gas that could cause climate warming. Methane, chloroflurocarbons (CFCs), nitrous oxide and other trace gases also absorb infrared radiation and warm atmosphere. Methane, for instance, absorbs twenty to thirty times as much molecule for molecule–as CO_2 and CFCs absorbs approximately 20,000 times as much. The following table explains the GHGs situations in this world.

Table 1 reveals that CO_2 had generated significant amount of Green house gases and follows Methane, Nitrous Oxide and CFCs, respectively. Developed Countries are the main contributors for green house gases by human activity.

Table 1
Green House Gases: Past, Present and Future Details

Parameter Concentration	CO_2	CH_4	N_2O	*CFCs*
1950	280 ppm	1150 ppb	285 ppb	0.0 ppb
1985	345 ppm	1790 ppb	305 ppb	0.4 ppb
Expected 2075	526 ppm	4402 ppb	478 ppb	3.8 ppb
Annual concentration increase %	0.4	1	0.2	5
Relative Green House efficiency CO_2	51	25	230	1500
Current Green house contribution %	57	12	6	25
Anticipated rate between 1985 and 2075%	0.57	1.0	0.5	25
Equilibrium temperature change 1850-2075 °C	3.12	0.62	0.28	0.93
Total				4.95°C
% total temperature change	63	12	06	19 = 00%
Life time year	100	10	150	100

Source: Y. Anjaneyulu (2004), Introduction to Environmental Science, BS Publications, Hyderabad, p. 576.

Impact of Global Warming

The potential effects of global climate change can be considered in terms of ecological systems, sea-level rise, water resources, agriculture, electricity demand, air quality and health effects. Due to of sudden change in climate many species will be extincted or loss of fresh water fish population, mixed effects on migratory birds, shorebirds would suffer. By rising sea level, increased loss will be on Coastal wetlands, inundation of Coastal lowlands, increased erosion of beaches, increase in salinity in estuaries. Coastal wetlands currently total 13.145 sq. million kms; with a 1 m rise in sea, 26 to 66% of these wetlands may be lost.

Even on inland water levels also the impact was there, such as changes in soil moisture, changes in floods and droughts, changes in water quality, changes in sedimentation process and changes in water demand. Temperature increases can decrease levels of dissolved oxygen in the water. Bio-chemical oxygen demand (BOD) also increase with temperature.

Global warming exhibits direct and indirect effects on Agricultural productivity. Frequency of heat waves alters the pattern of rainfall and also changes in top soil management practices. Dry land yields of corn, wheat shorten a crop's life cycle. Summer cooling electricity demands would increase, while winter heating demand would decrease. As a result of climate change, annual electricity demands are expected to increase by 4 to 6% by the year 2055, additional power plants will be required to meet peak demands.

Global climate change also has implications for ambient air quality. Increased emissions of SO_x, NO_x, Co are associated with power plants meeting increased electric demands.

Human health effects are manifested by changes in morbidity and increases in mortality, particularly for the elderly during hotter and extended summer periods.

Global mean sea level which has risen 10-15 cm in the last century may raise by another 10-20 cm by 2025 cm and 50-200 cm by 2100. The countries most at risk are the river delta areas of Bangladesh, India, Egypt, Thailand, and China but many small Islands will also suffer. 20% of the most populated areas of India and Bangaladesh would be inundated. July 1998 was the hottest July in the history of the World since Meterologists started keeping records more than 118 years ago.

Measures to Control Global Warming

In the United States, $ 1 billion were earmarked to combat the potential of global warming, by starting Global warming Research per year since 1991. U.S. Could reduce its green house gas emission by 25-35% of 1990 levels using existing technology at low or no net cost. Billions of trees will be planted around the world to help combat the excessive production of CO_2, especially since the trees absorb CO_2 in the air. Another important sink is the biomass, viz. living green plants.

Despite the complexities that climate change poses to the agricultural sector in India, there are a lot of opportunities to leveraging the right kind of technologies and policies that reduce the losses and contribute in improving the livelihoods of millions. Land use management and adoption of green accounting frame work to help in making genuine investment decisions.

Optimal use of energy based on our daily needs is perhaps a first step. Additionally, the use of clean energy technologies and appliance will go a long way in mitigating impacts. The threat of global climate change is indeed upon us and if we are to save this beautiful planet, the world community should take collective and meaningful actions for the present and future generations to come.

India has many progressive forest conservation, afforestation, wildlife protection and community forestry policies and programmes. It is possible to explore how climate change consideration could be incorporated into the on going forestry programmes and policies.

State government agencies, State utility companies and regulatory commissions all need to participate in the mainstreaming of climate considerations. Indeed, raising consumer awareness will be the key to arresting climate change globally with local actions that permit its migration, and the adoption to its impacts. Political will is needed to implement it at all stages i.e., from grass roots level to parliamentary level.

Conclusion

Environmentalists feel that globalization is a threat to globe. Due to too much industrialization, urbanization, population explosion had raised the Green house gases especially developed countries. 1°C increase in heat, certainly brought many health problems, extinction of flora and fauna. Kyoto protocol has given a clear warning that emissions have to be checked before 2015 year. Elinino effect has changed the life styles of fish and sea birds. Fossil fuel consumption alone is responsible for the annual release of 5 billion metric tons of carbon into the air. The world has already warming up by about 0.5°C. It is expected to get 4°C warmer up by the year 2030.

Forests are the areas where a great deal of photosynthesis occurs through which they act as sinks for wetlands, inundation of coastal low lands, increased erosion of beaches, increase in salinity in estuaries.

Consumption of energy is the root cause of CO_2 emission, which is to be reduced drastically. States have to take stern and pursue the policies to reduce Green House gases at grass root level. It is time to "think globally and act locally" by everybody to make this as good earth.

Notes

1. The atmosphere may be broadly divided into four regions–Troposphere stratosphere, Mesosphere and Thermosphere. The transphere contains 70 per cent of the mass of the atmosphere. The stratosphere is layer having a poositive lapse rate.

   The mesosphere shows negative lapse rate. The thermosphere gives a positive lapse rate (max. temperature 1200°C).

   Weather: The weather means at any given place and time on earth the troposphere has a set of physical properties including temperature, pressure, humidity, precipitation, sun shine, cloud cover and wind direction and speed which is called weather.

   Climate: The climate means the average long term weather of an area, it is a regions general pattern of atmospheric or weather conditions, seasonal variations and weather extremes (such as hurricanes, or prolonged drought or rain) averaged over a long period (at least 30 years).

2. The intergovernmental panel on Climate change (IPCC), an international body of over 3,000 experts, projects that the global mean temperature may increase between 1.8 to 4°C by 2100. More importantly, a warming of about 0.2°C per decade, almost double the annual increase over that last 50 years, is projected for the next two decades.

   Industrial countries need to assume leadership to reduce their own emission and also assist developing countries such as India in reducing their emissions. Countries of the European Union, Japan and Canada have committed to reduce their emissions of six GHGs by about 7.5 per cent under the Kyoto protocol compared to their 1990s levels. The US and Australia have assumed no mandatory Commitment. Carbon buyers in industrialized countries that have to meet Kyoto targets have created a market through the clean development mechanism (CDM) for the sale of carbon that is saved or requested in developing countries.

Notes and References

1. Jagadish Bhagawathi (2007), Environment in Peril? In Defense of Globalisation, OUP, New Delhi.

2. Paul Krugman's Column (2008), Dealing with the Dragon, *The Hindu,* Jan. 5, p. 11.
3. Jayant Sathaye (2007), Climate Change and India; Policy Response, *The Hindu Environment Survey 2007,* p. 7.
4. David Brown (2008), Climate Change, *The Sunday Express,* Jan 6, p. 13.
5. Planning Commission (2002), 10th Five Year Plan 2002-2007, Vol. II, p. 1076.
6. Pothik Ghosh (2007), New Protocol to Lack Teeth Pollu-shun, *The Economic Times,* December 31, p. 18.

Section–V

Democracy and Human Rights

18

TWELFTH FINANCE COMMISSION FOR FISCAL DEMOCRACY

The Finance Commission (FC) mandated by the Constitution to be appointed by the President periodically to mediate revenue sharing between Centre and States is a key pillar of India's federal structure. Transfers mediated by the FC, and its recommendations in responses to matters additionally referred to it have a profound impact on the budget, of all States and Union. Article 280 of the Constitution, which specifies the functions of the Finance Commission, stipulates that the Commission should make recommendations to the president on: (a) the shares of the Centre and the States of the taxes that are to (b) Principle which should govern the grants-in-aid to be given to the States in need of assistance. Late Guhan felt that Finance Commission can only bark at the Centre but bite the States.[1]

The Eleventh Finance Commission (FFC) has recommended an overall share of 37.5 per cent of the Centres gross revenue receipts as transfers to States, fiscal transfers to the States, through all channels. As percentage of the gross revenue receipts of the Centre increased from an average of 31.4 per cent in the period of the Sixth Finance Commission to 38.1 per cent for the Seventh Finance commission. It further increased further to 40.3 per cent for the period covered by the Ninth commission.

The two principal modes of fiscal transfers viz., tax devolution and grants have certain distinguishing features. Tax devolution has a built-in-flexibility as it can increase automatically if the Central taxes are more buoyant. Grants-in-aid are mainly targeted towards achieving a degree of equalization. That is why many of the better- off states assessed to be in revenue surplus do not get article 275 grants[2]. Prior to the 80th Constitutional amendment, two main central taxes are found other than corporation tax and the union excise duties. With the 88th amendment of constitution, article 268A, provides that "Taxes of services shall be levied by the Govt. of India and the States......" It also further specifics that the principles of collection and appropriation will be determined by parliament.

Good Governance and States

The better-off states have represented that their share has steadily fallen in the overall concern.

The plan assistance is given to the States as consisting of grants and loans. The grants-loan ratio for the States in general is 30:70 whereas for the special category States, this ratio is 90:10. In normal Central assistance, 30 per cent is earmarked for the special category states.

The Mastricht Treaty role of 3% of GDP as the fiscal deficit target and 60 per cent as the desired debt-GDP ratio are well known. In U.K. a 'golden rule' of limiting borrowing only to finance capital expenditure has been followed since 1997 as a sustainable investment rule.

To strengthen the basic idea of promoting a fiscal domain for the local bodies as being the key to effective local self-governance. The provision of local goods requires that the link between local service and the responsibility of financing it by the potential beneficiaries is appreciated.

Gadgil-Mukerjee Formula

Distribution of plan assistance to States is governed by the Gadgil Mukerjee formula. According to the formula, 60%

weightage is given to population of a state-the state with large share. States which have been successful in birth control have been complaining that they are being penalised for better performance. Under the Gadgil-Mukerjee formula, performance criteria, such as per capita income of a State gets (25%) weightage. Other criteria are tax efforts (2.5%), fiscal management (2%), population control (1%), female literacy (1%) completion of on going externally aided projects (0.5%) and land reforms (0.5%). Quantum of assistance also depends on special performance of a particular state (7.5%) experts opine that there is an urgent need to change this formula.

Very recently, National Advisory Council (NAC) chairperson Sonia Gandhi has called a meeting of experts to redefine Central fund allocations to states by reducing population weightage from 60% to 25%. States under attack are U.P. Bihar and Madhya Pradesh.[3]

Fiscal Responsibility and Budget Management Act, (FRBM) 2003

The FRBM Act marks a watershed in fiscal reforms. The Act provides an institutional framework binding the government to purpose a prudent fiscal policy. The Act casts responsibility on the Central government to ensure inter-generation equality in fiscal management and long term macro-economic stability by achieving sufficient revenue surplus, removal of fiscal impediments in the effective conduct of monetary policy and prudential debt management through limits on borrowings and deficits. (a) The main features are to take appropriate measures to reduce fiscal deficit and revenue deficit so as to eliminate revenue deficit by March 31, 2008, and there after build up adequate revenue surplus. (b) Rules are to be made to specify the annual targets for reduction of fiscal deficit and revenue deficit. (c). The revenue deficit and fiscal deficit may exceed the targets specified in the rules only on grounds of national security or national calamity or such other exceptional grounds. (d). The Central government shall not borrow from the Reserve Bank of India except by way of advances to meet temporary excess of cash disbursements over cash receipts. (e). Reserve Bank of India not to be subscribed to the primary issues of the Central government securities from the year 2006-07. (f). Central government to take suitable measures to ensure greater transparency in its fiscal operations. (g). Central government to lay in each financial year before both houses of parliament three statements Viz., medium term fiscal policy statement, fiscal policy strategy statement and macroeconomic framework statement along with the Annual financial statement and Demands for grants. (h). Finance Minster to make a quarterly review of trends in receipts and expenditure in relation to the Budget and place the review before both houses of parliament[4] The award of 11th and 12th Finance commissions have shown relative differences in the values of variables over time. The States are classified into three groups-gainers, losers and no change. Debt written of scheme has the right set of incentives in some ways it is more stringent.

Finance of State Governments

The deterioration in the finances of State governments has been sharper than that of the Central government. All the major fiscal indicators reveal a worsening of the fiscal situation as compared with the position obtaining in 1990-91. Fiscal deficit of states as a proposition of GDP increased from 3.3 per cent in 1990-91 to 4.7 per cent in the revised estimates for 2002-03. Revenue deficit witnessed a sharper deterioration from 0.9 per cent of GDP to 2.5 per cent of GDP in the same period. The factors responsible for such a deterioration include growing burden of interest payments, pension liabilities and administrative expenditure. Losses of State owned public enterprises, in appropriate user charges and deceleration in central transfers compounded the problem. In recent years, the need for state level fiscal reforms has been well recognized. The problem of fiscal consolidation cannot be addressed unless reforms encompass both the Centre and States. With the worsening of the fiscal situation, particularly since 1998-99, a number of states have taken up fiscal reforms in right earnest.

Finance commission transfers have in recent years accounted for between and 60 per cent of total transfer to states from the Centre. The remainder was transferred through the Planning Commission through assistance for state plans[5].

Tax Devolution and Grants under Twelfth Finance Commission

The notable departures made by the Twelfth Finance Commission (TFC) in the scheme of Tax devolution and grants from that of its predecessor, the eleventh finance Commission (FFC) are:

- Enhancing the share of the States in the net proceeds of the shareable Central taxes of 30.5 per cent from 29.5 per cent.
- Raising the limit of the revenue transfers to the States to 38 per cent of the Centre's gross revenue receipts from 37.5 per cent.
- Changing the formula for tax devolution in the re-allocation weights in favour of population and efficiency factors.
- Application of norms in the assessment of non-plan revenue gap for determining the amount of grants-in-aid to States.
- Applying the equalization principle to provide grants for education and health to States which are relatively deficient in their revenue capacity, provided they maintain their normal expenditure on these heads at the current level.
- Providing grants for maintenance of roads and bridges, heritage conservation, state specific needs local bodies an calamity relief on a larger scale.
- Enlarging the grants to local bodies substantially and modifying the, formula for their allocation among States, to take account of deprivation in the provision of drinking water and sanitation, the index of decentralization which was used by EFC as one of the criteria has been dropped[6].

Chelliah argues for a new an scientific approach to federal financial relations in which the States should be treated as autonomous units and should be asked to determine for themselves the levels of revenue and expenditures. A key point is to keep the States' share in Union taxes, once fixed, unchanged for a larger period at least 15 years, unless there is a clear shift in their responsibilities.

To cure these deficiencies, a composite Index of fiscal performance (FPI) made up of three major components,. Viz., deficit index own revenue effort index and expenditure and debt repayment index. These are derived by combining eight indicators reflecting various aspects of fiscal performance. By using the data of 1990-99 years, Gujarat and Maharastra improve dramatically and those of Bihar, Madhya Pradesh and Uttar Pradesh worsen if the proposed indices are used instead of the TFCs,

Finances of even some of the better-of states turned alarming, with payments on salary, pension and interest accounting for 75 per cent of their revenue receipts, crossing 100 per cent in some states and the outstanding debt doubling, every five years beginning 1995 reaching nearly Rs. 9,00,000 crores in 2005 (Contingent liabilities accounting for another Rs. 2,00,000 Crore) clearly the debt situation of the states cried out for relief.

The urge to control fiscal policies in order to please international capital markets must not lead to strategies that undermine economic democracy and social cohesion, especially in counties that are as heterogeneous and federal as India.

Rakshit questions the TFC focus on saving as the engine of growth. In a demand deficient economy, he argues, it is investment which drives sowing and not the other way round. Even in a full employment economy, creation of investment opportunities through fiscal policy, such as investment infrastructure helps to raise savings by inducing investors to plough back a large share of their income/profits.

Investment in human development and environmental improvement considered as composition of government expenditure, which certainly changes shape of economy positively.

Loan Council

TFC also stresses the need to have an independent body like loan council to decide the borrowing limits to the states and oversee their implementation. Union government is not much concern over it. However, Finance Ministry has constituted a "Central Monitoring Committee" consisting of officials to consider the details of the States' fiscal correction paths, examine their waiver. Claims from the States and recommend the quantum of the waiver. The task of fixing caps on the States' borrowing also rests with the Ministry of Finance. Clearly these go against the spirit of the TFC's recommendations. In the interest of federalism, sooner the transition is made to market based discipline the better. The Centre should help the disadvantaged State's if they find it difficult to access the market, as the TFC has suggested.

Chelliah was cautious that fiscal consolidation cannot be sustained unless some of the root causes of the states' fiscal distress are addressed. In particular, it is necessary to review the planning process and do away with the plan/non-plan dichotomy as the TFC has urged.

The future of federalism in India will depend very much on how the transfer system reconciles equality with efficiently while respecting the fiscal anatomy of the State.

The virtuous cycle of reforms, robust government finances, and an equlising system of fiscal transfers, should help establish a sound federal fiscal system in India[7].

Government Employment Policy and Pay Commissions

In federal structure, a state government has to formulate its policies on government employment, levels of employee's remuneration, the relative size of the government sector. Keeping its own economic conditions in view, State had to decide the numbers to be employed. The federal government cannot underwrite equal salary levels in the government sector across the country. Equalization grant given to a State would strengthen its capacity to pay wages. The Central government in India has no systematic policy of controlling or regulating the size of its work force. But it follows the policy to rising upward, periodically, the real wages and pensions of its employees. This is done on the basis of the recommendations of a pay commission appointed at intervals of 10 to 15 years. By all means, the real wages of government employees have to be increased with the growth of the economy and the rise in per capital income. Generally, senior civil servants in "*ad hoc*" way increase the salaries in *lump sum*. Substantially, Central government raises the salary bill by Trade unions pressure and its impact fall on State governments, which approaches Finance Commission to support the gap by grant. The revision of salaries of employees could be linked to the rise in real per capital income of the Centre and also individual States. This can be done within three or four years.

The states should be treated as autonomous units and be asked to determine for themselves the levels of revenues and expenditure[8]. The Twelfth Commission recommended performance budgeting, doing away with the distinction between plan and non-plan expenditure, and transparency including elimination of hidden subsidies[9].

Conclusion

Finance Commission (FC) mandated by the Constitution to be appointed by the President of India periodically to mediate revenue sharing between Centre and States is a key pillar of India's federal democracy.

In course of time, good governance States' lost their share from Finance Commission devolution of resources. The grants-loan ratio for the states, in general is 30:70, Currently, National Advisory Council's Chairman has interested to reduce the population weightage from 60% to 25%. The FRBM Act 2003 has made the States have made the States to eliminate fiscal deficit as on March 31, 2008. State level fiscal reforms are highly needed. Enlargement of grants to local bodies for drinkable water, sanitation etc was considered as top priority. States should not mould the fiscal policies to please international capita and undermine economic democracy.

Sooner or later, the federal structure is to be made to market based discipline. The Centre should help the disadvantaged

States, if they find it difficult to access the market. Chelliah suggested that the revision of salaries and pensions of employees could be linked to the rise in real per capital income of Centre and individual States.

Notes and Reference

1. M. Govinda Rao, Pratap R. Jena (2005), Balancing Stability Equality & Efficiency, *Economic & Political Weekly,* July 30, p. 3405.
2. Govt. of India (2005), Reports of the Finance Commission of India, Academic Foundation, New Delhi, p. 13.
3. (Rajeev Jayaswal (2006), For Sonia, Big Aim't Beautiful: Calling for Slashing Population Weight in Central Fund Allocation, *The Economic Times,* Feb. 17, p. 1.
4. Govt. of India (2004), *Economic survey,* 2003-04, p. 36.
5. Indira Rajaraman, D. Majundar (2005), Equity and Consistency Properties of TFC Recommendations, *EPW,* July, 30, p. 3419.
6. Amaresh Begchi (2005), for Sonia Big Aint' Beautiful: Calling for Slashing Population Weight in Central Fund Allocation, *The Economic Times,* Feb. 17, p. 1.
7. C. Rangarajan (2005), Approach and Recommendations, *Economic and Poli weekly,* July 30, p. 3398.
8 Raja J. Chellaiah (2005), Malady of Continuing Fiscal Imbalance, *Economic and Political Weekely,* July 30, 3403.
9 Mihir Rakshit (2005), Some Analystics and Empirics of Fiscal Restructuring in India, *Economic and Political weekly,* July 30, p. 3448.

19

NEHRU: A VISIONARY FOR DEMOCRACY AND DEVELOPMENT

Origin of Parliamentary System

The Institutions of parliament is the greatest political inventions of man, Parliament should reflect the will of the people of the country as a whole. Parliament democracy will fail, unless we learn to work together in national interest. Democracy without discipline leads to *mobocracy* and chao, and discipline without 'democracy leads to slavery'. In the 14th century parliament began to present petitions (bills) to the king, which with his assent would become law. Legislative Assembly of Britain and of other governments modeled after it. The British Parliament consists of the Monarch, the House of Lords and the House of Commons, and its roots to the Union (C.1300) of the Great Council of the Kings Court, two bodies that treated with and advised the King. In the 14th century, Parliament was split into two houses-with the lords spiritual and temporal debating in one and the Knights and burgesses in the other. Robert's Walpole was the first party leader to Head the Government as Prime Minister (1721-42). Rules of parliamentary procedure originated in Britain in the 16th and 17th centuries and were subsequently adopted by legislatures around the world., Roberts Rules of order, codified in 1876 by

U.S. General Henry M. Robert (1837-1923) and regularly refined and enlarged, is the standard set of rules used by legislatures in the U.S. Generally accepted rules, procedures and practices used in the governance of deliberative assemblies. They are intended to maintain decorum, ascertain the will of the majority, preserve the rights of the minority, and facilitate the orderly transaction of business. Nehru, the Prime Minister of India laid solid foundation for democracy and development in India.

A Brief Bio-data of Jawaharlal Nehru

(Born Nov. 14, 1889, Allahabad died May 27, 1964, New Delhi). He was the first Prime Minister of India (1947-64), Son of Independence, advocate Motilal Nehru (1861-1931). Nehru was educated at home and in Britain and became a lawyer in 1912. More interested in Politics than law, he was impressed by Mohandas K. Gandhi's approach to Indian independence. His close association with the Indian National Congress began in 1919; in 1929 he became its president, presiding over the historic Lahore session that proclaimed complete independence as India's Political goal. He was imprisoned nine times between 1921 and 1945 for his political activity. When India was granted limited self government in 1935 the Congress Party under Nehru refused to form coalition governments with the Muslim league in some provinces; the hardening of relations between Hindus and Muslims that followed ultimately led to the partition of India and the creation of Pakistan. Shortly before Gandhi's assassination in 1948, Nehru became the first Prime Minister of Independent India. He attempted a foreign policy of non-alignment during the cold war, drawing harsh criticism if he appeared to favour either camp. During his tenure India clashed with Pakistan over the Kashmir region and with China over the Brahmaputra River valley. He wrested Goa from Portuguese. Domestically he promoted democracy, socialism, Secularism and Unity, adapting modern values to India conditions. His daughter Indira Gandhi became Prime Minister two years after his death.[2]

Vital Economic Issues

In Agriculture, large scale State intervention in the shape of extinguishing or modifying rights in property, controlling farm practice and regimenting the peoples' way of life from a prior considerations may be ever disastrous. Talk of a socialist pattern of society has been very much in the air. Nehru couples it with the welfare state as a twin objectives which congress party has accepted. Of course *Sarvodaya* group was against Socialism as a goal. Nehru has discounted the importance of the communist, Communal and Praja Socialist parties. He realizes that there can be no socialism on the basis of a pauper economy, which production is the key to progress. For elimination of inequality social ownership or control of the principal means of production is not an inescapable necessity. On the contrary from the point of view of rapidly increasing production without adapting totalitarian coercion, there is everything to be said for an enlightened policy to encouraging private industry. Maulara Azad gave cogent reasons why nationalsation is no panacea, and British experience seemly fully to bear this out. But a far more potent reason which was weighted with countries bred in-the democratic tradition against going in for socialism or for a socialistic pattern is their rooted faith in liberty as the very life breath of democracy. We in India who have accepted the democratic way of life cannot afford to jeopardize that supreme value.

Move to Socialistic Pattern Society

Britain had welfare state without socialism and doing very well on it. Nehru had painstakingly sought to explain that they are not thinking of that kind of socialism at all that they contemplate something which will be as distinct from the Marxist-Leninist conception of socialism as from capitalism. Nehru's instincts are essentially democratic. He realizes that socialism of his dream can not be realized in a day. He knows that means are no less important than ends. If confronted with the choice between socialism and democracy, we have no doubt he would prefer the latter any day.

The Hindu in November 1958 wrote that our failure to reach the plans food targets shows that not enough was invested in agriculture. Industrialization is not an end in itself what should be aimed at is the reconstruction of the whole country from the village up. Today we have roads and railways which link the big towns, we have business and industry and education mainly sited in the towns. But the purchasing power of the villager does not rise. The villagers want schools, bridges, markets, improved tools and machines, fertilizers as well as irrigation and electricity.

Mixed Economic System

Mixed economy is an inescapable consequence of the political and economic character of the country. *The role of the state should be that of a catalyst. It should not become an octopus that seeks to control every thing.*

Our plans have failed so far mainly in this latter aspect. There has been too much dependence and Central Government direction and too little of local initiative and inspiration. Neither the progress of agriculture, which is so vital for the solution of the food problem nor the diversification of industry which is essential for providing employment, will be possible unless the impulse for improvement and organization comes from the bottom, from the village and district level[3].

Rainbow of Secularism

Nehru felt that secularism did not mean something opposed to religion or "a state where religion as such is discouraged. It means freedom of religion and conscience, including freedom for those who may have no religion". And it means a "State which honours all faiths equally and gives them equal opportunities and does not allow itself to be attached to one faith or religion[4].

Delhi is the eternal city, as the ruins of its forerunners-Indraprastha and Hastinapur–testify. It is the heart of India only a nit-wit can regard it as belonging to the Hindus or Sikhs alone. From Kanyakumari to Kashmir and from Gujarat to Assam, all Hindus, Muslims, Sikhas, Parsis, Christians and

Jews who people this vast sub-continent and have adopted it as their dear motherland have an equal right to it. No one had the right to say it belongs to the majority only and that the minority can remain only as the underdog. Whoever serves it with the purest devotion must have the first claim[5].

Kashmir and India

On the eve of Independence, All India Congress Committees (AICC) stand as declared in its resolution of June 15, 1947 was that "the people of the States must have a dominating voice in any decisions regarding them". In contrast Mohammad Ali Jinnah asserted on July 30, that the ruler would decide which of the two States to accede to" or to remain independent. When a dispute arose with Pakistan over Kashmir's accession to India on Oct 26, 1947 following a tribal raid from Pakistan, Nehru said repeatedly the people would nonetheiess, decide the issue in plebiscite. The international agreement that was used by V. K. Krishna Menon's words on the modalities of a plebiscite in the form of two resolutions of the U N Commission for India and Pakistan (UNCIP) dated August 13, 1948 and Jan, 5, 1949. Shaik M. Abdullah, Prime Minister (from 1947 till 1952) had a strong disapproval of plebiscite. On August 8, 1953 Shaik Abdullah was sacked from the office of Prime Minister of Jammu and Kashmir and put him behind the bars. Nehru felt that why would they live in a country where the Jan Sangh (presently Bharatiya Janatha Party) and the Rastriya Swayamsevak Sangh are constantly beleaguering them. Nehru was always preaching the Mission of Secular democracy

At present, Kashmir is an integral part of Indian Union on the basis of 'Accession' and as a symbol of Indian Secularism Bharatiya Janata Party demanded that Kashmir is an integral part of India by removing article 370[6]. Even today, Kashmir became a burning problem. Which has swallowed lot of wealth, men and energy, we are looking for amicable solution in this decade

The Kamaraj Plan

In August 1963, an attempt was indeed undertaken to enhance the party influence over the government through, what came to be known as "the Kamaraj Plan". The idea was to revert back government Ministers to party positions after certain tenure and *vice versa*. Jawaharlal Nehru sympathized this theory, but hardly put his weight behind its implementation. Instead, his colleagues like Morarji Desai alleged that he used the Kamaraj plan to remove all possibie contenders" from the path of his daughter, Indira Gandhi". Besides, the Kamaraj plan created a new dispossessed group within the congress who had been deprived of their Ministerial positions. This increased intra-party factional squabbles. The spirit of the Kamaraj plan was thus greatly lost[7].

Democracy and Development

Development involves investment. It naturally involves savings, private and public. Both are necessary. He would not like to spend a large part of resources in making more and more weapons. The industrial background has to grow, which means that we should provide for this process of development all the more. In planning, you must have clear social imperatives. In a democratic country like India, we cannot think of any social objective which does not touch the vast masses of the people. We want to produce more and more wealth and also have it properly distributed. We should continue with democracy, functioning in as wide a measure as is possible, even though the shadow of war and other troubles have hovered over us. Democracy is a complicated way of functioning and sometimes it involves delays. I think we should get rid of these delays. India is not merely a land of mountains, rivers, forests, cities, towns; it is a mass of human beings, many of them struggling for a bare pittance. We have to have perspective planning, that is, we must plan for the next 15 years or 20 years.

Ever since we become free, we have been absorbed in this major war against poverty, ignorance, illiteracy and all that. The democracy we profess and practice has not substantially grown in most countries. We established the democracy largely taken from the British and partly from the American practice[8].

Conclusion

Nehru-multifaceted personality, had introduced Parliamentary Democracy and Five Year Plans for development. Which became solid and strong roots for fast development. Villages were founded as 'engine of growth' for all round development. Mixed economy was considered as a competitive boon system!" Secularism was treated in Constitution and in practice, as a backbone. Even under globalization era, Kashmir is even today become a bone of contention for both countries. Democracy and development were interdependent for curing all ills, and pushing economy for welfare of all.

Notes and References

1. Britannica (2005), Britannica Ready Reference Encyclopedia, New Delhi, Vol. 7, p. 218.
2. Britannica (2005), Britannica Ready Reference Encyclopedia, Vol. 7, New Delhi, p. 84.
3. Rangaswamy Parthasarathy (1978), A Hundred Years of *The Hindu*, the Epic Story of Indian Nationalism, Kasturi & Sons Ltd., Madras, pp. 703-714.
4. S. Gopal (1980), Jawaharlal Nehru: An Anthology (Ed. Vol.) OUP, Delhi, pp. 327-330
5. *The Hindustan Times* (1948), Delhi Belonged to Everyone. January 18.
6. A. G. Noorani (1999), How and Why Nehru and Abdullah Fell Out, *Economic and Political Weekly*, pp. 268-272.
7. Suranjan Das, (2001), The Nehru Years of Indian Politics Edinburgh Papers, *Centre for South Asian Studies*, No. 16.
8. Publication Division (1983), Jawaharlal Nehru's Speeches 1963-64, Vol. V, 49.

20

NEED FOR EMPOWERMENT OF TRIBALS IN INDIA

Costa Rica development a fairly just working model for payment for tribals and farmers to ecosystem services (PES) which helped take the forest cover in the country from about 30 to about 50 per cent in just three decades, has helped reduce poverty and has given Costa Rica a new identity as the Switzerland of Latin America.[1] Amartya Sen, felt that development can be seen as a process of expanding the real freedoms that people enjoy.

Sage of the Tribals in India is a story of the struggle of the weak against the powerful, of the oil lamp and the storm. It is said that a lamb connot lie beside the Lion even with a fence between them, for long, and will ultimately land up inside the lion.

Now–almost 70 years later–National Tribal Policy Draft, shows that very little had changed for the tribals of this country.

According to the 2001 census, the total population of STs is 84.3 million, which constitutes 8.20 per cent of the country's population of these about 1.32 million (1.57 per cent) belong to primitive Tribal Groups (PTG's).[2]

10th Five Year Plan Objectives

The Tenth Five year plan objective of empowering the tribals is being achieved through a three pronged strategy of social empowerment, economic empowerment and social justice.

Economic Empowerment

Cultivation is the main occupation of 45 per cent of the tribals and 37 per cent of them are agricultural labourers, according to the 2001 census. Forty-six per cent tribals in rural areas and 35 per cent in urban areas were living below the poverty line, according to 1999-2000 figures. Various schemes to empower the tribals through employment and income generating activities and food security are being implemented through the National Scheduled Tribals Finance and Development Corporation (NSTFDC), Tribal Cooperative Marketing Development Federation of India Limited (TRIFED) and State Scheduled Tribes Finance and Development Corporation (STDs).

Social Justice

Constitutional guarantees ensure justice to the tribals. The protection of civil Rights Act 1955 (Per Act) and Scheduled Castes/Scheduled Tribes (Prevention of Atrocities Act 1989 (POA Act) are two important legal instruments to protect the tribals from all kinds of social discrimination like untouchability, exploitation and atrocities. The POA Act provides for special courts and disposal of the cases. Nineteen States have appointed Special Cells/ squads/ officers to ensure effective implementation of the Act. In order to enable the tribals to participate in the decision making process, provisions of the Panchayat (Extension to the Schedule Areas) Act, 1996, has been extended to the Scheduled areas empowerment them to formulate plans, implement and monitor Schemes.

Social Empowerment

The Flag ship Scheme of Post-metric scholarship, which is a vin to the post-matric scholarship scheme for SCs, ware revised in 2003 on similar times. Till 2004-05, 2 million tribals students availed of scholarships. The Ashram Schools in Tribal Sub-plan (TSP) area scheme was launched in 1990-91 to promote educational development in tribal areas through the creation of residential facilities, especially focussing on ST girls and children of PTG's, migrant and nomadic STS. The scheme is being implemented in 21 States and two Union Territories.

Low Literacy Pockets Scheme for the development of girls and women's literacy was introduced in 1993-94 in 136 districts of 14 States, where the literacy rates arrange ST females are less than 10 per cent. The scheme is being implemented through NGO's, institutions se up by government and autonomous bodies as well as registered cooperative societies.

The construction of Hostels for Scheduled Tribe boys and girls scheme was started during the third plan. A separate scheme for construction of Hostels for Scheduled Tribe boys was launched in 1989-90 and both the schemes were merged into one scheme during the Tenth plan. (163). A new scheme of Rajiv Gandhi National Fellowship for ST students to pursue higher education was launched during 2005-2006 and entrusted to UGC for implementation.

In spite of the various educational and vocational training programmes in operation, the literacy rate, enrolment rate, health and other indicators of the tribal population remains poor. Delivery system has failed, which is to be re-designed and implemented.

Primitive Tribal Groups on Extinction

There are about 5000 forest villages predominantly inhabited by the tribals, especially Primitive Tribal Groups (PTG's), which lack basic minimum services. There is need to undertake development of these forest villages. Efforts have already been initiated to prepare comprehensive projects for their development, initially in Assam, West Bengal, Madhya Pradesh, Gujarath and Chattisgarh, where 80 per cent of the forest villages are located. The PTG's live in the in accessible pockets of forests, with declining sources of sustenance. The National Forest Policy 1988 stipulates Certain measures to involve tribals in forest development activities.

Tribal Rehabilitation

A National Policy on Relief and Rehabilitation of project Affected families (PAFs) has been notified on 17 February 2004 with a relief package of 17 parameters to be fulfilled before permitting dislocation. This needs to be effectively implemented.

Missing Tribals

The problem of nomadic and semi-nomadic tribes are distinct and there is no authentic tribes are distinct and there is no authentic data on them. As they do not have permanent residency due to their mobility, suitable welfare and development programmes need to be devised for their benefit.

Forest Dwellers Rights

To address the problems of tribal communities, who are dependent on forests and to undo the historical injustice done to them, the scheduled Tribes and other Traditional forest Dwellers (Recognition of Forest Rights) Bill, 2006. This Act recognizes the forest rights of forest dwelling scheduled tribes and other traditional forest dwellers over the forest land under their occupation for self-cultivation, rights over minor forest produce and traditional rights.[3]

Kalrayan Hills: Northern Tamilnadu Tribals Economic Situation

The Malayalis (hillmen) inhabiting the Kalrayan hills are found in northern Tamilnadu, especially shevaroys, Panchaimalais, Namakkal District Javadis of Thiruvannamalai District. They are Tamil specking Karala vellalars who migrated to the hills with their god, Karia Ramar. Despite intensive efforts, there turns to agriculture are low and forest foraging for gall nut and curry leaves is an occasional activity. There tribals live in abject poverty. Malayalis produce inferior millets (Varagu, Samai, ragi etc.) by means of rainfed cultivation on hill-tap land. Tribals land rights have been violated by the forest Department, when classifying agricultural land, tribal owned land, revenue Purambok land and forests. Tribal dialect has the work 'Kadu' for cultivation land. Though centre and State in support of Tribal land demarcation, forest officials were seized by forest Department. With connivance of local government officials, tenurial contracts to tribals are similarly transferred and confiscated. Voluntary organisations have expedited land alienation through seizure of large tracts. Threats of physical harassment prevent complaint by tribals. Plain land people always cheats tribals. Poor transport also hinder production and commercialization. Money interest rates vary widely that is, Rs. 5 to Rs. 10 for a month for every Rs.100. Within the community the interest rates month for every Rs. 100. Within the community the interest rates are around 36 per cent. Although a lower interest may be explained by trust, full information and mutual obligation, the higher interest is experienced not as reflecting the opposite higher interest is experienced not a reflecting the opposite conditions but as the usurious expression of unequal power.

Intervention of State

Large sized Agricultural Multipurposes Cooperative Society (LAMPs) was initiated to cater to a wide set of needs of tribal people. The LAMPs objective is to give remunerative price to the forest produce and make tribals to live without exploitation. Political pressure made the LAMPs not to work actively, so that private traders can go for exploitation. State employees Forest Department Officials and private traders are cheating and exploiting tribals in all possible schemes like-Housing, sericulture, horticulture, Livestocks, Sheep rearing. Forest Officials were always harassing the tribals for sake money that is corruption. Tribals are being living in fear of officials. Tribal School attendance is very low than plain school. girls are allocated to child care to release parents for agriculture. Education was seasonal and sporadic. Un-education and unemployment were the root cause of poverty.[4]

Tragedy of Tribals in Telangana

It had more plateau area, so that more tribals to end in Telangana region.

Gonds

In 1930-40 the Gonds, Adilabad District were dis-advantaged by the system of village officers, who kept accounts in Marathi and there was falsification of records and large scale wresting of land from the Gonds by Patwaris themselves. There was also alienation of Gonds lands by new settlers. The reservation of forests was the greatest single threat to the prosperity and well being of the Gonds. Lands held by Gonds on patta were brought under Reserve forests. The hostility between clash. The confrontation known as the Babhijheri incident was on too small a scale to be classified as a tribal rebellion. Eleven tribals died in this conflict. The traditional authority of the Gonds was lost to the Deshmukhs and the Karnams and later to the Panchayats. The second Gond rebellion was triggered off by the recognition of the forward tribe Lambadas as Scheduled Tribe in Telangana area.

Koyas

A similar process took place in a different context but similar circumstances among the Koyas of Eturunagaram Agency of warangal District and in the Bhadrachalam Agency of Khammam District. Ownership of land signifies livelihood, culture and identity in a tribal economy. The STs usually possess lands have also been going out of tribal possession on account of appropriation by exogenous forces. Poor land record systems in tribal areas coupled with illiteracy, poverty and ignorance of tribals and the greed of others have resulted in the continuous transfer of resources from tribals to non-tribals for several decades. Diminishing access to natural resources and dispossession has led to their exclusion and economic impoverishment after reducing them to the status of migrant labour, rickshow pullers and head loaders and socio-psychologically setting them adrift.

Value System of Koyas

Their greatest handicap has been and continues to be their value system, the paradigm of which is guilelessness, truth, honesty, loyalty and adherence to their word on commitments like the Raghuvamsi value. In Eturunagaram agency, much of tribal land was under the settlers hand. Forest Department is disputing the 50 years continuars cultivation by tribals. Even in Bhadrachalam Agency also the same story of occupying the tribal lands by plain land people. The tribals were pushed deep or vertical into the forests by non-tribals as we have seen from 1930 onwards upto a point where non-tribals could not reach. Even radical groups, (Naxalites) whom they host willingly or otherwise, say that they are not interested in specific problems of any tribals in any area as they would not like to be bagged down to local problems. They have a wider ideological agenda, which does not include the interests of the tribals in any particular local area. The tribals cynically feel that they are the protectors rather of the predators. Thus Matsya nayaya (Low of Fish), might is right, prevails in the scheduled areas of Telangana.

One is reminded of the position of the last Moghal Emperor, Bahadur Shah zafar after 1847, who lamented that he could not even get two yards of land for his burial in his own country, India and was buried in Burma, where he spent his last days.[5]

Chenchus in Nallamala in Rayalaseema

The fleet footed Chenchus are known to escape from wild animals they often encounter in the thick Nallamala forests, but when it cames to diseases they succumb meekly, thanks to Government apathy. Two deaths from suspected diarrhoea in a span of few hours sent shivers down the spines of the otherwise hardy Chenchus, the dwindling primitive tribal group, in tiny hill top gudem off the Srisailam - Dornala road. Going by the insurance claims with Integrated Tribal Development Agency, Srisailam, there were 178 deaths during the years 2005 and 2006, mostly from diseases, a high mortality rate, considering the declining population of about 30,000 Chenchus.[6]

Tribals Under Clutches of Naxals in Andhra–Orissa Border

It is like living under the shadow of the gun for the tribal youths in the interior hamlets and villages in the Andhra-Orissa border area. If the tribals do not follow the instructions of *annalu* (Naxals), they get maimed or killed, if they follow their instructions and supply them with food supplies and other needs, they come under the police scanner with all attendant suffering. Sandwitched between the Naxals and the crops, many tribals youth are leading a wretched life.

Many tribal youths in the borders of East Godavari and visakapatnam districts of Andhra Pradesh-Orissa borders (AOB) have been suffering a lot with pressures from the police and Naxals and ultimately forced to help Naxals. Many tribal hamlets are under developed due to the negligence of the Tribal welfare and ITDA officials. Some hamlets have no roads even. If drink water, electricity, education and medical facilities. The police can wean away tribals from joining *dalams*. Infact Naxals are spoiling the lives of the innocent tribals.[7]

Conclusions

Saga of the Tribals in India is a story of the struggle of the weak against the powerful, of the oil lamp and the storm. The Tenth plan had an objective of empowering the tribals is being achieved through strategy of socio empowerment and social justice. Economic development like major issigation projects, Hydel power projects, Major industries, forest based industries, on one side and other side, plain people bulldozing tribals rights and lands made the varied tribal lives into umpteen miseries. Of course, ignorance, poverty, unemployment, ill-health, uneducation among tribals were worst suffers in Indian Society. All government Schemes like ITDA were helped a little for their welfare. A strong political will is needed to overcome the perennial problems of Tribals even after sixty years of freedom.

Notes and References

1. Rohini Nile Kani (2007), Payments for Ecosystem Services, *The Hindu*, August 3, p. 11.
2. Planning Commission (2005). Mid-Term Appraisal of 10th Five Year Plan 2002-2007, p.162.
3. Government of India (2007), *Economic Survey 2006-2007*, p. 226.

4. S. Ramachandran (2005), Tribal Poverty in Tamilnadu: The Case of Kalrayan Hills, Monograph.
5. J. M. Girglani (2007), The Tragedy of Tribal in Telangana Feb.27, 5th Annual, Prof. B. Janardhana Rao Memorial Lecture, Warangal.
6. K. Venkateswarlu (2007), Chenchus in Nallamala Under Siege, *The Hindu*, August 9, p. 4.

21

HUMAN RIGHTS AND PUBLIC–PRIVATE HEALTH POLICY: NEED FOR PARADIGM SHIFT

It was once said that the moral test of Government is how that government treats those who are in the dawn of life, the children; those who are in the twilight of life, the elderly and those who are in the shadows of life, sick, the needy and the handicapped. (Hubert H. Hamphrey). Amartya Sen, Nobel prize winner, felt that development can be seen as a process of expanding the real freedoms that people enjoy.

I

The basic objective of development is to create an enabling environment in which people can enjoy, long, healthy and creative life. people are the real wealth of nations.[1] Upholding human rights and the dignity of all human beings and adoption of an intergenerational approach are important pre - requisites for improving public health and ensuring sustainable development. Government have the obligation to respect, protect and fulfil human rights. They have a responsibility for their people's health which could be fulfilled only through providing adequate health and social measures. Public health officials have dual responsibilities of protecting and promoting public health and respecting, protecting and fulfilling human rights. Application of the new synergy of public health and human rights requires additional efforts to create consultative mechanisms, as well as education, training and research in health and human rights.[2] Health and development in various parts of India have progressed unevenly. Healthcare expenditure is the second most common cause of rural indebtedness. Of course, nutrition is a cornerstone that influences and defines people's wealth. "Human Rights" means the rights relating to life, liberty, equality and dignity of the individual guaranteed by the constitutions or embodied in the International covenants and enforceable by courts in India.[3] Health and Human rights are interdependent and have to go for achieving health for all.

Macro–Health Variables

In the South East Asian Region (SEAR), 40 per cent of under-five children were underweight and out of this 43 per cent stunted, 30 per cent a low birth-weight, 23 per cent of the population had Iodine Deficiency Disorders. 1.3 million persons had clinical vitamin A deficiency, and two thirds of pregnant women had iron-deficiency anaemia. Among the priority areas for action are growth monitoring/promotion, nutrition surveillance, promotion/support of breast feeding, food security and safety net, and anaemia prevention and control strategy.

Health and Human Rights experts have a collective responsibility to conceptualise and carry forward these agenda for a better and healthier society.

The goal of extending the benefits of sustainable health over an expanding life span, to all members of the human family, is the cardinal tenet of public health. The declaration of Human Rights eloquently upholds the right to life as an inalienable entitlement of all human beings. Right to health, defined in the preamble of the World Health organization (WHO) Constitution projected a vision of the ideal state of Health as an eternal and universal goal. The Alma-Ata Declaration 1978 called all nations to ensure the availability of essential primary health care. For ensuring provision of health services, four essential features-availability, accessibility, acceptability and quality of services are highly needed.

Health Status in SAARC Countries

The health expenditure *per capita* is the sum of public and private expenditure divided by the population. Health expenditure includes the provision of health services - preventive, curative, family planning activities, nutrition and emergency aid designated for health. Private Health expenditure is direct household out of pocket spending. Public Health expenditure is current and capital spending from budgets. A brief on health expenditure is given below.

Table 1
Commitment to Health in SAARC Countries

	Health Expenditure			
Country	*Public 2003 (% of GDP)*	*Private 2003 (% of GDP)*	*Per capita (PPP, US$) 2003*	*Physicians 1990-2004 (Per 100,000 people)*
Bhutan	2.6	0.5	59	5
Bangladesh	1.1	2.3	68	26
India	1.2	3.6	82	60
Maldives	5.5	0.7	364	92
Nepal	1.5	3.8	64	21
Pakistan	0.7	1.7	48	74
Srilanka	1.6	1.9	121	55

Source: UNDP, Human Development Report 2006, p. 301.

The Table 1 gives a bird's eye view of concerned nation's expenditure on health. Maldives–an Island found as a top nation which spends 5.5 per cent of GDP from budget and very low from citizen's pocket. The *Per Capita* expenditure is very high as $ 364 and number of physicians are around 92 per one lakh. By all means, Pakistan spends very low government expenditure, but physicians are more around 74 for one lakh population. In India, state's contribution to health is very low, but private expenditure is treble times more, whereas physicians number is in better position of 60 per one lakh population.

Globalisation and Sharing Health and Human Rights

Dr. Brudtland had drawn attention to the new set of human rights issues arising from globalization. While globalization along with privatization could contribute to advancing health through sharing of information, technologies and resources, and providing higher quality services, it could, also, stimulate the spread of health hazards and diseases, and widen inequalities and inequities. The role of non-State actors-mainly NGOs and Multi-national Corporations (MNCs), whose accountability were poorly defined and inadequately monitored. The universal need for governments is ensure that actions taken by the private sector and other actors in civil society complied with human rights principles. The desirable forms and extent of responsibility for multinational actors within the international legal system were also yet to be defined from a health and human rights perspective. Health experts are to be collaborated with experts in human rights in conceptualizing these agendas and carrying this work forward. NGOs and civil society also had a very vital role to play in advancing the urgency to include the human rights dimension in all of health development work.

Given the current ethical standards and the free market technology-driven operational principles, the private sector had not provided quality health care at reasonable cost. This necessitated introduction of participatory regulatory norms. It is better to create an enabling climate for the growth of the voluntary sector, which was reaching out innovative and quality healthcare in remote areas of the country. The government has to take immediate assertive action to arrest the current situation i.e., continuous neglect of the health of the nation may cost the nation dearly.

As Prof. Amartya Sen, the Nobel Laureate, had remarked one cannot approach Public Health without keeping human rights in view. People active in Public Health and Human Rights had a Collective responsibility to move the agenda forward for a better and healthier society.

People Empowerment and health

It was people's empowerment that made all the differences in health outcomes. Such approach would take care of everything that we want to correct. The past experience had shown that better health record was not always relatable to the stage of economic development. Southern states could advance in health field because of the education of girl child.

With proper planning, we could avoid starvation deaths or minimize the ill-effects of a super cyclone. Thailand, when confronted with the HIV/AIDS epidemic, had developed and implemented a well-planned strategy with political commitment at the highest level, and was successfully over coming this challenge. National Human Rights Commission has to work as a catalyst to promote humane governance at all levels of society. Free legal and wealth aid are to be extended for below poverty line classes and make them empowered. "Family Doctor" concept is to be adopted in India also like England.

The Right to Health

As defined in the preamble of the WHO Constitution, health is a state of complete physical, mental, and social well being, and not merely the absence of disease or infirmity. The enjoyment of the highest attainable standard of health was one of the fundamental rights of every human being and that governments have a responsibility for the health of their people, which can be fulfilled only through the provision of adequate health and social measures.

Rights relating to autonomy, information, education, food and nutrition, association, equality, participation and non-discrimination are integral and indivisible parts of the achievement of the highest standard of health.

Rights and Responsibilities of Patient

The World Medical Association had in its Declaration on the Rights of the patient explored the recent significant changes in the relationship between physicians, their patients and broader society. While a physician should always act according to his/her Conscience, and always in the best interests of the patient, equal effort must be made to guarantee patient's autonomy and justice. The patient has a right to medical care of good quality without discrimination, freedom of choice of physician and hospital, self determination, information, confidentiality, and health education. The declaration referred to dignity and privacy and to religious assistance. It also covered care of the unconscious patient, the legally incompetent patient and diagnostic or therapeutic procedures against the patients will. Health plan, choice of health care, emergency services, relief of pain to accept or refuse treatment, treatment options non-discriminate care, privacy, medical record, fair review of complaint, second opinion on case, free from restraint, to raise ethical issues, access to visitors, information of research, care at the end of life are the basic rights. The responsibilities are to be on right time of appointment, help the hospital staff without violence, follow the directions of staff, finish the course of treatment, give feed back forms, use emergency services in a real emergency, provide all information correctly, observe procedures and accept financial responsibilities i.e. settle bills promptly.[4]

Health Insurance

This system for the advance financing of medical expenses through contribution or taxes paid into a common fund of Pay for all or Part of health services specified in an insurance policy or law. The key elements are advance payment of premiums or Taxes, Pooling funds, and eligibility for benefits on the basis of contributions or employment without an income or asset test. Health insurance may apply to a limited or comprehensive range of medical services and may provide for full or partial Payment of the costs of specific services. Benefits may consist of the right to certain medical services or reimbursement of the insured for specified medical costs. Private health insurance is organized and administered by an insurance company or other private agency; public health insurance is run by the government. Both forms of health insurance are to be distinguished from socialized medicine and government medical care programmes, in which doctors are employed directly or indirectly by the government, which also owns the health-care facilities. E.g., Britain's National Health Service.[5]

II

Neglected Health Sector in India

Health was considered as one of the leading sectors that colonial rule forward in Nineteenth Century in India.

Healthcare is important not only for reaping the demographic dividend, having a healthy productive workforce and general welfare, but also, for attaining the goal of population stabilization. Population stabilization is proposed to be achieved by addressing issues like child survival, safe motherhood and contraception. There has been some improvement in the quality of health care over the years, but wide inter-state, male-female and rural-Urban disparities in outcomes and impacts continue to persist. While population stabilization is in concurrent list, health is a state subject. The reproductive and child health services reach community and households levels through the primary Healthcare infrastructure. Empirical studies suggest that education, income and the overall quality of the State Administration are often more important than specific public health interventions in explaining the differences in demographic and health indicators. India's position on health parameters compared even to some of its neighbours continues to be unsatisfactory, which are given below.

The Table 2 proves that India compares poorly, not only, with China and Sri Lanka, but also, with Bangladesh and Nepal with respect to some indicators.[6]

Want of Charity Like More Bill Gates for Health and Welfare

India has made great progress in healthcare over the last 20 years mainly in the private sector. Though the public spending in health care in India is among the lowest in the world, India is in the top league for private spending, among the top 20

Table 2
Some Health Parameters: India and its Neighbours

Country	*Life expectancy at birth (years) 2000-05*	**MDG Under five mortality rate (Per 1000 live births 2004)*	**MDG Infant Mortality rate (Per 1000 live births 2004)*	**MDG Maternal Mortality ratio (Per 100,000 live births) 2004*
China	72	31	26	51
India	63	85	62	540
Nepal	61	76	59	740
Pakistan	63	101	80	530
Sri Lanka	74	14	12	92
Bangladesh	63	77	56	380
South Asia	64	84	62	N.A.

**MDG:* Millennium Development Goal, N.A: Not available.

Source: UNDP, Human Development Report, 2006, p. 315

countries in the world. This has encouraged Medical Tourism from wealthier countries including USA and UK. Unfortunately, high quality healthcare is unaffordable for the local population and the average person is not covered by private insurance and hence ordinary people have to sell their assets to get treatment if they develop life threatening ills. The concept of welfare state remains a dream for most developing countries. Probably the world needs more Bill Gates models of charity to save the developing Countries and the poorer section of the developed countries. Bill Gates has given big charity for prevention and curation of AIDS in the world.

The idea of 'Welfare State' means different things in different countries. In the ideal model the state accepts responsibility for the provision of comprehensive and universal welfare for its citizens. This includes: social services, social security, Health care and old age pension.

In Europe, Germany was the first country to start a social security under its first Chancellor Otto Bismarck in 1879. Inspired by the Social Changes in Germany, Loyd George, Prime Minister of Britain from 1916–1922 laid foundation of British Welfare State by starting health and unemployment insurance through National Insurance Act. But the architect of the post World Was II welfare state of Britain is William Beveridge. National Health Service is considered to be the jewel in the crown of British welfare State. In Britain, about 50 per cent of the national budget is spent on health, social security and local government services.

British healthcare system is based on the family doctor principle. Every citizen in UK has to be registered under a family doctor otherwise called as General Medical Practitioner. Average list size of general practitioner is 2000 patients in England. The general practitioner in average, sees about 30 patients per day. Average waiting time to see a specialist is 2-3 months with the exception of suspected cancer, heart disease and urgent cases. In the USA healthcare is funded by private insurance which is usually done by employers. Recently, President George Bush, USA declared that the poorest Americans are getting for better health services than Canadians or the British; can wave away the desperation of un-insured Americans, who are often poor and voiceless. A cross national survey conducted by the Common wealth Fund that America ranks near the bottom among advanced countries in terms of how hard it is to get medical attention on short notice, and that America is the worst place in the advanced world if you need care after hours or on a weekend.[7]

Lifelong learning and annual appraisal is a requirement now and five yearly revalidation is going to be mandatory for all practicing doctors.[8]

Chennai based Star Health and Allied Insurance, the first standalone health insurance in the country, plans to roll out an exclusive policy for HIV-affected people. The annual premium will be Rs. 3,000 and the insurance cover against treatment will be Rs. 50,000. For above 55 years, star has introduced two policies-senior citizens red carpet and diabetes safe insurance policy.[9] The Health Insurance Venture of Apollo hospital with DKV of Germany will take of on August 8, 2007.[10]

Indian Railways also introduced Helpline Express-a hospital train, which will provide medical services to the poor in remote rural areas.[11]

Institutionalize Public-Private Partnerships in Healthcare

Since government resources have been unable to maintain existing health systems, increase access to health services for those not covered by current systems and improve the quality of care provided government is no longer viewed as the necessary "engine of development", or the main provider and financier of health services. The co-existence of the public and private sectors in the health sector is not new. This interdependence is centuries old. Since 68 per cent hospitals, 37 per cent of hospital beds and over 80 per cent of the provisioning of healthcare is attributed to the private sector, the private sector is beginning to occupy centre-stage. The private sector is increasingly, also a significance source of new investment (Particularly across tertiary healthcare, pharmaceuticals and R&D). The private sector has gained a dominant presence in medical education and training, diagnostics and technology, Pharmaceutical manufacture and sale, hospital design, construction and management of ancillary services. The objective of government is to direct more resources at primary Health levels, where private sector is not available.[12]

Public and Private Health Mix

Most Industrial Countries started with private health systems. In low and middle income countries out of pocket spending represents a large share of health spending even in countries with well functioning public system. Worldwide, richer groups generally resort more to the private sector, but the situation differs by country. Richer groups also use public facilities more–which indicates that subsidies are not well targeted. The public–private mix varies by type of service. The private sector is involved in many critical services, including disease control and child and reproductive health. But immunization, family planning, and skilled delivery care are more often provided by the public sector. Even in India, poor people, who turn mainly to private providers to treat illness, rely on the public sector for vaccination (93 per cent) and antenatal care (74 per cent). The boundaries between public and private services have blurred. Many governments subsidize privately provided services-all high income countries do and so, increasingly, do middle and low income countries, as in the Thai land social security scheme.[13]

Expenditure on Medical Services

In India every state's total expenditure is an indicator of its spending capacity on peoples welfare. Probably, it is found that more the expenditure on peoples welfare programmes, more the benefit to them. Of course, the expenditure on public health differs from state to state, depends upon it allotment and priority. Earmarking of funds is first step, but reaching the right patient, without corruption is an uphill task for state. The following table gives a comprehensive view over it.

The Table 3 proves that Maharastra, U.P, A.P, Tamilnadu, West Bengal, Karnataka are the top ranking states allotted big budgets of health expenditure. Simultaneously they spent on Medical and public health are 3.89 per cent, 3.49 per cent, 3.65 per cent, 4.12 per cent, 4.53 per cent, 3.42 per cent, respectively. In fact, Delhi, capital of India, was spent 11.5 per cent its budget as a topmost one.

The least ranking in seven sisters budget States like Arunachal Pradesh, Manipur, Megalaya, Mizoram, Nagaland, Sikkim, Tripura spent from its budgets as 5.71per cent, 3.92 per cent, 5.10 per cent, 4.69 per cent, 3.70 per cent, 2.81 per cent and 3.91 per cent, respectively. Neither leading States nor least developing States spent more than 6 per cent of its expenditure budget on Health. In fact, poverty represents social institution which affects all aspects of life including health, illness related behaviour. It is a major causative factor in disease developing countries.[14] With out removing poverty, sound health may not touch the door of house hold.

The National Accreditation Board for Hospitals and Healthcare Providers (NABH)

NABH will soon start certifying small health care delivery Centres such as nursing homes, blood Banks, diagnostic centres (for radiology) and the dental clinics based on their quality of

Table 3
Expenditure on Medical Services, 2004-05 (Budget Estimates)

(Rs. in Crores)

State	*Total Expenditure*	*Medical, public Health, Family welfare water supply and sanitation*	*% of Total Expenditure*
Andhra Pradesh	34,151.54	1245.31	3.65
Arunachal Pradesh	1,165.06	66.58	5.71
Assam	14,982.89	463.62	3.09
Bihar	16,341.49	545.58	3.34
Chattisgarh	7,605,73	272.56	3.58
Goa	2,635.06	107.99	4.10
Gujarat	23,786.33	774.56	3.26
Haryana	11,684.02	354.17	2.95
Himachal Pradesh	5,791.07	260.28	4.49
Jammu & Kashmir	7,967.63	439.18	5.51
Jharkhand	7,844.24	266.53	3.40
Karnataka	25,437.48	870.65	3.42
Kerala	18,971.09	895.16	4.72
Madhya Pradesh	18,261.16	779.99	4.27
Maharastra	47,904.39	1670.88	3.49
Manipur	1686.83	66.04	3.92
Meghalaya	1617.13	82.42	5.10
Mizoram	1183.74	55.51	4.69
Nagaland	1753.31	64.82	3.70
Orissa	14,083.91	528.81	3.75
Punjab	19,120.90	704.77	3.69
Rajasthan	19,588.25	939.59	4.80
Sikkim .	1754.87	49.31	2.81
Tamilnadu	28,128.73	1160.03	4.12
Tripura	2215.70	86.66	3.91
Uttaranchal	5863.58	227.75	3.88
Uttar Pradesh	42,785.71	1663.22	3.89
West Bengal	27,798.44	1259.60	4.53
National capital Territory of Delhi	5,952.34	686.79	11.54
All India	4,18,062.62	16,579.36	3.97

Source: State Finances, 2004-05, Reserve Bank of India, Mumbai.

medical facilities and professional competence. Quality Council of India (QCI) and NABH are putting standards from August 2007. They are planning a nationwide Campaign through media and conferences to appraise consumers and the medical fraternity about the need for such accreditation. NABH will check the medical parameters such as clinical competence, credibility of practitioners, and equipment provided at the centre. NABH is a member of the International Society for Quality in Healthcare. Standards are considered the highest in the World. Insurance Regulatory Development Authority (IRDA) is already mulling medical reimbursement for treatment in hospitals to be allowed only from NABH-accreditated hospitals. So far, seven hospitals, mostly corporate owned, have got NABH certification, while another 6-7 hospitals are expected to get the accreditations in the next two months.[15]

The European Commission has alleged that nearly 30 per cent of the fake drugs coming into the EU are from India. This insinuation could severely impact the India pharmaceutical industry's exports and contract manufacturing ambitions.[16] State and industry should take it seriously and challengingly for not getting such an allegation in future development.

Conclusions

The basic objective of development is to enjoy long, healthy and creative life. Health and development in various states in India have progressed unevenly. NGOs and civil society had a very vital to play in advancing the urgency of human rights dimension in Health development. Healthcare position in India, Considering all parameter, it is in quite un-satisfactory even among neighboring SAARC Countries. The private sector is emerging very stronger in India than Public Health. Private health insurance cover is spreading out fastly to secure health of aged and sick. Rural health needs more support from State, NGOs and private players. Still Indian drug industry is facing a block mark of 30 per cent fake which is to be over come to by political will. Human touch is the need of the hour for every health provider.

Notes and References

1. Mahbub Haq (1990), Human Development Report 1990.
2. NHRC (2001), Regional Consultation and Public Health and Human Rights, Report and Recommendations April-10-11, 2001, p. 3.
3. Gopalan (1998), India and Huma Rights, Lok Sabha Secretariat, p. 26.
4. PRO, (2007), Brochure of Apollo Hospitals, Hyderabad.
5. Britannica (2005), Britannica Ready Reference Encyclopedia, New Delhi Vol. 4, p. 276, II
6. Government of India (2006-07), Economic Survey, pp. 215-216.
7. Paul Krugman's column (2007), The Waiting Game, *The Hindu* July 17th, p. 9.
8. M. A.Varghese (2007), Economics and Health, Manorama Year Book 2007, pp. 560-562.
9. Bureau (2007), Star Health to Offer Cover for HIV Patients, *The Economic Times*, July 6, p. 12.
10. Staff Correspondent (2007), Apollo's Health Insurance by Aug. 8, *The Hindu*, July 20, p. 19.
11. Correspondent (2007), Sonia Gandhi Inaugurates Hospital Train, The Hindu, July 13, p. 12.
12. Govt of India (2005), Mid-Term Appraisal of 10th Five Year plan (2002-2007), pp. 114-117.
13. The World Bank (2004), World Development Report 2004, pp. 136-138.
14. A. Ranga Reddy (1995), Healthcare System for Under Privilezed Moving from the State to Corporate Culture, (ed.) by A. Ranga Reddy on Healthcare Services Management, Delta Publishing House, Hyderabad.
15. Khomba Singh (2007), Hospitals to be Subject to Minimum Quality Standards Now, *The Economic Times*, July 24, p. 6
16. Editorial (2007), Crack Down on Fake Drugs, To Protect India's Pharma Ambitions. *The Economic Times*,, July 20, 2007.

Appendix

Relevant Laws of Human Rights

1. Indian Slavery Act 1843.
2. Universal Declaration of Human Rights, Dec.10, 1948, U.N.O.
3. Protection of Civil Rights Act 1955.
4. International Covenant on Civil and Political Rights, 1966.
5. International Covenant on Economic, Social and Cultural Rights 1966.
6. Bonded Labour system (Abolition) Act 1976.
7. Convention on Elimination of all Forms of Discrimination Against women 1979 (CEDAW).
8. Child Labour Prohibition & Regulation's Act 1986.
9. Scheduled Castes and Scheduled Tribes (Prevention of Atrocities) Act 1989.
10. National Commission for Women Act, 1990.
11. National Commission for SCs & STc Act, 1990.
12. National Commission for Miorities Act, 1992.
13. Vienna Declaration and Programme of Action, June 25, 1993.
14. Protection of Human Rights Act, 1993.
15. Fourth World Conference on Women, Beijing, Sept. 1995.

Relevant Laws of Healthcare in India

1. The Drug and Magic Remedies (Objectionable Ads) Act, 1954.
2. The Prevention of Food Adulteration Act, 1954.
3. The Spirituous preparation (Inter-State Trade & Commerce) Control Act, 1955.
4. The Indian Red Cross Society (Amendment) Act, 1956.
5. The Indian Medical Council Act, 1956.
6. The Medical Termination of pregnancy Act, 1971.
7. The Drugs and Cosmetics (Amendment) Act, 1972.
8. The Maternity Benefit Act, 1961.
9. The Ear Drums ad Ear Bones (Authority for use for Therapeutic purposes) Act, 1982.

10. The Eyes (Authority for use of Therapeutic purposes) Act, 1982.
11. The Mental Health Act, 1987.
12. The Transplantation of Human organs Act, 1994.
13. The Pre-Natal Diagnostic Techniques (Regulation and prevention of Misuses) Act, 1994.
14. The persons with Disabilities (Equal opportunities, protection of Rights and full participation) Act, 1995.

22

CHINA: TOWARDS MARXIAN DEMOCRATIC MODEL

The Community Party of China (CPC) has decided to build a "harmonious Society of Socialism and uphold Marxism as the guiding ideology[1].

Stages of Reforms Implementation

Reforms first introduced in agriculture (1978-93) foreign trade and investment sectors (that too in limited Coastal regions) and later extended to industry. The initial reforms in agriculture brought prosperity to a vast number of poor people, created conditions for the subsequent phenomenal growth in rural industries and built up a big political support base for more reforms.

The Chinese relied more on introducing competition. The rapid growth of new enterprises mostly Township and Village Enterprises (TVEs) and some private firms) created competitive pressure on the State Owned Enterprises (SOEs). The monopoly of the Central State Trading Corporation was replaced by a large number of regional trading Corporations competing with one another[2]

The Chinese leaders realised the dangers of nationwide experiments suited to local conditions, gradual reforms, pragmatism instead of dogmas and the importance of the rule of law. China followed dual pricing. In the transition from plan to market, farmers and industrial units were required to buy and sell fixed quantities of inputs and outputs through the planning mechanism at Government controlled prices. The remaining part could be bought and sold at market prices. There were few incentives for farmers and SOEs to improve productivity and profits as these would be expropriated by the government.

Perhaps the most significant difference between the Chinese reforms and those in Russia and east Europe in the 1990s is that China did not destroy old institutions without building new ones. In the period after the catastrophe of the *Great Leap Forward* China's leadership remained divided about economic strategy. Although self-reliance was a shared aim, one group, that included Zhou Enlai and Deng Xioapang, sought to restore what was in effect, an import substituting strategy that had brought important gains during the 1950s. (Gautam sen (2000), Post Reform China and the International Economy, *Economic and Political Weekly,* March 11, p. 929.

Maintaining macro-economic stability (low inflation, exchange rate stability and avoiding financial crisis) through 'financial dualism'. This involved a combination of controls on international capital flows, keeping the deposit interest rate low for state owned banks and increasing money supply at a fast rate.

In the *second stage* of reforms (1994 onwards), China has made significant progress towards building a rule-based marked system and Western style institutions and practices but again with distinct Chinese characteristics. In certain respects, China has reversed some of the initial policies. China has downsized government bureaucracy, introduced tax reforms with internationally accepted practices, made State owned banks more commercially-oriented, introduced prudential regulations on the financial system, started privatisation and restructuring of SOEs resulting in big layoffs. Unfixed the exchange rate and introduced current account convertibility, incorporating private property rights and the rule of law explicitly in the Chinese constitution (which is indicative of a big ideological shift for the ruling communist party).

China's increasing inequality is largely caused by the rising urban-rural gap and inter-regional disparities. Government policies have contributed to this as 'Social policies favour urban over rural areas and economic policies favour the coast over the interior. State owned enterprises suffer from a few basic problems in all Countries, such as soft budget constraint, multiple objectives, multiple control authorities and absence of incentives for managers and workers to improve performance. China is no exception.

The Chinese pension system is entirely by the current contribution of employers and employees. The seriousness of the crisis can be from the fact that at the outset of reforms there were 30 workers contributing to the pension system for each retiree but by 1995 were fewer than 5.

Fast Foreign Direct Investment Flow

China's share in the total World trade went up from 1 per cent to about 4 per cent and is projected to go up to 10 per cent by 2020 to make China the second largest trading nation in the World. Foreign Direct Investment (FDI) flow into China jumped from near zero in 1978 to more than 355 billion yen in 2003 and China became the second largest recipient of FDI after the US. The 21st Century is widely projected to be China's Century just as the 20th Century was Japan's.

The export boom of China was facilitated by the re-location of intensive steps of production from Hong Kong and Taiwan to the Adjacent Special Economic Zones (SEZs) in the Chinese Coastal Provinces. Labour Unions, though officially allowed in China, mostly played a cooperative role with the management, instead of the collective bargaining role practiced in non-communist countries. Managers were given the right to hire and fire workers in the export-oriented factories in the SEZs.

The saving rate in China was quite high 35 per cent of GDP in 1979 whereas in 1994 it was 44 per cent of GDP.

It is earlier to transform a small country (like Singapore or Vietnam) than a very big, over populated country like China. FDI flows in 1999 have been $ 38.8 billion against the peak level of $ 44.2 billion in 1997.

Chinese reform strategy-its contents, timing, sequencing and implementation-which was un-conventional in many respects. the reforms initiatives were bottom-up (Crossing river by touching stones-Deng's Celebrated phase).

Most of the FDI inflows to India came from the original neighborhood (US, UK and Germany). Interestingly, Mauritius is the second largest source of FDI inflows to India in recent times. It is interesting to note that unlike China, the fuel and power sector dominates (about 28 per cent of total investment) in India. The Telecommunications sectors too contributes about 19 per cent of that total investment during the period 1991-2000. India has excelled in the area of Computer software and has evolved as an information technology hub for the world market.

It is now open as to why some economies have attracted large FDI flows and grown fast (for example, east Asia and now China), over the last 40 years and others have not. The Latin American and Caribbean economies are geographically closer to the highly developed economies. Yet, these regions could not take advantage of this physical proximity. Their economies could not become part of the original, intermediate or even extension of the intermediate neighborhoods. Perhaps due to the fact that most people came from cultures where neighborhood was too weak.

Expansion of Exports

Mao Zedong and Lin Biao were intended upon Semi-autarchy with only very limited engagement with the capitalist world economy. Both groups considered the latter hostile and a dangerous adversary, but important differences of opinion obviously existed.

The goal of export promotion was formally adopted in August 1979, by assigning top priority to fulfilling export contract obligation. As far as foreign investment was concerned, investment by overseas Chinese had been regarded by China's communists as some how genuine, indeed, local in terms of national loyalties. The success of China's export efforts is evident in the rise of its trade GDP ratio. According to one estimate, China's trade/GDP ratio rose from 10 per cent in 1975-79 to 36 per cent in 1990-94. In current US dollars the value of exports had risen from approximately $ 16 billion in 1978 to $ 138.4 billion in 1995. Export volumes, which had doubled between 1970-78, rose more than eight fold between 1978 and 1997.

China's low wage work force has provided the basis for Chinese over seas firms to persist in productive activities in which their own home country had lost comparative advantage. Labour intensive processes and production have generally moved to China while more capital intensive and knowledge intensive parts of the production process are located elsewhere in the more advanced economies of the region-mainly Hong Kong and some parts of South East Asia[3].

Basically, overseas Chinese foreign investors are largely in the export sector of China's economy. Hong Kong itself exports 200 per cent of its GDP, most of which originates in China[4].

Much of the activity of Chinese overseas investors has been concentrating regionally. Twelve coastal provinces and municipalities have absorbed 90 per cent of foreign direct investment. The principal recipients of inward flows are Guandong, Shanghai, Fujian and Jiangsu. The investment was mainly in export activities and real estate and gradually diversified from light industries to electronics, telecommunications and transport.

The noteworthy feature of Overseas Chinese foreign investment in China is the shift from labour-intensive to capital intensive sectors in the 1990s. The Chinese Overseas Community engaged in a profitable economic relationship in China, but one that is also moulded by unique cultural and political factors specific to their relationship with China.

Entry into World Trade Organization

China may no longer have the luxury of taking a cautious approach to reform. For instance, with China, set to open up its banking sector to foreign banks by 2007 under *World Trade*

Organization (W.T.O) accession commitments, foreign competition for domestic banks will soon be an inescapable reality[5].

Academic research has still not identified which institutions are the key ones for fostering growth. But there is an emerging consensus that a sound legal framework, strong financial sector supervision, good corporate governance, and low levels of corruption are conducive to growth. Having good institutions will help foster the expansion of the private sector, which has accounted for much of China's recent dynamism and the strengthening of the remaining state sector enterprises.

In China, like the Soviet Union, policies was supposedly all and the economic entirely subordinate to the political. With markets, the central ideology, communism decays and cannot provide the glue to hold Society together. Everywhere it has been replaced by nationalism, Xenophobia-hence Yeltsins's Russian nationalism defeated Gorbachev's Soviet internationalism, Milosevic's serb nationalism replaced Yugoslow internationalism it is no different in China. As the communist party decays, the cadres use their political position to support their efforts to make money through managing the (SOEs), starting new local authority business (TVEs) or private enterprise[6].

As the beginning of the 1990s, there were just over 1,00,000 private operations (those employing eight or more workers), employing 1.8 million workers; they now employ 24 million, with possibly 30 million more in units employing less than eight workers. Many of the party cadres are involved in private business, either directly or by using their political position to support private business.

Decline of Poverty Level

The headcount indices of 16 per cent and 35 per cent for China and India respectively for a common poverty line of approximately $ 1 per day at purchasing power parity (World Bank Development Indicators, 2003). Chinese economic performance since 1978 is a bigger miracle than the earlier east Asian miracle. In China, a massive systematic changes were being brought about in the World's most populated economy while at the same time maintaining a near double-digit growth rate, a huge build up of foreign exchange reserves, a sharp decline in Poverty and a wide participation of different sections of society in the benefits of economic growth, in most of the years over more than two decades. 80 million people are poverty stricken, largely distributed in the 592 poverty stricken counties, which are getting support from the State[7].

From the beginning, Deng made it clear that they would not follow any particular country's development model nor Would they move away from the single party political system maintaining tight control over society. Average life expectancy improved from only 32 in 1950 to 69 years in 1982, which was Maoist era.

By the international poverty line ($ 1 day, using 1985 Purchasing power parity), the percentage of rural poor declined from 60 per cent in 1978 to 11.5 per cent in 1999. Rural per capita real income more than quadrupled while urban per capital real income trebled over the period 1978-'97. The share of agricultural labour in total employment went down from over 70 per cent in 1978 to around 50 per cent in 1996. It took the US 50 years and Japan 60 years to achieve a similar structural transformation (Alok Ray, (2002), Op.cited p.3836). Unemployment reached 8 per cent of labour force by the mid 1990s. However, the official Chinese data give the unemployment including furloughs as 7.9 per cent of the labour force for 1998, as against 6.5 per cent in 1997 and 5.6 per cent in 1996. Clearly the urban unemployment rate has been steadily climbing in recent years.

Dense Corruption

Reforms turn out to make the problems even worse unless government is willing to move on to a full democratic system (with a multiplicity of competing parties). Implicit in all this is the most dramatic symptom of decay, the pervasive corruption, and the deep cynicism of the population about the integrity of its leaders. This is to leave aside spectacular scale of corruption-the giant quasi private Business Corporations of PLA, financing the largest part of the military budget outside the control of the Central government. There has always been a surprising amount of corruption in China-it does with the discretionary powers allowed at the local level. Mao's Socialist Education Movement in the early 1960s revealed some of the spectacular abuses around then. But the market economy along with the close relationship between the party, local government and public or private business has opened up an immense area for new money making. A series recent cases have shown a level of gangster-party rule in major cities-Shenyang, Xiamen, Xingtai - which may extend much further than the cases already cited. Hundreds of officials have been arrested. And despite efforts to protect the party's top leadership, this cannot always be done-a politburo member has been sentence to 16 years goal, two executed for corruption; a Vice minister is awaiting trial for accepting bribes from smugglers. Reform, privatisation and strong protectionist local government are a recipe for un-avoidable and dense corruption[8].

Environment Degradation

China's air and water pollution, especially in the cities, is considered one of the worst in the World. Air pollution alone is estimated to cause around 3,00,000 deaths annually in China. The economic cost of Air and water pollution in China has been variously estimated to lie at 3-8 per cent of GDP.

China's Investment in India

Trade links are strengthening, investment links are non-existent. Chinese firms are still finding tough to do business in India, adding for good measure that the Chinese companies have not got a very good arrangement in India. The NIIT already runs 112 Computer Training Centres in China. Aurobindo Pharma, Ranbaxy, Dr.Reddy's and Orchid Chemicals, Sundaram Fasteners were entered into China. Earlier India initiated the largest number of 153 anti-dumping cases against Chinese exports upto March 2003. Still India considers China as Non-Market Economies (NME). India will also need to modify its anti-dumping legislation in keeping with the global trends, international economic realities and need for intensifying the future potential of India-China Economic Cooperation[9].

Single Party Rule

Chinese leadership, by maintaining the single party communist rule and reform from within, had no need to pay attention to this political argument for rapid privatisation. Rather Political Considerations in China dictated a slower approach. All these imply that the Chinese strategy of SOE reforms at a slower pace, without changing the political institutions, has turned out to be a better strategy.

It is likely to go down as China's dependency ratio rises in future as children of the one child policy increasingly dominate the work force, the retirement population swells, and the one-child policy is relaxed under a more liberal political regime. The phase of shifting labour from low productivity agriculture to higher productivity manufacturing is nearly over in China.

Deng Xiaoping-A Visionary

Deng (Aug. 22, 1904-Feb. 19, 1997) introduced economic reforms in China much earlier in the late seventies. He is the first leader who visualised the impact of a stagnant economy. He argued vociferously that privatisation can be reconciled with socialism. Deng's popularity, power and prestige began decline within the Communist Policy of China (CPC) and Chinese Society after the Tiananmen episode (1989). He convinced that as long as the largest section of peasantry is well fed and well off, the CPC will remain in power. In India, all political parties against to this philosophy. Deng was convinced that the main conflict in Socialist China lay not between capital and labour but between backward productive forces and the advance industrial system. He allowed economic liberalism but restricted political choice. The ultimate goal of Communism is to develop the productive forces for which economic development is essentially developed.

Inspite of the so-called revival of Maoist fever and the anti-corruption speeches made by Deng, China had *"five million millionaires"* by the end of May 1993. In 1993, there were two million stockholders in China and each week the number grows by 50,000.[10]

Conclusion

China introduced reforms first in agriculture, where much of population is associated, then market based reforms. After USA, next nation is China in inviting FDI flow in the World. China's low wage work force has provided the basis for Chinese overseas firms. Entry into W.T.O. has taken as a challenge and choice. By taking series of anti-poverty measures, it reduced poverty to 11.5 per cent level. Corruption is very dense more millionaires are entered into the economy. Environmental degradation on Air and water are found deeper and wider. Unfortunately, India still observed China as a non-market economy.

Notes and References

1. P. S. Suryanarayana (2004), Chinese Party to Promote Socialist Market Economy, *The Hindu*, Sept. 9.
2. Alok Roy (2002), The Chinese Economic Miracle: Lessons to be Learnt, *Economic and Political Weekly,* Sept. 14th, p. 3839.
3. Gautam Sen (2000), Post Reform China and the International Economy, *Economic and Political Weekly,* March 11, p. 932.
4. Arindam Banik, Pradip, K. Bhaumik, Sunday O Iyare (2004). Explaining FDI Inflows to India, China and the Caribbean: An Extended Neighborhood Approach, *Economic and Political Weekly,* July 24, p. 3400.
5. Eswar S. Prasad (2004), Growth and Stability in China, *Economic and Political Weekly,* May 15, p. 2011.
6. Nigel Harris (2001), China: The Old Order Changes, *Economic and Political Weekly,* Oct. 13, p. 3897.
7. S. P. Gupta (1996), Chinese Economic Reforms, Allied New Delhi, p. 11.

8. Nigel Harris (2001), China: The Old Order Changes, *Economic and Political Weekly,* October 13, p. 3900, Aug. 22, 1904, Feb. 19, 1997.

9. Ravinder Goel, (2004), MFN Status for China on Cards, *Sahara Time,* Oct. 2.

10. Ravindra Sharma (2004), Deng Xiaoping: Reformer, Innovator, Visionary, Mainstream, Oct. 2, p. 21.

23

INCULCATE HUMAN RIGHTS AMONG LAW ENFORCING AGENCIES AND THE LOWEST STRATA

Human rights are the rights which are possessed by all human beings irrespective of their race, caste, nationality, sex, language, etc., simply because they are human beings. As pointed by FAWCETT, 'Human rights are sometimes called fundamental rights or basic rights or natural rights. A fundamental rights are those which must not be taken away by any legislature or any act of government and which are often set out in a constitution. LAUTERPACHT said that human rights are not created by any legislature, they resemble very much the natural rights. Any civilised country or body like the United Nations must recognise them. They can't be subjected to the process of amendment even[1]. The legal duty to protect human rights includes the legal duty to respect them. Laski, Hobbe's, Kant's views also offered significant insights into the understanding the implications of principles of justice, liberty, rights.

All human beings are born free and equal in dignity and rights, they are endowed with reason and conscience and should act to one another in spirit of brotherhood. It is noted that terrorism and its linkages in some countries to drug trafficking are aimed at the destruction of human rights, democracy, territorial integrity, security of states and de-stabilising of legitimately constituted governments. Ved Marwah, a former Commissioner of Police observes that brutalisation of the police occurs in response to rising crime graph including armed insurgency, terrorism and arson, etc., and the consequent hue and cry about police inefficiency. Human rights education has to be an input to consolidate democracy, which not mere form of Government, it is a set of values and a way of life.[2]

National Commission for Human Rights has rendered a signal service for the cause of protection, promotion and observance of human rights, especially in the field of civil liberties. For example, its work in the field of prevention of custodial death, rape and torture has been praiseworthy.

Time is riped to spread the tentacles of National Commission for Human Rights (NCHRs) as a apex organ at New Delhi should open its branches in State, District, Taluqs/ Mandals and Villages to bring awareness and practising rights day in day out. Human Rights violation were visible not only in metropolitan cities but also in village economies. Like mafias in urban areas, semi-feudal farmers have been crushing the minimum rights of Dalits, tribals, small farmers, tenants and farm labourers.

First and foremost, state apparatus especially police, is the biggest organisation, which is to be associated strongly in this venture. Generally, it is known that courts are accessible only to rich and influential class. Low cost, instant justice courts like family courts are to be established to monitor family issues at rural and urban areas.

The marginalised and dis-advantaged groups continued to be exploited and denied human rights like Daliths, Tribals, bonded labourers, economically poor.

Supreme Court and Public Interest Litigation

The Emergency (1975-77) period witnessed colonial nature of Indian legal system. During emergency, state regression and governmental lawlessness was widespread. Thousands of innocent people, including political opponents, were sent to jails and there was complete deprivation of civil and political rights. In post-emergency period political situation was changed, investigative journalism was began to expose gory scenes of governmental lawlessness, custodial violence. Public Interest Litigation (PIL)[3] emerged as a result of an informal nexus of pro-active judges, media persons and social activists. The first reported case of PIL in 1979 on the inhuman conditions of prisons and 40,000 under-trail prisoners in Bihar jails. It exposed failure of criminal justice. It generated a debate for prison reforms. In 1981, a news report revealed that about 33 suspected criminals were blinded by police in Bihar through pulling acid into their eyes and then their eyes were burnt. In response to a PIL, Supreme Court deputed its Registrar to visit Bhagalpur jail and investigate the truth. The Supreme Court condemned the police for their cruel act and directed the state government to bring the blinded men to Delhi for medical treatment. It also ordered speedy prosecution of guilty policemen. The Court found right to free legal aid as a fundamental right of every accused.

In a landmark judgement, the Supreme Court ruled that every injured person has a fundamental right to get immediate medical treatment and that a hospital cannot refuse to treat a medico-legal case. Five women prisoners in Bombay city jail were subjected to a custodial violence. The Supreme Court issued guidelines for it and also it should be applicable to whole of Maharastra requiring that only police women be used to guard or interrogate women suspects or prisoners.

A telegram was sent by an association of Delhi judicial officers to the Supreme Court alleging assault, hand-cuffing and brutal torture of the Chief Judicial Magistrate, Nadiad, Gujarat in the streets by certain police officers. Supreme Court condemned the police brutalities in the strongest terms and ordered their punishment in the exercise of its contempt power. A civil liberties group drew Supreme Court's attention to police attrocities committed against poor people, who were forcibly taken to a police station in Delhi to work there without wages. One person died in police beating. The Court awarded

Rs. 50,000 as an interim compensation to the next of kin of the deceased and ordered recovery of the amount from delinquent policemen. Compensation jurisprudence for custodial violence is one of the positive achievements of PIL but compensation awards seem to be arbitrary and look more like a charity. There is little evidence that guilty policemen have actually been punished. Even in those cases, where prosecution has been launched, the cases remain pending for years in absence of judicial monitoring of the proceedings.

Terrorism and Insurgency

In terroristic period of 1980s in Punjab many advocates were abducted and killed. The inquiry revealed the truth in the allegations. Referring to mass cremation of persons labelled as un-identified by the Punjab police, the court remarked: "Our faith in Democracy and Rule of law assures us that nothing of this type can happen in this country but the allegations in the press note are horrendous as they need thorough investigation. On December 13, 1996, the Court placed on record to report of CBI which confirmed that over 585 bodies of persons, who were subsequently been identified, had in fact been cremated after being labelled as unidentified. The Court held that families of those identified were entitled to receive compensation to be determined by NHRC.

The human rights problem in Jammu and Kashmir has always remained problematic. The situation of terrorism and armed militancy is more acute in this area than any other part of the country. Unfortunately, the violation of human rights in Jammu and Kashmir have not been litigated before the Courts.

There are few cases of army excesses. In one case, about 81 tribals lost their lives on account of Army Test Fire Range in a place in Madhya Pradesh. A PIL resulted in closure of the Test Range. The Assam Disturbed Areas Act, 1995 and the Armed Forces (Special Powers) Act, 1958 confer wide ranging powers to the Army, preventing judicial intervention in army excesses. Even the NHRC has no powers to hear the complaints against armed forces.

Violence Against Women

Women's issues have increasingly been brought before the Supreme Court with the growth of women's movement and investigative journalism and discrimination. It is widely perceived that investigation into crimes against women have been unsatisfactory and in some cases even the judges have shown gender bias. It is worthwhile to mention a case to show the deficiencies of the criminal justice system in handling sexual harassment at work place and rape cases.

One Guntaben was gangraped by policemen of Gujarat. She was stripped naked by policemen before a crowd and subsequently raped by several policemen in the cabin of a truck. The incident occurred in 1986. The investigation ordered by the Supreme Court took evidence of 504 persons. Even then CBI took many years to complete the investigation. The case was heard several times between 1986 and 1993 and two commissions were appointed. pending completion of enquiries by the State Government, Supreme Court awarded Rs. 50,000/- as compensation to Guntaben by its order in 1993. A news report revealed rape of 25 tribal women in certain areas of Western Tripure by Army personnel of Assam Rifles. In response to a PIL, the inquiry report confirmed rape of some of these women. The Assam Rifles and the State Government did their best to hush up the crimes. The case remained pending for long time.

Bonded Labour

The bonded labour system continues to be the most perinicious form of human bondage. Under this system, a worker continues to serve his master in consideration of debt obtained by him or his ancestors. Bondage can be inter-generational or child bondage or loyalty bondage or bondage through land allotment. According to an early study, there were 26,17,000 bonded labourers only in ten states. Most of these labourers came from lowest strata of the society, such as the untouchables, adivasis or agricultural labourers. It occurred to Indian Government only in 1976 to pass a central legislation, i.e., Bonded labour system (Abolition) Act, 1976. In these cases, there is no effort to punish the owners of these labourers. The government must ensure them a reasonable wage and better living conditions.

Child Labour

The child labour began in early 1980s in response to a large number of news reports exposing exploitation of children in factories manufacturing fire-works and matches at Sivakasi in Tamilnadu and carpet industries in Mirzapur, Uttar Pradesh. The investigative journalism coupled with PIL cases led to passing of child labour (Prohibition and Regulation) Act, 1986. This Act prohibits employment of children in the hazardous industries. Finally the Supreme Court advocated a scheme of compulsory Insurance for both adult and children employed in hazardous industries. Every employee had to be insured for a sum of Rs.50,000. In its final judgement Supreme Court delivered 1996, directed the offending employer of child labour in match factories will pay Rs. 20,000, which would then be deposited in a Child-Labour-Rehabilitation-cum Welfare Fund. The children illegally employed would receive education at the cost of the employer. This is a happy event. Some countries still continues to refuse to purchase goods made through the employment of child labour. By introducing economic recovery might withdraw their children from exploitation labour. Problem of child labour can't be eliminated by judicial activism alone in the face of capitalist development and global power relations. Nonetheless, data on which area is not available even today.

Human Rights Concerns are inseparable from the issues of good governance, democracy, social development, social policy, law and social justice. Modern societies are becoming increasingly criminogenic. Deviance, conflict, exploitation, regression and violence coexist with modernity and development. In fact, there is a direct, positive correlation between crime and deviance, on one hand, and development and modernity, on the other. Repeated and registered crime is only a tip of the iceberg of criminality of a society of third world countries, like India, Bangladesh, Sri Lanka, Pakistan, Nepal and Bhutan.

Police Excess and Custodial Deaths

Police excess are found common in many Indian states. It shows an undemocratic and un hormonious rule was prevailed. For instance, in Andhra Pradesh 10 deaths in Police Custody (PC) and 45 deaths in Judicial Custody (JC) took place in the year 1995-96. The corresponding figures for 1996-97 are 27 deaths in police custody and 70 deaths in judicial custody. The total custodial deaths rose in Andhra Pradesh from 55 in 1995-96 to 97 in 1996-97. In the entire country a total of 444 custodial deaths (PC + JC = 136 + 308) were reported in the year 1995-96 and the same in the year 1996-97 were reported to be 188+700, totalling 888. 12 per cent in 1995-96 and 11 per cent in 1996-97 of custodial deaths are alone found in Andhra Pradesh. NCHR has recorded in 1996-97 that 60 per cent of the admitted complaints (2,725) reported "other police excesses"-a finding highly revealing of the nature of the Indian Police.

Equity and Justice

The Indian Police system seems to oscillate between two poles-overreaction and inaction; between reckless use of force and insensitivity to the letter and spirit of law and indifference of response. Politicalisation of police may also be a factor in response failure. A news report in the front page of a Telugu daily, *Vaartha* dated June 12, 2001 that Police Commissioner announced strategy, reacting over mounting crime rate and activities of about 400 rowdy shelters and anti-social elements in the city of Vijayawada alone. Internal punishment of rowdy sheeter by Civil Society is not a crime. Parading of the arrestees and erstwhile criminals publicly in the streets not only deters crime but also re-assure confidence of the public in police system acting tough. This news report is used only for the light it throws on the intimate nexus of crime, law, Human Rights, State Agencies, Personalities and Civil Society and its culture of crime. Human Rights are moralistic and spiritual than legalistic. Religion, culture, education, leadership and the formal and informal institutions of society, all play a role in this sphere[4].

"Vienna Declaration of 1993 gained universal acceptance of human rights in industrial countries". There are three main characteristics of that approach to development. First, the right to development was the right to a particular process of development where all human rights and freedom are to be realised and those human rights were related to all dimensions of human development, to be realised in a manner that establishes not only the entitlements to food, health, education, poverty reduction and equitable distribution of the fruits of development but also the culpability for the non-achievement of those entitlements. Secondly, the development programmes should be based on equity and justice. Thirdly, delivering the rights to development to all individuals"[5].

Conclusion

Human rights are nothing but fundamental rights availing the principles of justice, liberty, equality. In third world countries, because of poverty, unemployment the rights are suppressed by rich cult and also supported by state wings. To some extent, judicial activism was played a positive and compensatory role for the victims. Unfortunately, states are becoming arrogant, proudish, militant way tries to crush weaker section, opponents, downtrodden, but they should learn value system at every level of development. They should honour the growth and development of aged, women and children especially lower strata. Fair democracy, good governance, social development, empowerment of women are to be given priority in developmental process, so that human rights can be understood and practised. Civil society is to be encouraged by civil liberties for bringing equity and justice.

Notes and References

1. S. K. Kapoor (2000), International Law and Human Rights, Central Law Agency, Allahabad.
2. K. K. Bajaj (1999), Human Rights and Higher Education, *University News*, May 10, pp. 1-5.

3. Paramanand Singh (1999), Human Rights Protection Through Public Interest Litigation in India, *The Journal of Public Administration*, Oct-Dec.

4. C. R. Prasada RaoV.Venkateswarlu &M.Lakshmipathi Raju (2001), State and Civil Society and Human Rights Scenario in India, *The Journal of Public Administration*, Oct.-Dec.

5. Arjun Sengupta (2002), Official Development Assistance: The Human Rights Approach, *Economic & Political Weekly*, April, 13.

24

UNEMPLOYMENT: TIME FOR CONVERSION OF CURSE INTO COMMON-WEAL

Introduction

Amartya Sen, Nobel laureate, felt that development can be seen as a process of expanding the real freedoms that people enjoy. Mugbul Huq' Pakistan economist, viewed that development is to create an enabling environment in which people can enjoy long, healthy and creative life. V.R. Panchamukhi observed that increasing role of market forces and competition, globalization etc will have to be suitably tempered so as give due consideration to the employment dimensions of development. The visionary perspective is India should achieve the full employment goal by 2020.[1]

Every household has to employ the people in positive productive use that State and Society has to support it.

Unemployment in paradoxical situation in Asia:

The latest 21st century development is that Asian countries will face emerging labour shortages and other social and economic consequences of their ageing workforces. Key challenge in these countries is to extend working life and enhance the employability of older workers through *lifelong learning* in such a way that promotes decent work at later stages in the life cycle, while also providing a mechanism for skills and knowledge transfer to the next generation of workers. Japan's labour force is projected to contract 7 per cent between 2006 and 2015 due to ageing[2].

Providing "gainful and high quality employment at least to addition to the labour force" is one of the monitorable targets of the Tenth Five Year Plan in India. However, in the first three years of the plan period (2002-005), the pace of creation of employment opportunities may not exceed the addition to the labour force. The Tenth Plan envisaged the creation of 50 million employment opportunities over the plan period, against a total addition to the labour force of 35 million persons. "Unemployment condition of a person who is able to work, is actively seeking work, but is unable to find any. Statistics on unemployment are collected and analysed by Government Labour Office in most countries and are considered an important indicator of economic health"[3].

Dream of Manmohan Singh, Prime Minister, on Employment

India at 60 is a nation of young people. To realise our true potential, we must invest in the health and education of every child. We must create new employment opportunities for all, especially for the less privileged sections of society, and for those living in rural areas. We must eliminate the rural-urban divide in development indicators. We must also ensure that the process of industralisation generates enough jobs for our youth, in urban, semi-urban and rural areas. In the past 60 years, people moved to where work was available; in the next years, work must move to where people live[4].

Solution of Unemployment by Mayawathi, Chief Minister, U.P.

Mayawathi's gesture of extending voluntary reservations to the socially excluded is definitely need of the hour. It is a tragedy that even after 60 years of independence the State failed to address the basic needs of education and employment of a large segment of society, despite all claims of socialism and welfare. If implemented in right earnest, will go a long way in evolving a new India where no one will be seriously disadvantaged. In this direction ASSOCHAM-an industry Association has already created a corpus of Rs.5 crore for skill development and providing basic higher education to children from backward Communities, including SCs/STs. Over the past couple of months they have already imparted skill training to over 3,000 youth from these sections[5].

Human Capital an Unrivalled Resource

Educated, skilled, hardworking and English speaking managers, scientists, engineers and workers, represent the greatest strength of India. The Country has the youngest workforce of any large economy, a status that will be maintained for long. According to a recent World Competition year Book prepared by IMD, Switzerland, India ranks 11th among 60 nations in terms of the extent that the University education system meets the competitive needs of the economy in terms of availability of skilled labour, especially engineers, India ranks 7th. India was ranked first for availability of qualified engineers (China is 57th and US ranks 9th). India ranks among the top three of 30 nations in terms of availability of skilled labour[6].

Employment and Unemployment in India

To the landless worker in an India village, of one of the world's most unfortunate individuals, unemployment is not even a misfortune. It is his normal fortune[7].

The National Sample Survey Organisation Survey, (NSSO) namely 61st round conducted during July 2004-June 2005 constitutes an important source of information on employment and unemployment. The 61st round of the NSSO survey reveals a faster increase in employment during 1999-2000 to 2004 - 05 as compared to 1993-94 to 1999-2000. The following table analyses it.

The Table 1 has proved that as labour force and workforce are raising, unemployment rate is also raising from 2.88 in 1983 to 3.06 in 2004-05, which is not significantly high. Female unemployment has increased both in rural and urban areas[8].

Table 1
Employment and Unemployment in India (By Usual Principal Status)

	1983	*1993-1994*	*1999-2000*	*2004-2005*	*1983 to 1993-1994*	*1993-1994 to 1999-2000*	*1999-2000 to 2004-2005*
	In million				*Growth in per cent per annum*		
Labour force	277.34	343.56	377.88	428.37	2.06	1.60	2.54
Work force	269.36	334.54	367.37	415.27	2.09	1.57	2.48
Number of unemployed	7.98	9.02	10.51	13.10	–	–	–
As a proportion of labour force in per cent							
Unemployment rate	2.88	2.62	2.78	3.06			

Source: Government of India (2007) Economic Survey 2006-2007, p. 208.

The share of agriculture in total employment has come down from 61.67 per cent in 1993-94 to 58.54 per cent in 1999-2000, and further to 54.19 per cent in 2004-05. With the declining share in agriculture in GDP, the scope for absorbing substantial additional labour force in agriculture appears limited. Employment in the organised sector, however, has decreased in 2001-2003 years both in Public and Private sectors[9]. Service sector employment opportunities are raising very fast in Indian economy than agriculture and Industry; as in advanced economies.

II

Employment and Unemployment in Andhra Pradesh

Labour force participation rates during the year 2004-05 increased when compared with 1999-2000. Labour force participation Rate of Andhraw Pradesh was higher when compared with all India. Which is presented in Table 2.

The Table 2 reveals that males and females labour Participation in rural Andhra Pradesh are found more than in all India rural level. Unfortunately, urban female labour participation is also higher than all India urban Population. This is a positive trend in Andhra Pradesh labour force.

Table 2
Labour Force Participation Rates

	Andhra Pradesh			*India*		
Year	*Males*	*Females*	*Persons*	*Males*	*Females*	*Persons*
1999-2000 Rural	582	387	484	515	220	370
2004-05 Rural	586	399	492	531	237	387
1999-2000 Urban	517	158	341	528	123	335
2004-05 Urban	567	210	388	561	150	364

Source: Govt. of A.P. (22007) Socio-Economic Survey 2006-2007, p. 248.

Raising Workforce in Andhra Pradesh

Work force participation rate among males and females in rural areas of Andhra Pradesh declined during 2004-05, when Compared to 1999–2000. Whereas in urban areas of Andhra Pradesh, it was increased. Work force participation rates in general are high in Andhra Pradesh when compared with all India. Which is analyed in Table 3.

Table 3
Work Force Participation Rates

	Andhra Pradesh			*India*		
Year	*Males*	*Females*	*Persons*	*Males*	*Females*	*Persons*
1999-2000 Rural	535	355	445	478	204	344
2004-05 Rural	528	350	439	488	216	355
1999-2000 Urban	480	144	315	490	111	309
2004-05 Urban	523	192	358	519	133	334

Source: Govt. of A.P. (2007) Socio-Economic Survey 2006-07, p. 249.

The Table 3 explains that both rural and urban work force participation is higher than all India level. Unfortunately, in urban work force participation is very little higher than all India level.

Unemployment Rate on Decline in Andhra Pradesh:

Higher the Unemployment rate leads to higher the violence and unrest in the Society. Naxalism is a bye product of it. Then violent organisation has emerged from this angle only. The uneven behaviour and Policy of employment also generated vengeance. Suppose upper caste got more jobs than BCs, SCs and STs. The unemployment gap between rural and urban also made Indian economy or Andhra Pradesh economy in an ugly and unfortunate situation. A.P.J. Abdul Kalam, formerly president often suggested public amenities for rural area (PURA) to fill the gap between rural and urban India. Caste and unemployment discrimination also added more woes in rural level. The following table gives a comprehensive picture of unemployment in State.

Table 4
Unemployment Rate (Current Daily Status)

	Andhra Pradesh			*India*		
Year	*Males*	*Females*	*Persons*	*Males*	*Females*	*Persons*
1999-2000 Rural	81	81	81	72	70	71
2004-05 Rural	100	122	109	80	87	82
1999-2000 Urban	72	89	76	73	94	77
2004-05 Urban	78	83	79	75	116	83

Source: Govt. of A.P. (2007) Socio-Economic Survey 2006-07, p. 251.

The Table 4 analyses that, in general, unemployment in rural and urban Andhra Pradesh is higher than all India level. At all India level, urban unemployment is found higher than Andhra Pradesh. It is found that in agriculture sector, women are even proferring crop cutting, harvesting and some menial Jobs, whereas men are liking non-farm jobs, to get higher wage rates. This is the late trasition in Andhra Pradesh Agriculture labour marketing.

Dominance of State in Public Sector

Employment is a birth right of every citizen and constitutionally guarenteed. State should be more liberal in generating employment potential in private sector than public sector. Wage rates are to be enhanced to compensate their standard of living. The following table provides a bird's eye view of it.

Table 5 denotes that Government of Andhra Pradesh in the last four decades consistently added more employees in public sector than private sector. Even after economic reforms 1991 also public sector was a leader in providing regular employment. Private sector offered only below fifty per cent in public sector. Comparing 7.5 crore population for the 2001 census, creating 20 lakh persons employment is highly insignificant. State has to encourage more rural private institutions for generating more size and quality employment.

Table 5
Employment in Public and Private Sectors in Andhra Pradesh

Years	*Public Sector*	*Private Sector*	*Total*
March 1966	656003	300738	956741
March 1976	933878	258391	1192269
March 1986	1259098	340339	1599437
March 1996	1464097	484580	1948677
March 2006	13,74,735	6,26,719	220,01,454

Source: Govt. of A.P. (2007) Socio-economic Survey 2006-07, p. 250

New Initiatives of Andhra Pradesh

The State computerised all Employment Exchanges by providing online services to the job seekers and employers. In view of slowly decreasing public employment, four new initiatives were taken up.

(a) 8670 candidates were placed under pre-recruitment training for Defense and Para–military forces during the year 2004 and 1052 upto September 2006.

(b) 1132 candidates were placed through *job melas* during 2004 and 1281 during 2005 and 1739 candidates in September 2006.

(c) 6554 candidates were guided under adoption of one Government High School and one Junior college in each district for providing career guidance to the students of terminal class during 2004 and 61,227 during 2005 and 24,109 candidates in September 2006.

(d) Training was arranged for 994 Urban unskilled unemployed during 2004 and 609 during 2005 and 652 in September 2006.

When private sector was emerging in the State Private Employment Exchanges were also entered by taking premiums, especially Information Technology areas.

An overseas Manpower Company has been launched in Andhra Pradesh in March 2006 to help the unemployed youth and to bring Overseas Employers and the aspirants together. 2128 candidates have registered till 30th September 2006 at this company. Two programmes have been organised in English Language proficiency for the Job seekers desirous of going abroad. Two Malaysian Induction Training programmes have been organised by the Company so far for the Job seekers desirous of taking up job in Malaysia[10].

In 2006, Government of Andhra Pradesh introduced *"Udyogshree"*. In this connection, a Job *mela* was organized on August 19, 2007 to give employment for 6464 jobs. Around 40 thousand unemployees attended. Finally they failed to interview the candidates, because of organizational lapses[11].

Further State proposed a Employment Generation and Marketing Mission (EGMM) to provide employment to rural youth by constructing Transit homes in and around city. Specialised Training will be provided through 86 Industrial Training Institutes. The Mission will provide employment for 10 lakhs youth.[12]

Suggestions for reducing Unemployment

(a) It is right time to educate the girl child compulsorily first and make the family to trim it. It reduces population growth in long term.

(b) Under the globalisation wave, agriculture is going towards Corporatisation and farmers are to be shareholders, especially marginal and small farmers.

(c) Special Economic Zones (SEZs) are indicators for transforming the disguised unemployees to productive employees and transferring the ownership and agriculture.

(d) Rural industries are to be promoted like Agri-business, Textile, Dairy.

(e) Rural infrastructure facilities like *pucca* roads, power, education, health, water, transport, internet are to be guaranteed.

(f) Rural greenery is to be promoted and protected i.e. eco-system at any cost. Mass afforestation programmes with wildlife protection are to encouraged at every village level.

(g) People participation through Non-governmental organisations, (NGOs) Voluntary Organisations, (V.O) Charity Trusts, Educational ad Health Institutions are encouraged, than State employees.

(h) State should play the role of low-maker and monitor only, than provider. Producer private sector is to be encouraged with proper guidelines.

(i) Unfair, dishonestry and corrupt practices are very much in Political hierarchy, outdated rule minded bureaucracy, middlemen involvement at all levels have made the development into complex, not encouraged meritorious products to generate any innovative and inventive ideas.

(j) Quality Training Institutions are to be established and nurtured with incentives.

(k) Collaboration with foreign–institutions, investors, banks, industries are to be promoted.

(l) People are to be motivated as positive thinkers and workaholic in day to day life.

(m) Able bodied, skilled, professional employees should *have lifelong employment* opportunities like in Japan economy, to fill the generation gaps for making strong knowledge society.

(n) NREGP, IRDP, Self employed programmes are strengthened and encouraged. Ethics ad *Nyaya panchayats* are to be established to oversee the development both inn rural and urban areas.

III

Conclusion

Development fruits should have to percolate to all sections of Society, especially rural. Through Quality education and training people are to be made workaholic. It is found that female empowerment and workforce is very low at all India level. As share of agriculture in the GDP is falling very sharply, the employment opportunities are also, fallen drastically. Andhra Pradesh is a leader in many economic indicators also fallen very low in creating employment. More unemployment is found in rural areas than urban even among women workforce. State has not encouraged employment potential in Private sector. State initiatives for generation of jobs are very insignificant. Rural development through people participation and NGOs, VOs is highly needed. Next sixty years, Jobs have to knock the door of the unemployee, convert chronic curse into common-weal.

Notes

Current Daily Status (CDS)

The CDS indicates the Unemployment status of a person without gainful employment and seeking employment during all the seven days in a week. The rate of unemployment is the ratio of unemployed days per week to the total labour supply per week.

Labour Force Participation Rate: (LFPR)

Is defined as the number of persons in the labour force per 1000 persons. Persons categorised as working (employed) and also those who are seeking or available for work (unemployed) together constitute labour force.

Work Force Participation Rate (WFPR)

Persons who were engaged in any economic activity constitute work force. The number of persons employed per 1000 persons

Unemployee

Persons who owing to lack of work has not worked but either sought through employment exchanges, intermediaries, making applications to prospective employers were considered as unemployed. Unemployment rate is defined as the number of persons unemployed per 1000 persons in the labour force.

Types of Unemployment

1. Voluntary unemployment, 2. In voluntary unemployment, 3. Disguised unemployment, 4. Cyclical unemployment, 5. Seasonal unemployment and 6. Frictional unemployment.

Underemployment

It is used to describe the situation of those who are able to find employment only for shorter than normal periods–for example, part-time workers and seasonal workers and may also describe the condition of workers whose education or training makes them overqualified for their jobs.

Full Employment

Is conventionally defined not as zero unemployment but as that level of employment where unemployment has fallen to the irreducible minimum.

PURA

Providing Urban Amenities in Rural Area (PURA): APJ Abdul Kalam's intervention made to introduce this programme by Planning Commission at All India level in Tenth plan.

Notes and References

1. V. R. Panchamukhi (2000), India: Vision 2020, 4th *Annual Conference of the Economic Association of Bihar,* May 27-29, p.19.
2. Kyodo (2007), Japanese Labour Force to Shrink 7%, *The Economic Times,* Aug, 17, p. 14.
3. Britannica (2005), Britannica Ready Reference Encyclopedia, Vol. 10, p. 52.
4. Manmohan Singh (2007), India @ 60, *The Economic Times,* August 15, p. 2.
5. D. S. Rawat (2007), Is UP Job Quota Policy Sensible? *The Economic Times,* August 15, p. 18.
6. G.Vijaya Raghavan and U. S. M. Nair (2007), The Great Indian Boom–The Remaissance of Manufacturing, *Manorama year Book* p. 48.
7. John Kenneth Galbraith (1958), The Affluent Society, Mentor Books, New York, p. 91.

8. Planning Commission (2007), *Economic Survey* 2006-07, p. 208.
9. Planning Commission (2006), Mid-Term Appraisal of 10th Five Year Plan (2002-2007), p. 264.
10. Government of Andhra Pradesh (2007), Socio-economic Survey 2006-07, p. 161.
11. Correspondent (2007), Unemployed India, *Andhra Jyothi,* Chittoor edition, August 20, p. 9.
12. Correspondent (2007), Transit Homes for Rural Youth, *The Hindu,* August 21, p. 4.

INDEX

D

Q & R

S